The New School Executive

The New School Executive

A Theory of Administration

Second Edition

THOMAS J. SERGIOVANNI
University of Illinois, Urbana-Champaign
and
FRED D. CARVER
Southern Illinois University, Edwardsville

1817

HARPER & ROW, PUBLISHERS, New York
Cambridge, Hagerstown, Philadelphia, San Francisco,
London, Mexico City, São Paulo, Sydney

Sponsoring Editor: George A. Middendorf
Production Manager: Jeanie Berke
Compositor: Port City Press

Art Studio: Vantage Art Inc.

THE NEW SCHOOL EXECUTIVE, A Theory of Administration
Second Edition

Library of Congress Cataloging in Publication Data

Sergiovanni, Thomas J.
  The new school executive.

  Includes bibliographical references and index.
  1. School management and organization. I. Carver, Fred Donald, joint author. II.
Title.
LB2805.S53 1980   371.2   79-18195
ISBN 0-06-045906-9

Contents

v

Preface to Second Edition

The first edition of *The New School Executive* was concerned primarily with aspects of administration and organization internal to the school. During the past decade, however, we have witnessed the rapid decline of the autonomous local school district with its entrepreneurial administration in favor of more complex and interdependent, albeit restrictive, administrative and governance arrangements. The first edition viewed the school as a Janus professional and bureaucratic organization and gave attention to reconciling these images. In the second edition, a third face is added to professional and bureaucratic images—the political system. Attending to this new emphasis is Part IV, which contains two new chapters: Chapter 12, "The School as a Political System," and Chapter 13, "The School Executive and External Relations."

A second significant addition is an emphasis on contingency theory as a construct and mechanism for resolving seemingly contradictory prescriptions and findings in the literature of educational administration. Theorists and researchers who construct this literature often work from specializations which enhance and blind at the same time. Further, ideologies play an important role in the work of literature development. Contingency theory offers a way by which administrators might navigate through this sea of apparent controversy, selecting insights and prescriptions from a variety of sources and matching them to the unique value characteristics and problem situations. Contingency theory is considered informally throughout the book and formally in a new chapter entitled "Administrative Values and Decision-Making: A Contingency Approach."

A further addition of significance is our modest proposal for a social humanities view of educational policy and administration.

The proposal, which appears in Chapter 16, seeks to integrate more fully and systematically issues of science and value.

For their help and encouragement, we thank our students and colleagues at the University of Illinois, Urbana-Champaign and elsewhere. The list of those to whom we are indebted has grown too large for individual recognition. Thomas J. Sergiovanni assumed major responsibility for Parts I and II and Chapters 12, 15, and 16. Responsibility for Part III and Chapters 13 and 14 fell to Fred D. Carver. This division of labor does not reflect the communion we share for the book's ideas.

THOMAS J. SERGIOVANNI
FRED D. CARVER

Preface to First Edition

Administrative effectiveness in education is ultimately determined by the human condition which exists in the school. Among formal organizations, the school is unique, for both its process and product, its means and ends, are basically human. It is not likely that schools will be successful in developing awareness, creativity, respect, sensitivity, responsibility, a desire for learning, a spirit of inquiry, a capacity for love, and similar conditions in youngsters unless schools are organized and operated in such a way as to be able to champion and nurture these conditions. One basic assumption of this book, therefore, is that those growth and development goals which we hold for youngsters are best achieved by teachers and other adults who are committed to these goals also for themselves—both as persons and professionals. The extent to which teachers will be committed to growth and development, moreover, depends upon the health of the school as a human organization.

The orientation of this book is behavioral and reflects a deep commitment to increasing the administrator's capacity to humanize the schools. In this effort, we describe and analyze three critical sets of forces which must be dealt with by school administrators. We think of these forces as systems which comprise screens through which educational decision-making takes place—each system, furthermore, forming part of a larger system which comprises the context of the school executive as he works toward administrative effectiveness.

One set of forces, the Belief System, is examined in Part I. Here we are concerned with the interface which exists between values, attitudes, goals and objectives, and administrative action. Both the art and the science of administration are described in this part, and an attempt is made to join them into an applied science of administration unique to education. Part II deals with a second set of forces, which we describe as the Human System. Our concern here is in helping school administrators work more effectively with people. In this effort, we consider job satisfaction, human needs, motivation, and commitment. Care is taken to differentiate our approach to human resource development from traditional human relations approaches, which we believe to be quite superficial. In Part III, the Organizational System, we examine certain environmental and situational forces which often exert enormous power over educational decision-making. The sociological manifestations of the school are examined in this part. Of particular interest and importance in the discussion is the seemingly unending struggle which takes place when the school as a formal organization works to achieve its own goals of survival, stability, reliability, and control while at the same time its human inhabitants (teachers, students, and administrators) struggle to form this formal organization into their own images of effectiveness. Part IV [now Part V], the Action System (the larger system which contains the Belief System, the Human System, and the Organizational System as subsystems), deals operationally with educational decision-making. Each of these systems is an important component of the work of school executives.

This book is intended to have a number of uses. Our intent was to write a book for those initially studying educational administration at the master's or advanced certificate levels. Since programs at this level are typically strong in emphasizing technical skills and focusing on roles and tasks, we hope that our book will provide a needed behavioral and conceptual perspective to such programs. Students in more advanced courses may find the book useful as an introduction to the systematic study of administrative behavior and educational decision-making. Our hope also is that practicing school executives will find the book helpful in relating and integrating problems of value, people, and organization into a meaningful whole which will permit them more confidently and humanly to engage in educational decision-making.

We do not pretend to have written an objective book about administration. Indeed, we have doubts about whether educational administration ought to be discussed *only* as an abstract and pure science. Our value system—especially with reference to the purposes of education and to the forms, processes, and ways in which these purposes should be pursued—permeates our efforts in describing administrative effectiveness for school executives. To those who find the introduction of our value system distracting, we apologize. For those who disagree with our value system but who can use it as a counterpoint to their own views perhaps we have provided a useful service. Our hope is that most readers will find our value perspectives to be compatible with their own.

THOMAS J. SERGIOVANNI
FRED D. CARVER

The New School Executive

Part I
THE BELIEF SYSTEM

Chapter 1
Educational Administration as an Applied Science

In the decade of the sixties efforts toward the development and establishment of a science of administration intensified. This trend was evidenced by movements (1) toward interdisciplinary approaches to the study of administration; (2) to develop both a general theory and special theories of administration; (3) toward increased interest in the development of organizational theory as a means to understand the sociological, political, and psychological environments within which administrators must work; and (4) to increase efforts in programmatic research based on administrative and organizational theory. Changes in preparation programs for school administrators, the establishment of administrative-science centers in a number of universities, and the emergence of organizational science as a new discipline were further indications of increased concern for the scientific[1] study of administration.

The quest for a science of administration remained with us during the decade of the seventies though its thrusts and character differed from the previous decade. Praxeological approaches to administration based heavily on newer versions of old scientific management principles and on adaptation of management systems analysis could be widely observed, and as a counterpoint one also finds interest in developing theories of schools as political conflict systems. Interest in management by objectives, accountability systems and competence-based training, evaluation and in-service for teachers and administrators reflect the first thrust, and interest in the paradigms of political science and decision-making theory reflect the second.

Scientific approaches to the study of administration, however, have resulted in many problems for those who study and practice school administration. School executives in particular seem confused by the new emphases and often seem disengaged from advocates of more scientific approaches. Many observers feel that the rift between theory and practice in administration is such that theoretician and practitioner—though attached to the same roots— form two virtually unrelated professions. Many critics of administrative science react defensively because they fear or do not understand scientific approaches to administration. Other critics react analytically by suggesting that such approaches are often not in keeping with the goals of education or the purposes of educational organizations. Many advocates of administrative science, on the other hand, react dogmatically by insisting that their approaches are applicable in all cases and by making claims regarding the solution of educational problems which are wholly unwarranted. Other advocates more reasonably argue that the newer scientific approaches, though offering no panacea to school executives, provide them with analytical frameworks which help increase their effectiveness.

School executives themselves typically consider administration to be largely an intuitive enterprise. According to this approach, administrators are born, not made; and school administration is an art successfully practiced by those with an intuitive knack which is refined through experience. It is argued that the complexities of human nature are such that one might best administer by intuition and leave theories of administration to those with less to do. Followers of the art of administration view successful administrators as being characterized by having intestinal fortitude, a tenacity to survive, and common sense.

Many of the features of both administrative art and administrative science have validity, but we believe that the standard claims and charges made for and against each of these approaches are largely distorted. In this chapter, therefore, we shall explore both the scientific and artistic nature of administration. These dimensions taken together form the basis for an integrated applied science of administration unique to education.

A SCIENCE OF ADMINISTRATION

Administration as a science is concerned with describing, explaining, analyzing, and predicting organizational phenomena and human behavior as they relate to the accomplishment of organizational goals. The scientific approach to administration is one of objectivity and neutrality. The focus of this approach is on the identification and articulation of principles which have wide application to administration in general. The approach therefore presents a panoramic view which includes methods of organizing, work flow, authority and power systems, leadership, control, coordination, planning, change, administrative behavior, group behavior, individual behavior, human adaptation, motivation, decision-making, and so on. Ultimately, those who seek a science of administration wish to examine each of these variables in cause-and-effect relationships so that action propositions may be developed to guide administrative behavior more effectively.

A number of general propositions about leadership developed from the research of Fiedler and his colleagues at the Group Effectiveness Laboratory of the University of Illinois[2] are illustrative of scientific efforts in this area. The propositions suggest that when the situation for exercising influence and leadership is very favorable or very unfavorable, task-oriented leadership styles are most effective. Those situations which are only moderately favorable for exercising influence and leadership lend themselves to relation-oriented leadership styles. The degree of favorableness of a given situation is determined by the extent to which leader and group have good relationships with each other, the position power of the leader is strong, and the tasks of the group are well defined and clearly structured. By combining each of these situational dimensions (leader-member relations, position power, and task structure), eight situations for leadership can be identified. Four of these situations, being either very favorable or unfavorable for exercising influence and leadership, require task-oriented styles. Four, being only moderately favorable, require relationship-oriented leadership styles. The eight situations which comprise the specific leadership propositions from Fiedler's research are summarized as follows:

1. Task-oriented, authoritarian leadership styles are more effective in group situations where
   a. leader-member relations are good, tasks are structured, and leader position power is strong.
   b. leader-member relations are good, tasks are structured, and leader position power is weak.

    c. leader-member relations are good, tasks are unstruc-
      tured, and leader position power is strong.
    d. leader-member relations are moderately poor, tasks are
      unstructured, and leader position power is weak.
2. Relationship-oriented, participatory leadership styles are
  more effective in group situations where
    a. leader-member relations are good, tasks are unstruc-
      tured, and leader position power is weak.
    b. leader-member relations are moderately poor, tasks are
      structured, and leader position power is strong.
    c. leader-member relations are moderately poor, tasks are
      structured, and leader position power is weak.
    d. leader-member relations are moderately poor, tasks are
      unstructured, and leader position power is strong.

Research such as Fiedler's leads to the development of propositions about the real world and the way it operates; this research
offers factuality and objectivity—two important features of scientific propositions relating to administration. Further, since the
Fiedler research on leadership and group effectiveness has
spanned a period of over 25 years and has included subjects from a
variety of occupational groups, the findings are considered reliable
and have wide applicability—two other important features of scientific propositions relating to administration.

    What should school executives do in light of this scientific
evidence about leadership? Should they adjust leadership styles to
accommodate given situations?[3] Should teachers be encouraged to
do the same? What are the short-term and long-term consequences
to the school and to the classroom in adopting one or another
leadership style or in arranging group situations to accommodate
style? Fiedler's measurements for group effectiveness were comprised of outputs which were readily quantifiable (e.g., team scores,
number of units produced). Highly quantifiable and concrete
measurements of school output are legitimate means by which to
judge effectiveness, but schools are also concerned with other
outputs, those from the affective domain, for example. What effects
do various leadership styles have on this domain? Are we willing to
forsake effectiveness in one domain in order to increase effectiveness in another?

    As school executives work with teachers—and as these profes-
sionals in turn work with students in unstructured task situations[4]—they need to be sure that their leadership styles are consistent with the broader goals of education rather than simply
with those which will result in increased measurable output at the

moment. Yet the science of administration does not permit us the luxury of evaluating its propositions in terms of a value system unique to education. Herbert Simon, for example, one of the pioneers in developing a science of administration, reminds us that belief systems have no place in science: ". . . an administrative science, like any science, is concerned purely with factual state-ments. There is no place for ethical assertions in the body of science. Whenever ethical statements do occur, they can be sepa-rated into two parts, one factual and one ethical; and only the former has any relevance to science."[5]

Scientific approaches to administration—although able to pro-vide invaluable inputs to educational decision-making in the form of hard knowledge, concepts, and fundamental understanding— offer little direct help in formulating operational strategies for school administrators. The problem of deciding which scientific propositions are appropriate to school administration is further compounded by the presence of unanticipated consequences of administrative acts. Thus administration may be scientific in that one can make fairly accurate initial predictions based on theory and propositions, but administration is also artistic in the sense that once action is implemented, the variability and complexity of human behavior produce unanticipated consequences which defy systematic decision-making.

The strengths of a science of administration—objectivity, neu-trality, and wide applicability—are also its weaknesses. The ab-sence of values, the lack of goal emphasis, and the difficulty in developing carry-over in particular situations require that school executives continually assess and modify scientific propositions in the light of a value system unique to education and of goals unique to their schools. Therefore, although it would be unwise to ignore scientific findings, it seem equally unwise to accept them without evaluation and modification.

BASIS FOR AN APPLIED SCIENCE

It is our position that educational administration is an applied science based on the interdependence between science and art. A science of administration, being value free, is not readily useful to school executives. An applied science, however, enhanced by scientific appreciation and understanding of human and organiza-tional phenomena but dependent upon value sets as additional inputs to educational decision-making, is most useful to school executives. An applied science of administration, then, unlike a science of administration, has the ability to absorb and use values as criteria for evaluating and influencing decision-making.

Unfortunately, school executives often confuse an applied science of administration with the development and cataloging of "practical strategies." Being practical, though, involves using the most efficient[6] way to achieve school goals and, as such, often sacrifices means in order to achieve ends. A true applied science of administration, on the other hand, is concerned with means as well as ends and, therefore, focuses on quality of process as well as quality of goal achievement. For example, deviously manipulating students and teachers may be most practical for the efficient achievement of school goals. A school executive may justify the practicality of such manipulation by suggesting that in the long run *his or her* goals are better for subordinates and, further, that they should be achieved with a minimum of cost and fuss. Devious manipulation, however, often requires subordinates (teachers or students) to be dependent upon superiors, denies them growth and expression, and may be damaging to their self-concepts. As a long-term strategy, this "practicality" causes effects which usually diminish administrative and organizational success. It is our view, then, *that educational administration is basically an ethical science concerned with good or better processes, good or better means, good or better ends, and as such is thoroughly immersed in values, preferences, ideas, aspirations, and hopes.*[7]

Though a pure science of administration largely ignores ethical considerations, even the best-intending school executive cannot possibly hope to approach administrative effectiveness by ignoring theoretical and empirical models, schema, and propositions emerging from the science of administration.

DECISION-MAKING

Previous sections focused largely on the importance of a value system for evaluating scientific evidence for use in education. One should not overlook, however, other purely human limitations of administrative science. March and Simon's now classic book entitled *Organizations*[8] has as its subtheme the importance of human cognitive and affective limitations on rational behavior. The authors suggest that decision-making in organizations should be viewed as approximating an irrational rather than rational model of executive behavior.

Rational decision-making models typically rely on the scientific method and are based on such fundamental rational assumptions as:

1. The exact nature of the problem to be solved is delineated, and clear goals are formulated.
2. The decision-maker identifies and specifies all possible alternatives to the problem.
3. The decision-maker anticipates and specifies all possible outcomes of each alternative.
4. Each of the outcomes is weighted and ranked from best to worst.

These assumptions specify the nature of rational decision-making strategies. Such strategies require that search does not cease until all alternatives are identified, weighted, and ranked in relation to goodness of fit with clear goals. Action-oriented administrators, at least because of the time constraints they face, are more likely to substitute *workable* decision-making strategies for those described as *rational*. That is, although school executives and others seek solutions to problems which are best, they settle for solutions which are satisfactory. It would be nice indeed to have the best needle in a haystack, but any needle that works will do.[9]

Using workable decision-making strategies, school executives:

1. identify simple objectives with manageable goals.
2. outline several alternatives which occur to them within the limits imposed by time, their experience, and other constraints.
3. make comparisons among these alternatives using theory, conceptual knowledge, opinion, past experience, judgment, and intuition.
4. select feasible alternatives which seem most consistent with the original problem or goal.

Since any course of action is likely to modify the original goal and since no course of action is likely to solve the original problem completely, the school executive sees his or her decision as one which is modifiable in an endless succession of patterns such as those described previously.

Although we may be unduly critical of the scientific method of rational decision-making, by no means does this imply sanctioning the "flying by the seat of our pants" or the "fireman" methods so often used by school executives. The model of workable decision-making strategies is a hybrid which relies on artistic and intuitive impulses in the sense that once a problem has been identified, the range of search for alternatives is restricted. The bases for restriction are not always clear but often include financial constraints, past experience, and administrative judgment. The model is scientific in

that problems and goals are evaluated conceptually and the restricted alternatives are compared against criteria (step 3). The
model does not require elaborate delineation of all possible outcomes, for it recognizes that each initial outcome provokes unanticipated consequences which in turn modify the original goals and
objectives, and retrigger the decision-making cycle. One thing
remains clear. The school executive's intuition throughout the
decision-making process is important. *This intuition, in turn, is
informed by his or her value system.*

FORCES WHICH INFLUENCE EDUCATIONAL DECISION-MAKING

In the previous section we discussed a model for decision-making
which, being extremely general, does little more than specify loose
stages of action as the decision-making process evolves. In this
section we discuss and outline four sets of inputs or forces which
have a pronounced effect on educational decision-making, administrative effectiveness, and subsequent school success: (1) forces
within the administrator, (2) forces in the human system, (3) forces
in the organization, and (4) forces in the environment.

Forces Within the Administrator

In reality, decision-making might best be understood under the
rubrics of preference theory rather than rational theory. In noting
the importance of personal preference in decision-making Rowe
notes:

> *In any complex decision where personal or behavior factors apply, the
> individual's preference will dominate the results. . . .*
> There are two corollaries to the rule that might also apply in this
> case. The first is: *A single factor usually forms the basis for a personal
> preference decision.*
> And the second states that: *While a decision is often based on
> personal preference, the analysis is usually a rational process. . . .*
> Perhaps one of the strongest cases against the belief in rational
> decision making emerged from an international study I conducted
> among 496 managers. I asked them to rank ten characteristics in order
> of importance to the decision maker. Rationality appeared eighth on
> the list.
> Perception, or the ability to correctly formulate problems, was
> ranked at the top of the list by 82% of the managers, while compulsion,
> the need to get the job done at any cost, was the least regarded
> characteristic. . . .
> This is not to say that all decisions are purely subjective. Rational

decision making does exist and its survival and propagation should be encouraged. Nor do I mean to suggest that a subjective decision is necessarily a bad one. If an individual has a high personal stake in a decision, he is more likely to carry it through successfully. . . .

Decision makers respond to forces and influences. Their behavior is the result of interaction between what they want to do and what they are expected to do. Whenever there is a conflict between personal needs or preferences and organizational pressures, and the decision maker is in a position to do so, personal preferences will dominate.[10]

Administrative preferences are influenced and shaped by a variety of organizational and environmental factors. The organizational history or culture of the school-community, its previous successes and failures, and the dominant philosophical tradition espoused by previous administrations are examples. Administrative behavior is also influenced by assumptions which school executives hold for themselves, their subordinates, and for human nature itself. Thus beliefs which school executives hold about schools and society, educational goals, school management, authority, and organizational arrangements are modifiers of behavior. A value system which arranges beliefs and preferences in some systematic way is an additional force within the administrator which affects his educational decision-making behavior. Personality idiosyncrasies which are developed as a result of socialization as a child, adult, educator, and school executive are another such force.

To understand how one's value and preference system influences decisions, consider the metaphor of a political platform applied to educational administration. School executives bring to their organizations educational and management platforms which serve as governing theories for their action and decision. Faced with a new question or situation, administrative action can be expected to be consistent with one's platforms.

To what extent are school executives aware of their governing platforms? Arygris believes that most are not well informed and indeed finds that executives often talk one platform but operate from another, often contradictory, platform. In his words:

When someone is asked how he would behave under certain circumstances, the answer he usually gives is his *espoused theory* of action for that situation. This is the theory of action to which he gives allegiance, and which, upon request, he communicates to others. However, the theory that actually governs his actions is his *theory-in-use*, which may or may not be compatible with his espoused theory; furthermore, the individual may or may not be aware of the incompatibility of the two theories.

We cannot learn what someone's theory-in-use is simply by asking him. We must *construct his theory-in-use from observations of his behavior.* In this sense, constructs of theories-in-use are like scientific hypotheses; the constructs may be inaccurate representations of the behavior they claim to describe.[11]

Forces within the administrator including his or her educational and management platforms assume a critical role in understanding educational decision-making.

Forces in the Human System

Earlier in this chapter we suggested that educational administration is basically an ethical science. The importance of linking administration and ethics is evidenced by the fact that schools are basically human organizations. As such, forces in the human system—needs, wants, aspirations, hopes and beliefs of teachers, students, and administrators—are modifiers of administrative behavior and educational decision-making.

Forces in the Organization

Forces in the organization which are potential influences of educational decision-making include structural characteristics of the organization which contribute to its mode of operation. Although schools as organizations are similar, no two are alike. Schools develop organizational personalities, conceptually similar to the human personality, which include unique organizational styles, authority styles, and interrelated organizational dynamics.

Forces in the Environment

The broader political and cultural context of the school as exemplified in its interaction with its school-community historically and presently, its interdependent posture as but one legal entity in a broader matrix of regional, state, and federal government, and its vulnerability as a public organization responsive to a variety of pressure groups comprises the forces in the environment which help to shape the nature of educational decision-making.

These four forces—which we believe provide the study content for an applied science of educational administration—form systems which are treated in this book as the belief system (Part I), the human system (Part II), the organizational system (Part III), and the political system (Part IV). They are, furthermore, connected and interwoven into an action system (Part V) which includes planning, coordinating, communicating, negotiating, deciding, leading, and other administrative-process functions. The forces and their integrating action system can be understood as a science of administration, but their effective articulation in educational settings and on behalf of educational goals is dependent upon an applied science of educational administration.

SKILLS OF EFFECTIVE SCHOOL EXECUTIVES

One approach to mapping what a school executive needs to be successful is to identify and list traits of successful school executives. This approach, however, fails to provide us with insights into the scope of administrative work and the skills one needs for success. Katz has identified three basic skills upon which he feels successful administration rests—technical, human, and conceptual.[12] All of these skills are related and, therefore, most difficult to separate in practice. They are treated separately, however, for analytical purposes.

Technical skill assumes an understanding of and proficiency in the methods, processes, procedures, and techniques of education. In noninstructional areas it also includes specific knowledge in finance, accounting, scheduling, purchasing, construction, and maintenance.

Human skill refers to the school executive's ability to work effectively and efficiently with other people on a one-to-one basis and in group settings. This skill requires considerable self-understanding and acceptance as well as appreciation, empathy, and consideration for others. Its knowledge base includes an understanding of and facility for adult motivation, attitudinal development, group dynamics, human need, morale, and the development of human resources.

Conceptual skill includes the school executive's ability to see the school, the district, and the total educational program as a whole. This skill includes the effective mapping of interdependence for each of the components of the school as an organization, the educational program as an instructional system, and the functioning of the human organization. The development of conceptual skill relies heavily on a balanced emphasis of administrative theory, organizational and human behavior, and educational philosophy.

Katz suggests that although each of these skills is important to school administration at all hierarchical levels, technical skills are most important to administrators at lower levels, and conceptual skills are most important to those at the upper levels. He suggests that each of the skills can and should be developed by those seeking advancement as school executives.

The relative importance of these skills seems to vary with the level of administrative responsibility. At lower levels, the major need is for technical and human skills. At higher levels, the administrator's effectiveness depends largely on human and conceptual skills. At the top conceptual skill becomes the most important of all for successful administrators.

This three-skill approach emphasizes that good administrators are not necessarily born; they may be developed. It transcends the need to identify specific traits in an effort to provide a more useful way of looking at the administrative process. By helping to identify the skills most needed at various levels of responsibility, it may prove useful in the selection, training, and promotion of executives.[13]

The emphasis on technical and conceptual skills may vary with management level, but human skills are the common denominator that appears to be crucial at all levels. By contrast the business manager's job is more technically oriented than that of the superintendent of schools. Yet each position requires competence in human skills; the former as he or she supervises nonacademic personnel and acts as a staff consultant to various line administrators and the latter as he or she works with the administrative team, the teacher organization, the school board, and various community groups. On numerous occasions superintendents have remarked that top administrators rarely fail for lack of technical know-how. They attribute forced executive succession to interpersonal and other human skill problems.

The importance of human and conceptual skills is further enhanced by the difficulty one encounters by adopting a predominantly *training* mode in preparing educational administrators. Learning experts suggest that training is the process of learning sequences of programmed behaviors. Training is most appropriate for occupations whose job tasks can be precisely defined and analyzed in a fashion which permits "one best way" to be determined. Education, by contrast, instills reasoning processes and fosters understanding and interpretation of knowledge.

Training aspects for the preparation of educational administrators exist and are important but should be considered secondary to educational aspects. Educational administration is an applied science that is complex and situational, offering few laws or principles. Leavitt reminds us, "There is no such thing as *the* right way for a manager to operate or behave. There are only ways appropriate for specific tasks of specific enterprises under specific conditions, faced by managers of specific temperaments and styles."[14]

THE DOMAIN OF EDUCATIONAL ADMINISTRATION

We have described four sets of forces which are key influences of educational decision-making and three skills which are fundamental to administrative effectiveness. We believe that each of these forces can and must be analyzed, related, and exploited from the perspective of an applied science of educational administration. This book examines human and conceptual skills in depth as they relate to the four forces and to the action system of administrative process. Light emphasis is given to technical skills, for they are adequately covered in a number of more specialized books. Indeed, these are the skills most appropriately learned on the job and through clinical experiences.

It seems appropriate to conclude this introductory chapter by emphasizing the fundamental interdependence between theory and practice. In many respects the study of theory is the practicing school executive's best friend and the study of practice is the theoretician's best friend. That the two are interdependent is supported by the observation that theory often follows practice and that practice expands and blossoms as a result of theory. Each innovation, improvement, or refinement in practice is followed by theory which explains and extends the practice. This addition to theory in turn stimulates and extends new practice, and so on.

No general theory of administration is proposed. Our approach is to provide readers with a variety of middle-range theories drawn from the disciplines of sociology, psychology, political science, decision sciences, management, and social psychology. Tempered with philosophical and other value considerations unique to educational settings, these middle-range theories are applied to the school. Consider the analogy of a potential home purchaser as he or she comes upon a locked model home. As this person wanders around the home peering through each of the windows, a glimpse of reality is provided. Each window gives an additional perspective, but *alone*, each provides incomplete, even biased, insights as to what the house is really like. Like windows, middle-range theories can provide school executives with insights and understandings of the problems they face.

In the remainder of Part I, "The Belief System," we examine the role of value judgments in relation to an applied science of administration as we begin our analysis of the first of three forces—those which exist within the school executive.

Notes

1. Our current preoccupation with science in education and in discovering scientific approaches to the study and practice of educational administration is a transfer of a larger societal value given to science.
2. Fred Fiedler, *A Theory of Leadership Effectiveness* (New York: McGraw-Hill, 1967), chap. 9, especially p. 146.
3. Fiedler argues that leadership styles should be taken as givens in people, for they are not readily altered. He suggests, instead, that situations should be manipulated so that they are consistent with the leader's style. Effectiveness, as defined by Fiedler, usually takes the form of some concrete output measurement.
4. Schools often and justly concern themselves with critically important structured tasks such as reading, spelling and math drill, physical education, skill development, music fundamentals, and the like; but they are also concerned with problem solving, discovery, knowledge usage, moral development, and other unstructured tasks. Indeed, the teaching of structured tasks is more easily accomplished by the use of workbook, programmed machine or text, computer, and other technical devices. We can hardly justify staffing schools with highly trained professional teachers, therefore, on the basis of structured tasks. The justification for a highly qualified teaching corps is based, of course, on the unstructured learning activities predominating in schools.
5. Herbert A. Simon, *Administrative Behavior* (New York: Macmillan, 1957), p. 253.
6. "Efficient" is used here in its more general meaning to suggest ease, least resistance, trouble free, quickest, least costly, and so on. Later we use the term in a more specific technical sense in our discussion of administration as a social process.
7. Beard feels that all of the social sciences are ethical sciences: "As ethical sciences they are concerned with good or better conduct and good or better material and social arrangements." See Charles A. Beard, *The Nature of the Social Sciences* (New York: Charles Scribner's Sons, 1934), p. 40.
8. James March and Herbert Simon, *Organizations* (New York: John Wiley, 1958).
9. We need to differentiate between the continuous search which all of us support for optimal solutions to educational problems, and the daily functioning and improvement of the nation's schools. School executives are more likely to leave the long-range search to philosophers and experts as they, the executives, focus on the ongoing enterprise. On the other hand, administrative effectiveness requires that decision-making be rich in conceptual capital and thus reflect progress made toward discovering optimal solutions. Charles Lindblom describes rational and workable decision-making strategies (he contrasts the "root" method with the "branch" method) in "The Science of Muddling Through," *Public Administration Review* 19 (1959):79–88.
10. Alan J. Rowe, "The Myth of the Rational Decision Maker," *International Management* 19, no. 4 (August 1974):38–40.

11. Chris Argyris and David Schön, *Theory in Practice: Increasing Professional Effectiveness* (San Francisco: Jossey-Bass Publishers, 1974), pp. 6–7.
12. Robert L. Katz, "Skills of an Effective Administrator," *Harvard Business Review* 33, no. 1 (1955):33–42.
13. Ibid., p. 42.
14. Theodore Leavitt, "The Management Merry-Go Round," *Harvard Business Review* 52, no. 4 (July–August 1974):121.

Chapter 2
Applied Science and the
Role of Value Judgments

Educators in general and school executives in particular perceive the role of values[1] in the educational enterprise as being of utmost importance. Harry Broudy summarizes this importance of values to education and administration as follows:

> The educator, however, deals with nothing but values—human beings who are clusters and constellations of value potentials. Nothing human is really alien to the educational enterprise and there is, therefore, something incongruous about educational administrators evading fundamental value conflicts. . . . The public will never quite permit the educational administrator the moral latitude that it affords some of its servants. For to statesmen and soldiers men entrust their lives and fortunes, but to the schools they entrust their precarious hold on humanity itself.[2]

In this chapter we explore the role of value judgments in relation to school administration and describe a number of frameworks for examining values. A useful value hierarchy for school administration is then proposed.

A PHILOSOPHY FOR SCHOOL EXECUTIVES

Harlan Cleveland has proposed that the public administrator can be differentiated from other administrators by three kinds of attitudes:

> His understanding of the web of tension of which he is a part.
> His consciousness of a responsibility to the public interest.
> His unwarranted optimism about the future.[3]

School executives, who comprise the largest single class of public administrators, do work in an environment characterized by a great deal of tension, requiring for success clear commitment to the public interest and an attitude of optimism for the future. Following Cleveland's analysis, therefore, we examine each of these attitudes as they relate to the school executive and his world of work.

Administration and the Web of Tension

With the enormous expansion of knowledge in education and in the content of the school curriculum, the emergence of specialization in the education professions, the trend toward differentiated and team teaching, the trend toward pluralistic power bases in controlling educational policy making, and the increased reliance on participatory administration, school executives often find themselves acting as brokers as they negotiate one group against another in attempting to utilize the best of each in order to approach school goals. Negotiated administration is not unique to the school's internal system. With the increased activity of formal and informal community power groups and with stronger governmental and organizational pressures, negotiated administration is also gaining prominence as the school relates and interacts with its complex external environment. It is too simple, however, to assume that students, teachers, and others can be charted, sorted, and understood as a means of regulating their behavior. This approach might be successful if one could control the variables of time and action. What is not readily chartable is the system of interaction of people with each other, groups with each other, factions and coalitions with each other. Once people are set in motion (time and action introduced), they form a complex system which is at the heart of the web of tension which surrounds the school executive's job.

Early movements in school administration sought to deny expression of this web of tension and its accompanying conflict. Paternalistic administration, based on human relations and happy-family-but-father-knows-best principles, was the popular school administration model. Conflict, dialogue, and disagreement were regarded as disrupters of the human relations approach and were not to be tolerated. Paternalistic administration continues to appeal to many school executives because it permits them to operate *superficially* in a manner consistent with the humanistic purposes of the school, while providing them with control over people, processes, and policy.

The new school executive recognizes the inadequacies of the human relations approach and favors an adequate degree of tension and disagreement as a stimulus to individual and organizational creativity. Administrative effectiveness in complex, growing, dynamic institutions actually requires that school executives manage tension rather than strive only for cooperation. The focus of administration is coordination rather than cooperation. Indeed, the two are not the same, for excessive cooperation leaves little to coordinate. Cleveland describes this difference by suggesting that "the muscles of an organization are like the muscles of a drunk: if they are too relaxed, he doesn't achieve much coordination."[4]

Tension should be considered as a stimulus to creativity but with calculated caution. An excess of tension in the school as an organizational system, like an excess of penicillin in the human system, can have damaging effects. Yet the absence of tension produces a stagnation which is equally damaging in the long run.

More critical than recognizing the tolerance limits for the absorption of tension by the school is recognizing the proper content of the tension itself. Disagreement, dialogue, controversy, negotiations, and the like should be as free from emotional content as possible. Teachers, parents, students, groups, agencies—and school executives as well—should be able to represent and present their views critically but constructively, vigorously but with personal impunity. The focus should not be on winning or losing in a personal sense but on the viability of one alternative over another—with the commitment of all participants to the improvement of education assumed. A healthy web of tension is one which is task and problem centered, rather than people and feeling centered.

THE PUBLIC INTEREST

School executives are first and foremost guardians of the public interest. "The public interest" is, however, a very broad term encompassing the needs of youth, of each student one at a time, of society, of the community, and of the profession. The problem of deciding what is in the public interest is even more complex when one considers it with respect to time. It is necessary to consider what is in the public interest at the moment, over a span of years, of decades, and of generations. Deciding what is in the public interest is, in the final analysis, a decision which the school executive must make based upon an identifiable value system.

Fortunately, school executives need not tackle the task of determining the nature of the public interest alone. Governmental agencies, professional organizations, university scholars, philosophers, and fellow executives are engaged in continuous debate and study as they seek to identify and operationalize short-term and long-term public interest. Since the public interest issue is of such great importance, school executives also supplement expert sources of information by continually seeking advice from citizen committees, teacher and student groups, and other relevant sources. But in the final analysis, efforts to determine the public interest and translate it into school goals are shaped by value preferences.

Optimism About the Future

The education professions have set formidable tasks for themselves and often work against incredible odds. Experts from both within and outside education are quick to suggest that many of the aspirations, plans, strategies, and programs of the schools are likely to fail and that the technology of education is too weak for the problems to be solved.

As educational problems increase, school executives find themselves more removed from the technology of the education professions. Teachers, specialists, consultants, and other educational workers have developed ability monopolies over various segments of the educational enterprise. These monopolies are characterized by sophistication and complexity, but the focus of the modern educator is narrowed considerably by his or her specialization. The multitude of directors, coordinators, assistant principals, deans, associates, deputies, and other middle managers both at the school and central office levels—all specialists of one kind or another—are evidences of the increased complexity of "keeping" school. As this complexity increases, school executives are becoming more dependent upon middle- and lower-level administrators as they seek and require technical advice and information. Moreover, since the training of specialists encourages them to be careful, calculated, and cautious, their advice tends to be somewhat pessimistic. As the administrator works to coordinate and integrate the competencies of many specialists, he needs to exude a counterbalancing sense of confidence and optimism. It is this optimism about the future which we believe gives direction and stimulus to the development of meaningful educational programs which serve the public interest.

In commenting on optimism, March identifies three key elements which he considers the essence of education.

> First a failth in learning. A belief in the beauty and grace of knowledge, trained intelligence, and scholarly competence. We seek educated educators, not primarily in order to have them know something that can be transmitted to their students, but to assure us that they share a fundamental personal faith in learning. We have a library, not primarily because it is needed or used, but because books are a symbol of our faith.
>
> Second, a commitment to adulthood. Some might prefer to emphasize a love of children; but I think that is less essential. Education is a recognition that childhood is a precursor to adulthood, that children are tourists in adolescence. We declare that being an adult is different from being a child, that educators are adults, and children should develop beyond childish things and childish beliefs.
>
> Third, a fundamental spirit of optimism. Enthusiasm for life and pleasure in its manifest ambiguity. Education presumes not so much an outcome of success as a process of personal dedication and excitement. The injustice, pessimism, and cruelty of existence belong in the curriculum; but education is deeply optimistic. It proclaims a human will.[5]

Though March comments that the elements—faith in learning, commitment to adulthood, and fundamental optimism—are neither mysterious nor profound, they remain appealing as signs of faith for the profession of educational administration.

VALUE-ORDERING AND EDUCATIONAL DECISION-MAKING

Educational decision-making requires choices among viable alternatives. Selecting one from a number of alternatives involves the ordering of preferences based on a hierarchy of values, or "value-ordering." Many school executives are able to make explicit the value system under which they work. Others rely on implicit but nevertheless potent evaluative criteria. In this section we present a number of value frameworks which may be used by school executives, teachers, parents, student interest groups, and others concerned with schools. One useful classification, proposed by Dwayne Huebner,[6] classifies value systems according to the kind of educational purposes and means with which they are associated. He labels these as technical, political, scientific, aesthetic, and ethical value systems. Each of these value systems is then explored as possible sources of identity for school executives and as stimuli to value-ordering for educational decision-making.

Technical

The technical value system is particularly familiar to school executives, for it utilizes a means-ends approach in the form of an economic model. Following this model, end results are specified rather clearly, and activities and programs are rationally and economically designed to achieve them; education is valued in forms of measurable outputs of the system; and school executives work to achieve productive goals in the most efficient manner. As the school executive speaks of the need for individuals to read, write, compute, think in specific ways, and make a living in order to exist productively in society, so he or she works to regulate organizations, materials, and people to work, think, and act in certain ways in order for all to exist productively in the school.[7] Technical valuing and economic rationality are important inputs to educational decision-making, for school executives are required to meet community expectations for productivity and efficiency. That technical values may take precedence over values more central to the educational process, however, remains a haunting danger.

Political

The political value system relates to possession of control and influence, and includes prestige, rank, and social position as means used to achieve this control and influence. In suggesting the importance of this value, Huebner describes administrative behavior as follows: "He [the school executive] influences others directly or through the manipulation of resources. To remain in a position of effective power, he must seek the support of those in positions to reward him or influence his behavior in some way. His work, his teaching of educational leadership, becomes the vehicle by which people judge the worth of his influence and hence decide whether he is worthy of their support, respect, or positive sanction."[8]

The political value system is often accompanied by negative impressions. Yet power is a relatively neutral phenomenon which can be used for both good and bad. All educational workers need a certain amount of power if they wish to influence educational decision-making and have reasonable control over their work environment. Political valuing is therefore a necessity for school executives if they are to assume responsibility, exert influence, and develop action on behalf of school goals; but the danger of power being valued as an end in itself and of becoming centralized in the hands of a few cannot be overlooked.

Scientific

The scientific value system is perhaps more often found among specialists in teaching and administrative roles rather than among generalists. As school administration emerges as a profession in its own right,[9] however, the scientific value system is gaining more acceptance. Educators strong in this value orientation may be quite experimental in their views as they engage in action research and express interest in developing innovative approaches to organizing schools and teaching students. The focus of such activity is on gaining better knowledge about the educational or administrative process.

Scientific valuing is an essential input to school decision-making, for as new knowledge is discovered and new ideas are examined, the school increases its capability to respond to its environment. An overemphasis on scientific valuing, however, may result in the school's assuming a laboratory posture rather than a student-centered posture; that is, professional staff may center activities, efforts, and rewards on expanding the knowledge base of the education profession rather than on the development of students. It is true that scientific valuing needs to be placed in proper perspective, but it is unfortunate nevertheless that most schools tend to overlook this value completely.

Aesthetic

If school executives as a group largely overlook the scientific value system, they virtually ignore the aesthetic one. Our society tends publicly to appreciate technical and scientific valuing, and privately to respect—perhaps even prize—political values. Aesthetic valuing refers to beauty, wholeness of design, symbolic meaning, contentment, and peace, which are available simply as a result of engaging in educational activity for its own sake.

Schools are concerned almost exclusively with culturally defined meanings, technical valuing, and economic rationality. Youngsters are typically engaged in activities and experiences which are defined by the school as it interprets its obligation in meeting societal expectations. Emphasis is given to preparing people for something—to reaching predetermined goals such as getting a job, going to college, developing a sense of loyalty to country, and developing an awareness of one's obligation to society. In order to accomplish these ends, the value of most learning activities is decided by someone other than the learner—such as the teacher, curriculum expert, text writer, or administrator. However, although all of these culturally defined meanings are important, they cannot be exclusive if we hope to develop the basic human potential of students and to provide them with intellectual enrichment. Aesthetic valuing requires that personal meanings in learning be legitimized and encouraged. To enrich personal meanings, one must enter a learning encounter on a more equal footing and in a more dynamic relationship. Indeed, what one gets out of a learning encounter with respect to personal meanings is as valuable as that which the teacher hoped to achieve in terms of culturally defined meanings. Thus the value of any experience, school or otherwise, is ultimately understood in the richness which it brings to the person. Meaning in one's life is the result of engaging in activities best justified in terms of intrinsic satisfaction and personal enrichment rather than merely the traffic such activities bear in an extrinsic sense.

Ethical

The ethical value system deals with assumptions about the nature of man and standards concerning one's relationship with his or her fellowman. Ethical values are particularly important to school executives, for they are human values—and the school is basically a human organization.

Educational activity is seldom valued according to only one of the value systems we have listed. Typically, effective school executives utilize all five as they consider alternatives and preferences. Indeed, much administrative effort is expended in ordering these value systems in a hierarchy for all who are involved in or affected by educational decision-making.

School executives often view the value hierarchy in a more simple classification than Huebner's by grouping school goals into four categories. The first of these categories is concerned with providing for the needs of the school itself. The second category is concerned with community perceptions of needs which become expectations for the school. Categories three and four concern themselves with the needs of society and those of the individual. School executives have been inclined primarily to evaluate educational decision-making in terms of its meaning to the school as an organization and to the community which the school serves (categories one and two). Societal and individual needs (categories three and four) are given attention only if such attention does not contradict what is considered important to maintain the school as an organization and to meet community expectations. There are, however, many indications of shifts in this value hierarchy, with individual and society receiving precedence over community and school.

CHANGING VALUES AND EDUCATIONAL ADMINISTRATION

This discussion assumes that there exists in America a dominant value system with which most individuals identify. Beyond this dominant value system there exists a number of other values which in reality portray our actions and our behavior. The dominant values in American culture—democracy, individualism, equality, and human perfectibility or optimism—are referred to by Getzels[10] as "sacred" values and as such are generally considered to be unchangeable. Indeed, some argued that the sacred values are unachievable as well but, achievable or not, they represent the hopes and desires of most Americans.

The other values, referred to by Getzels as "secular" values, include the work-success ethic, future-time orientation, independence or autonomous self, and Puritan morality. In Getzels's view: "The sacred creed has remained relatively stable, and democracy, individualism, equality, and human perfectibility as ideas are as attractive now as they were 150 years ago. But the traditional operating or secular values—work-success ethic, future-time orientation, independence, and Puritan morality—have undergone, and are undergoing, crucial transformation and cleavage in our culture and our social structure."[11]

Spindler[12] describes the shift in American values as a change from traditional to emergent value orientation. He argues that the work-success ethic seems to be losing ground to a noncompetitive human relations syndrome. Further, the future-time orientation characterized by self-denial, postponement of reward, and planned future is giving way to a hedonistic immediate gratification, present-time orientation. Spindler also suggests that the traditional value of the independent-autonomous self is shifting to group conscious-conforming orientation and that Puritan morality is being replaced by consensus morality.

Spindler suggests that school boards are likely to be more traditional than the public they serve, the public more traditional than the administrative staff, school executives more traditional than older teachers, with younger teachers and students dominating the emergent end of the value continuum. (School executives in our classes place themselves further on the emergent end of the continuum than most teachers. Indeed, they contend that teacher conservatism is a problem. Interestingly, teachers often make a similar charge with respect to school executives.) By and large, the school seems to be urging its students to work hard because hard work is both worthwhile and profitable while the society at large—or at least the younger portion of it—asks why. Moreover, if current value trends continue, the emergent value orientation will soon dominate American society.

Patterns of sacred-secular values which characterize the unique cultural web for a particular community or community type (rural-farm, black-ghetto, Italian-ethnic, wealthy-suburb, bible-belt, etc.) influence greatly the boundaries of discretion afforded to school executives and define the normal ground rules for operating the schools. Peshkin's study of decision-making in Mansfield, a "typical" small rural community in the Midwest, vividly illustrates this effect.

> At the time my study began, Tate had been at Mansfield High School for twenty-one years, five as coach and industrial arts teacher and sixteen as superintendent. Though not of local origin, nor in fact of rural background, he was most comfortable with country life. He had been content to confine his career to Mansfield despite job offers from larger school systems. In their turn, Mansfielders and the school board were very pleased with him; he became a person of consequence in community life and an accepted agent of community values in his capacity as educational leader. The school board, guardians of the community, trusted him on matters of fact and judgment, secure in the knowledge that he served their interests.
>
> The seven-member board was presided over by a Mansfield-born farmer. Five of the other six members also were native Mansfielders and farmers, notwithstanding that most school district residents work in factories and live in town. In fact, over the twenty years this school board has existed, the president has always been a farmer and at least five of seven members have been Mansfield-born farmers. Because school board elections generally inspire a good turnout—about two hundred of a possible seven hundred eligible voters—the "right" candidates continue to get elected. (The right candidates are those without the kind of "axe to grind" that might disturb the status quo.) The credentials of the newest board member were his status as a native and the well-known fact that he loved Mansfield and had a deep regard for its traditions. He replaced a man of demonstrated skill, a six-year veteran on the board who had lived in Mansfield only ten years.
>
> One year after my study began, Superintendent Tate died. This misfortune required the school board to undertake a task they had long dreaded—selecting a new superintendent. They assembled in special session one hot August week to interview five candidates. Afterward, as they sat together to make a choice, their desiderata emerged.

"Should we talk about Hagedorn to see why we don't want him?"

"Yes, let's get the feeling of the board on him. I believe we have better men. Not quality-wise, though. He could handle the job and the P. R. [Public Relations]. I don't think he's the type we're looking for."

"I hate to say it, but his physical appearance is against him. You need to call a spade a spade."

"He's not stable like some of the others."

"I'm afraid he'd be the butt of behind-the-back jokes."

"He's carrying far too much weight. That's a strain on the heart."

"He was tired. A man that size gets physically tired. We shouldn't kid ourselves. Image is very important. That size is against him."

"The next one is Dargan."

"I was impressed, but I feel he is too big for our town and school. His ideas are for the city, for bigger schools. We're not ready for all that."

"I felt he would probably be anxious to start a lot of things I don't know if we're ready for. He's definitely for a nongraded system. He said he'd start slow but he wanted it pretty bad. Knocking down walls scares you just a bit."

"I was impressed. But then we had more fellows in. We learned more about this nongraded idea. He would be a pusher, I'm sure."

"He had too many ideas to start off with. You need to see what a school has before jumping in."

"I thought he might be a little slow with discipline problems."

"I saw dollar signs clicking around in my head when he talked. He may be too intelligent for this community. He may talk over the heads of the community.

"Another thing. He was emphatic about four weeks vacation."

"Salary-wise he asked for the most."

"Well, this Dargan, he said he wanted to come to a small community. I think he may want to bring too many ideas from the city with him. He may be more than we want."

"What did you like about Morgan? These next three are a hard pick."

"He gave a nice impression here, I believe, of getting along with the public and the kids. This impressed me more than anything."

"To me he talked generalities."

"He had a tremendous speaking voice. He's young."

"His voice got very nasal at the end when he got relaxed."

"He wouldn't stay."

"He's on his way up."

"I believe he'd be a forceful individual."

"Take this other man, Rogers, I had a feeling about him. He said, 'If you hired me and I accepted it . . .' I don't think he's too anxious for the job."

"I can see why he was offered a job selling real estate. He's got the voice. He'd have your name on the line. I'm inclined to believe he'd talk himself out of most situations. Getting down to brass tacks, he spoke in generalities. He admitted he didn't know too much about new things in education. We need more specific answers."

"More or less this leaves us with Reynolds."

"He's the man to put on top."

"I'd hate to pick any one of the top three over the others."

"Both Reynolds and Rogers said that they have no hours. They work by the job. Reynolds worked his way through college."

"He was on ground floor as far as salary goes."

"And he's country."

After rejecting candidates for adverse physical appearance and for holding city and big-school ideas, they selected Reynolds, who worked hard like a farmer, would settle for a "reasonable" salary, and was "country"—a designation that had never before been mentioned as a criterion for selecting their new superintendent, or anything else, for that matter. Perhaps it should have been self-evident that no one could be chosen superintendent of schools in Mansfield who did not appear "country," the board's shorthand description of a suitable candidate for their rural-dominated, traditionally oriented school district.[13]

Schools have not given serious attention to value instruction, the role of values, and value changes except as these relate to the sacred or dominant values of democracy, individualism, equality, and human perfectibility or optimism. The changing secular values are virtually ignored as inputs to educational decision-making and as formal components of the school's educational program. This is further complicated by a growing gap between what the schools purport to teach concerning values and how the school and its agents behave. Whereas school executives and other professional personnel focus on the former, students focus on the latter. As Getzels has said: "School personnel become significant figures for the child; they become primary objects of identification. And where values are concerned, it is not so much what people say the child should do as the kinds of models the significant figures provide that matters. One cannot so much teach values as offer proper models for identification."[14]

Administrative effectiveness for school executives depends upon the continuous examination of internalized value assumptions. This examination should include comparing and testing value structures for goodness of fit or for overlap with those held by other educational workers, students, and the society at large. School executives, however, too often avoid value confrontation as they apply the principle of "least principle." Broudy[15] describes this principle as the tendency for school executives to deal with value conflict at the lowest level of abstraction possible. Value conflict, for example, is treated at the interpersonal level and on a one-to-one basis rather than at the organizational level. The major value problems facing school executives, however, are at the organizational cultures. (A number of these—professional versus bureau-cratic, cosmopolitan versus local, the management system versus the technical system, and the student subculture versus the school establishment—are discussed later in this chapter and in sub-sequent chapters.)

As school executives examine the traditional-versus-emergent shift in the secular value structure of American society, they should avoid abandoning all of one to adopt all of the other. For instance, although the emergent value orientation (interest in aesthetic and ethical values, for example) has much to offer, much would be lost by abandoning many of the features of the work-success ethic, a traditional value. This ethic is a powerful motivator of performance and is self-renewing in that satisfaction derived is primarily intrin-sic. Perhaps school executives need to encourage evaluation of the entire value continuum in the hope that features which hold the greatest promise may be identified. Another important goal for school executives is putting into operation the sacred values of democracy, individualism, equality, and human perfectibility in an attempt to bring closer aspiration and reality for Americans.

Bureaucratic Versus Professional Values

Teaching and the school are becoming at the same time more bureaucratic and more professional. Particularly in the past decade dual bureaucratic and professional cultures have been evolving in teaching. As administering the financial, building, and mainte-nance functions of school operation have become more complex, responsibility and decision-making have become increasingly cen-tralized and specialized. Central office staffs have increased mark-edly, as have office personnel and these in turn have caused a proliferation of paper work. Computers are being used more fre-quently as a means to standardize, regulate, and program decision-making. All of these developments are symptoms of an expanding bureaucracy.

Parallel changes in complexity and sophistication have also occurred in the nature, scope, and breadth of education programs and in instructional learning systems. This expansion of knowledge in teaching, content, and instructional technology is combined with a renewed and vigorous sense of responsibility for student welfare. A drive for status for teachers and an interest in upgrading teaching are related phenomena. All of these are symptoms of profes-sionalism. Often they are expressed militantly as teachers seek to increase control over their work and seek to increase power in co-opting more responsibility and more authority.

Table 2-1 POINTS OF CONFLICT BETWEEN BUREAUCRATIC AND PROFESSIONAL VALUES

BUREAUCRATIC EXPECTATIONS	PROFESSIONAL EXPECTATIONS
1. Stress on uniformity of students' problems and needs: standardized inputs	1. Stress on uniqueness of students' problems and needs: variable inputs
2. Stress on rules and regulations: programmed decision-making	2. Stress on research and change: problem-centered decision-making
3. Universal application of rules: fairness	3. Particularistic application of rules: fairness
4. Stress on efficient accomplishment of operational tasks	4. Stress on achievement of goals
5. Skill based on practice: experience differentials in status and rank	5. Skill based on knowledge: merit differentials in status and rank
6. Decisions focus on application of rules to routine problems	6. Decision focus on application of policy and knowledge to unique problems
7. Hierarchically legal authority	7. Ability-professional authority
8. Loyalty to the school, its administration, and trustees	8. Loyalty to the profession and students

SOURCE: This table is adapted from Ronald Corwin, "Professional Persons in Public Organizations," *Educational Administration Quarterly* (1965): 1–22.

As teachers intensify, formalize, and consolidate their interest and authority in matters which relate to the instructional system of the school, they in turn move further away from the management system of the school. Indeed, concern with the management system seems limited to occasions when bureaucratic or managerial requirements intersect or interfere with the instructional learning system. Traditionally teachers have seemed completely submissive to the management system, but today they are selectively submissive. Rules and regulations, for example, which increase the teachers' influence over students are gladly accepted, but those which increase the school executives' influence over the teachers' relationships with students are not. Teachers may seek bureaucratic interference which insulates them from hostile parents, but resist bureaucratic interference which insulates them from decision-making regarding educational programs, professional standards, or instructional implementation. In Table 2-1 points of conflict between bureaucratic and professional values are examined.

Points of conflict include all aspects of organizational activity from sources of authority, through methods of organizing, to modes of operation. Since we treat sociological and psychological dimensions and effects of bureaucratic-professional conflict more specifically in Part II, "The Human System," it seems sufficient to mention here that these different value systems generate conflict requiring the attention and understanding of school executives.

The role of the school executive in dealing with conflict of this kind seems relatively clear. He or she faces no problems with the two value systems as they coexist as long as the bureaucratic (or management) and the instructional learning systems do not intersect. At points of intersection, he or she assumes a broker's role, negotiating between advocates of the two systems in the hope of moving the school closer to its professional goal of offering better service to the student and society and to its bureaucratic goal of maintaining and strengthening itself as an organization.

(This analysis is simplified by our assuming that school executives identify with bureaucratic aspects of the school, and teachers with professional aspects. The pattern in reality of course is mixed, with administrators more likely to express bureaucratic values, and teachers professional values.)

ORGANIZATIONAL VALUES

To this point values as they apply to society as a whole, to groups within society, and to individuals have been discussed. Organizations also have value systems. These are composites of values and beliefs which individuals both bring to the organization and attribute to the organization by virtue of its role, reputation, or tradition. In this section the individual's relationship to collective values expressed by the school are examined.

Collective values fall into two general categories: those which form the hard value core for the school and those which form the boundary of a "freedom zone" of values for the school. The core values are accepted by all but the most deviant members of the school's society. The values which define the school's freedom zone boundary, on the other hand, are subscribed to by most members of the school's society, but the level of commitment varies for individuals, cliques, or groups within the society.

In situations where there is considerable overlap between an individual's value system and the value system held by the school, conflict is low. In situations where there is little overlap, value conflict is high. An individual may continue to enjoy effective school membership so long as there is sufficient overlap between his or her values and those of the school. If the degree of overlap, for example, does not include all or most of the sacred or core values of the group, the individual is physically or psychologically dismissed from the group comprising the school membership. The less overlap between individual and collective values, the less effective the individual will be in normatively influencing the school, its goals, and its behavior manifestation—and, conversely, the less effective the school will be in influencing the individual.

One important component of administrative effectiveness for school executives is the liberation and expansion of the zone of freedom so that the collective value system of the school is able to accommodate an assortment of individual belief systems. This expansion is particularly necessary, since many of the values which new teachers bring to the schools and with which students seem to identify vary from those usually attributed to the school.

New Breed of Teacher

The declining employment market for teachers in many areas notwithstanding, teaching as an occupation remains attractive to young people choosing careers. This popularity is due in part to changes in the conditions of work and in pay scales which make education jobs more attractive and in part to increases in the quantity and quality of preparation for entry to the education professions. Another major contributor to the popularity of the education professions as a career choice is the changing value system emerging from the culture of the young. Central to this shift in values, at least as far as occupational choice is concerned, is an interest in a career with meaning, one which provides an opportunity for self-enrichment and for societal improvement. Given a choice between a career offering more extrinsic potential for satisfaction or one offering more intrinsic potential, recent evidence indicates that more young people will choose the intrinsically satisfying career.[16]

But choices of occupations in general are becoming more restrictive in today's job market, and in recent years person-power needs in the education profession have undergone severe reduction. We are now in a period of entrenchment in education, of teacher surplus in many areas, of declining enrollments, and of fiscal conservatism. Some letup of this pressure can be expected in the decade of the eighties, but the effects on teacher temperament will likely remain for some time.

Two trends seem clear as one examines the new breed of teacher and the supply pool of students from which he or she comes. One trend suggests that the new teacher is and will continue to be more assertive, more aggressive, more abrasive, and more autonomous while being less respectful of authority, less conforming, and less malleable. This trend is causing and will continue to cause considerable difficulty for school executives unless present assumptions about administration, control, and organization change.

The second trend suggests that despite the fact that teachers are becoming increasingly "less manageable," they will be more interested in school development, in school learning, in growing professionally, in serving society, and in developing student self-actualization. That commitment to educational purposes and to the educational profession seems to be increasing among teachers, particularly newcomers, at the same time that teachers appear less manageable, seems contradictory on the one hand but complementary on the other. Whether the trends are actually contradictory or complementary in a given case depends upon what constitutes the focus for administrative behavior. If school executives view control over people and their activities as necessary in order to regulate and obtain conformity to schools' goals, the trends are contradictory and the future holds promise of continued and accelerated conflict and unrest for school administration. The trends are complementary in those situations where the focus of administrative behavior is viewed as control over the achievement of school goals and the maintenance and development of an organizational environment which encourages, stimulates, and motivates human talent.

It may be helpful to supplement our discussion of hopes and aspirations of college students and young teachers by examining similar feelings expressed by high school students. The conclusions of a *Life* poll taken in the late sixties by Louis Harris[17]—comparing perceptions and opinions of teachers, parents, and high school students about their high schools—reveal that:

1. More than one-half of the students who comprise the high school generation are impatient with the limited participation available to them in running educational affairs. Parents are in much less sympathy with this view than teachers.
2. Teachers are our best bet for helping the school keep abreast of the times and for promoting understanding between the generations.
3. More students than teachers feel that education today is valuable and stimulating—teachers are not complacent.
4. Students and teachers seem more satisfied with each other than with the way the school is run as an organization. Both groups seek and want more participation and involvement.[18]

Though generally teachers seem more in tune with student values and perspectives than parents, this suggestion should not

mask the fact that different subculture and competing value systems exist within the school. Willower notes that, "As organizations, schools are characterized by unselected and perhaps unwill-
ing clients, high population density, an exceptional stimulus
overload especially in the case of teachers, a host of logistical
problems, vague and diverse goals, ambiguous criteria of success,
lack of a widely accepted work technology, and a tangible degree of
political vulnerability.

This setting spawns adult and student subcultures which
coexist in a state of uneasy, sometimes inimical confrontation.
These collectivities tend to be distinguished by quite different
normative structures. The teacher subculture is marked by an
emphasis on pupil control and the maintenance of social distance
between teachers and their clients while the student subculture
typically is committed to its own world and its own set of values,
often in stark contrast to what adults think best. Hence the student
group has evolved methods to cope with and, if possible, gull the
system. Predictably, each side performs in ways that preserve and
enhance its status and autonomy relative to the other."[19]

Administrative and educational problems associated with shifting values are enormous and need continuous study. Yet such
problems, although perhaps more serious today than ever before,
are hardly new. Consider this statement issued well over 30 years
ago by the American Council of Education:

> Since Adam, there have been but two generations—the young and the
> old. And one of the most ancient and venerable human pastimes is the
> business of one of these generations looking with a quizzical and none
> too sympathetic eye upon the activities and the philosophies of the
> other ... while some adult spectators are inclined to see our youth
> going hell-bent to perdition, other observers will see them as develop-
> ing into a freer, stronger, more intelligent, and self-reliant generation
> than has ever appeared upon the stage of human affairs.[20]

This astute observation is remarkably contemporary.

In summary, education is a human activity characterized by
human goals held for human clients and pursued by a human
organization. The humanness of education, however, makes it a
public activity subject to pressures and opinions from a number of
sources. In this chapter we have examined the role of value
judgments and the relationship of those value judgments to an
applied science of administration. In this effort we examined or
proposed (1) a philosophy for school executives; (2) a taxonomy of
values for evaluating educational decision-making; (3) the broker-
age role for school executives; (4) organizational values and their
relationship to individual values; and (5) some characteristics of the

belief system of the new breed of teacher. Our purpose in the next chapter is to map out more specifically the field of educational administration as an applied science.

Notes

1. The term "value" is defined as proposed by Clyde Kluckhohn: "A value is a conception, explicit or implicit, distinctive of an individual or characteristic of a group, of the desirable which influences the selection from available modes, means, and ends of action." See Kluckhohn et al., "Values and Value—Orientations in the Theory of Actions," in *Toward a General Theory of Action,* Talcott Parsons and E. Shils, eds. (Cambridge, Mass.: Harvard University Press, 1952), p. 295.
2. Harry S. Broudy, "Conflicts in Values," in *Educational Administration–Philosophy in Action,* Robert Ohm and William Monohan, eds. (Norman: University of Oklahoma, College of Education, 1965), p. 52.
3. Harlan Cleveland, "A Philosophy for the Public Executive," in *Perspectives on Public Management Cases and Learning Designs,* Robert T. Golembiewski, ed. (Itasca, Ill.: F. E. Peacock, Inc., 1970), pp. 12–33. Although Cleveland addresses himself to executives in government, his comments have relevance to school administration. In the following sections we apply his attitude formulation to the work of school executives.
4. Ibid., p. 16.
5. James March, "Education and the Pursuit of Optimism." Invited address Commemorating the Fiftieth Anniversary of Texas Tech University, Lubbock, Tex., October 18, 1974. Published in *Texas Tech Journal of Education* 2, no. 1 (1975):16.
6. Dwayne Huebner, "Curriculum Language and Classroom Meanings," in *Language and Meaning,* James B. MacDonald and Robert R. Leeper, eds. (Washington, D.C.: Association for Supervision and Curriculum Development, 1966), p. 14.
7. Ibid., p. 15.
8. Ibid.
9. It seems to us to be more useful and indeed more realistic to view school administration—like teaching, counseling, and so on—as one of many interdependent occupations comprising the education professions.
10. Jacob W. Getzels, "Changing Values Challenge the Schools," *The School Review* 65, no. 1 (1957):92–102.
11. Ibid., p. 98.
12. George Spindler, "Education in a Transforming American Culture," *Harvard Educational Review* 25 (1955):145–56.
13. Alan Peshkin, "Whom Shall the Schools Serve? Some Dilemmas of Local Control in a Rural School District," *Curriculum Inquiry* 6, no. 3 (1977):187–89.

14. Getzels, "Changing Values Challenge the Schools," p. 100.
15. Broudy, "Conflicts in Values," p. 50.
16. See, for example: "What They Believe: A Fortune Survey," *Fortune* 79, no. 1 (January 1969):181; Jeffrey Hadden and Victor Thressen, "CRM Poll: Anything for a Buck? Forget It Baby," *Careers Today* 1, no. 2 (February 1969):14; "Reinforcements to Reform, a Special Report on Youth," *Fortune* 79, no. 7 (June 1969):73–74; and Bruce J. Biddle, J. Paschal Twyman, and Earl F. Rankin, Jr., "The Role of the Teacher and Occupational Choice," *The School Review* 70 (1962): 191–206.
17. "What People Think About Their High Schools," *Life* 66, no. 19 (May 1969): 29.
18. Perceptions of parents as compared with teachers suggest important differences in value orientation. (These are summarized from the *Life* poll by Louis Harris cited previously. The percentages of responses favoring the item for each group are given.) School should function to maintain discipline as opposed to promoting self-inquiry (parents, 62 percent; teachers, 27 percent); consider homework memorization good and useful (parents, 70 percent; teachers, 46 percent); feel that students are justified in perceiving school as drudgery (parents, 32 percent; teachers, 54 percent); open the school to outside speakers and lecturers (parents, 46 percent; teachers, 74 percent); expand the school curriculum and instructional program to include more field work and community activity (parents, 48 percent; teachers, 77 percent). With regard to unruly students, the Harris poll indicates that parents are more apt to recommend cracking down rather than understanding causes. Teachers are less likely to recommend cracking down preferring to emphasize understanding and treating the causes of unruly behavior. School administrators are more understanding than both teachers and parents.
19. Donald Willower, "Schools, Values and Educational Inquiry," Paper presented at the Ontario Institute for Studies in Education, June 1972.
20. *Youth Tell Their Story* (Washington, D.C.: American Council on Education. 1938), p. 4.

Chapter 3
A Belief Pattern for
Decision-Making

Perceptions play a major role in determining how one behaves. What kinds of assumptions do school executives typically hold for people, education, administration, and organization? How do these assumptions influence administrative activity and school effectiveness? These questions are examined as we build and explore suitable value criteria for evaluating scientific and intuitive knowledge about administration—the basis for an applied science of educational administration.

In this effort a value direction which shows the interdependent relationship between instrumental and substantive goals for schools is proposed and a set of management assumptions is offered as a basis for developing a humanly oriented applied science of educational administration.

GOALS AND OBJECTIVES

Over the years hundreds of commissions and committees at every level of the educational enterprise have debated, clarified, and articulated the goals and objectives of American education.[1]

The basis for modern programs of education, for example, can be traced to statements by the Commission on the Reorganization of Secondary Education, which was appointed by the National Education Association in 1914. The following statements from this commission seem comfortably contemporary:

> The purpose of democracy is to so organize society that each member may develop his personality primarily through activities designed for the well-being of his fellow members and of society as a whole.

> Education in a democracy, both within and without the school, should develop in each individual the knowledge, interests, ideals, habits, and powers whereby he will find his place and use that place to shape both himself and society toward even nobler ends.[2]

The main objectives of education, according to this commission, are health, command of fundamental processes, worthy home membership, vocation, citizenship, worthy use of leisure time, and ethical character. In concluding, the commission states: "The doctrine that each individual has a right to the opportunity to develop the best that is in him is reinforced by the belief in the potential, and perchance unique, worth of the individual. The task of education, as of life, is, therefore, to call forth that potential worth."[3]

Twenty years later the Educational Policies Commission of the National Education Association and the American Association of School Administrators, in a document entitled "The Purposes of Education in American Democracy," concluded that education should be concerned with (1) maximum development of the learner and, therefore, the schools should pursue goals of *self-realization;* (2) home, family, and community life and, therefore, schools should pursue goals of *human relations;* (3) economic demands and, therefore, the schools should pursue goals of *economic efficiency;* and (4) civic and social duties and, therefore, the schools should pursue goals of *civic responsibility.*[4]

Nearly three decades later the Commission of Imperatives in Education of the American Association of School Administrators, after two years of study, identified nine imperatives:

> To serve this generation of youth, to make every youngster know that he is really important and has a job to do, to make reason supreme and dominant over coercive force in every walk of life and to develop in everyone whom the school reaches and serves the understanding and the power needed to keep the economy productive and to keep democracy working in the years ahead as well as better than it has worked in the past, it is imperative:
> To make urban life rewarding and satisfying

To prepare people for the world of work.
To discover and nurture creative talent.
To strenthen the moral fabric of society.
To deal constructively with psychological tensions.
To keep democracy working.
To make intelligent use of natural resources.
To make the best use of leisure time.
To work with other peoples of the world for human betterment.[5]

Two observations can be made here about goals. First, for the most part goals can be separated into two categories—those which are explicit and those which are implicit. Explicit goals are formally stated and pursued. Implicit goals are often not stated at all and are informally pursued. Generally speaking, the more compatible are the two types of goals, the more successful the school will be. Explicit goals may be read in a formal document, but implicit goals are inferred by observing how people behave, assumptions that people have, sources and modes of expression of authority, organizational climate, leadership style, decision-making procedures, and communication facility. Second, fundamental to each of the statements of goals for education included here, and fundamental to most such statements generated locally, is the importance of student self-actualization in three areas of development—intellectual, social, and emotional. Curriculum content, course structure, and other formal learning efforts are important contributors to student self-actualization, but most observers agree[6] that process experiences such as critical thinking and problem solving, affective learning, and aesthetic appreciation are also necessary.

Educators have long agreed that how one works to achieve an educational objective (process) is as important as what is achieved (content). Teaching youngsters to think critically and independently requires using discovery and inquiry teaching methods. Interpersonal competence for youngsters is achieved through teaching methods characterized by warmth and acceptance. Mechanical mathematical operations, on the other hand, are taught and proficiency is encouraged through programmed and drill-teaching techniques. School executives readily accept the importance of compatible means-ends relationships for teachers and teaching, but they have not accepted the concept as it relates to school operation and school effectiveness. For example, school executives may work with teachers to provide flexible learning activities for youngsters as a means to achieve creative learning and development objectives, but they often insist on operating a relatively inflexible school which emphasizes smoothness and reliability. Many school executives do not recognize the contradiction of expecting youngsters to achieve intellectual enrichment, interpersonal competence, and personal self-actualization in high control, relatively closed schools primarily concerned with smooth, orderly, and efficient operation. Indeed, one of the major weaknesses in American education today is the incompatibility between how schools are operated and managed administratively and the self-actualization goals which schools hold for youngsters.

SUBSTANTIVE AND INSTRUMENTAL GOALS

Explicit and implicit goals in education can be characterized also as substantive and instrumental goals. The substantive goals of the school are what differentiates the school from other organizations and institutions of our society. Not only do they represent the hopes and aspirations of society, but they provide the blueprints which guide curriculum development and implementation, as well as the criteria against which the school is ultimately evaluated. The instrumental goals are more specific—indeed, more earthy and achievable—goals. Whereas substantive goals prescribe purpose, instrumental goals guide action. Generally speaking, the closer action is to purpose (compatibility), the more likely it is that purposes will be carried out.

We have suggested that goals of intellectual enrichment, interpersonal competence, and personal self-actualization can be achieved only accidentally in anything less than schools which hold these goals for teachers as well as students. Indeed, as teachers progress in their own development (instrumental), the development of youngsters is enhanced (substantive). Therefore, school executives who are interested in student self-actualization should decide, communicate, and plan in ways which facilitate and enhance teacher growth and development. Some will argue that teacher gains in growth and satisfaction are only organizational outputs rather than means to student cognitive and affective gains. Acceptance of this argument assumes a closed system which denies using today's teacher gains as tomorrow's organizational inputs. The school instead is best viewed as a dynamic and open organizational system which readily accepts yesterday's outputs as today's inputs and which cannot be fixed in time.

The interdependent nature of substantive and instrumental goals are summarized from an administrative point of view in Figure 3-1. Here instrumental concerns, those over which the administrator has relatively direct control, are listed along with substantive concerns which represent the school's *raison d'être*. Corresponding characteristics and concepts, most of which are discussed later in the book, are also included.[7] From a substantive point of view the school executive is interested in promoting effectiveness in his school or district's educational program. Characteristics such as goals and objectives, curriculum, learning climate, program dimension, and teacher behavior represent this domain. But instrumentally, educational programs are housed in organizations and are governed within these organizations by administrators who provide and coordinate resources, control work flow, implement decisions and evaluate progress. The manner in which these executive responsibilities are articulated over time constitutes the school's management climate. This climate is largely influenced by the management platform or philosophy of school executives. They, in turn, function within an organizational setting which, like climate, takes on an identity over time. Each of these levels of analysis and activity influences the other with the predominant patterns of influence likely to be top down. Though explicitly goals of an educational program may take on a certain character (for example, to provide youngsters with opportunities to develop self-responsibility), implicitly goals are greatly influenced by management and organizational factors. In the preceding example, a rigidly operated organizational structure and a management system which requires that teachers and students be passive might implicitly honor instead the goal "to help youngsters follow directions and avoid taking risks."

The concept of interdependence between school and classroom learning climates is important to this discussion. Generally, classroom learning climates reflect organizational climates which exist in the school as whole.[8] Indeed, improving the climate for learning depends upon improving the organizational climate of the school. Excessive interpersonal friction among teachers and between teachers and administrators, low morale, a feeling of powerlessness on the part of teachers, and coercive compliance strategies cannot be kept out of the classroom by closing the door. These environmental conditions have potent effects on what teachers do, how teachers relate with each other, as well as on student achievement and other gains. In order to understand this relationship one needs to examine the crucial role human factors play in the school. These human factors, often referred to as the school's human organization, provide the means through which the school achieves its goals. The human organization of the school is examined in Part II of this book. It seems sufficient to suggest here that the effectiveness of administrative behavior is evaluated largely in terms of the worth and condition of the school's human organization. Further, it

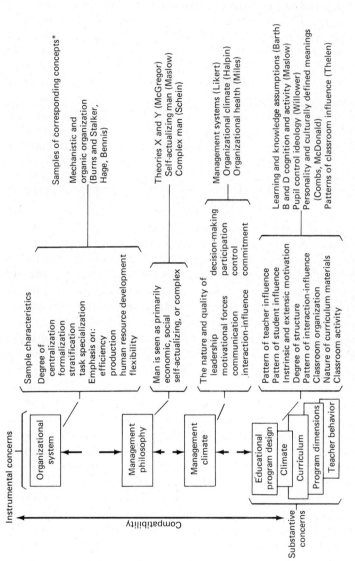

Figure 3-1 An administrative perspective on substantive and instrumental goals. (Source: Adapted from T. J. Sergiovanni "Synergistic Evaluation," *Teachers College Record* 75 no. 4 [1974]:549.)
* See note 7 at the end of Chapter 3 for references.

is improvement in this human organization which ultimately affects the achievement of school goals.

CONTROL AS A FOCUS FOR ADMINISTRATION

The most important means to school ends is power. This statement becomes more acceptable if one recognizes that political valuing is a neutral phenomenon which may be used in positive and supportive ways as readily as it may be misused. Alfred de Grazia states:

> The most important instrumental objective is power, specially defined within administrative situations as control. Since the actions of many are involved and the actions must be coordinated so as to present a deduced quality from the sponsored substantive goals, executives strive for control, by whatever means they have of influencing the decisions of others. . . . It may be granted externally to the participants by the symbols of authority and the sanctions of power; internally, control is dependent upon morale.[9]

Control is an important instrumental objective for school executives, but its focus is often misunderstood or distorted. School executives for example, often seek control directly over people. Substantive goals for schools are such, however, that instrumental goals which seek direct control over people actually can work against certain school ends. In this section ways in which school executives achieve compliance are examined and three power strategies are discussed: the coercive, the utilitarian, and the normative. The normative power strategy is then examined in further detail as we compare human relations management with human resources management.

Compliance

The means that one uses to gain commitment to goals and to stimulate activity toward these goals, according to Etzioni,[10] depends upon three conditions—the nature of the goals[11] to be achieved, the kind of involvement one wishes from those who are to do the work, and the nature of the tasks which define this work.

Etzioni proposes that if the primary goal of the organization is *order* and tasks are largely *routine,* the most efficient means to compliance are *coercive.* The price one pays for this efficiency, however, is that involvement of participants is *alienative.* Prisons are characteristic of this kind of organization. If the goal of the organization is primarily *economic* and the tasks are seen as largely *instrumental* means to this end, then the most efficient means to compliance is *utilitarian*—that is, to purchase participation. In this kind of organization, *calculative involvement* predominates. One's involvement is linked largely with what one perceives participation will bring materially. Business organizations are characteristic of this type. School goals are generally considered to be *cultural* in nature. Cultural goals are pursued largely in *expressive* ways as teachers and students define, legitimize, and strengthen commitment to the cultural goals of the school. Cultural goals and expressive tasks, according to Etzioni's formulation, require *moral* commitment from teachers and students. These are achieved through *normative* compliance strategies. One engages in the activities of the organization because they are good, professionally sound, can be rationally defended, make sense, and so on, rather than because one is commanded to engage, paid to engage, or coerced to engage.

Schools are very much concerned with the ways in which students, teachers, and others are involved in the educational enterprise. They cannot, for example, operate for long periods of time with alienated teachers or students—the risks of coercive compliance strategies. Schools can function with teacher and student involvement on the utilitarian basis of "what's in it for me," but most agree that this sort of involvement is less than desirable. The goals of the school, although largely cultural and achieved through normative compliance strategies, do however include economic considerations and reasonable manifestations of order. This problem has been discussed elsewhere:

> The appropriateness of a given compliance strategy will depend largely on organizational costs in relation to goal achievement. If, for example, the goal is order, and the task routine, the most efficient compliance strategy is coercive. Yet before one chooses this strategy he must be prepared to pay the price of alienated subordinates. If the price is worth the accomplishment of the goal, then the coercive strategy (at least within the limits of this formulation) is legitimate. The key, of course, rests with the variable time. Any system can absorb short periods of alienation by subordinates but, over time, alienation results in a collapse of the system. Schools, for example, can hardly operate as dynamic learning institutions with alienated students, parents, or teachers.[12]

Each of the goals (order, economic, cultural) and strategies (coercive, utilitarian, normative) of compliance may be legitimate given unique circumstance; but only the sets of goals and strategies, cultural and normative, can be considered as the focus of primary attention for school executives. The cost in morale and the discontent among staff and youngsters are too great to risk more than occasional reliance on coercive and utilitarian compliance strategies.

HUMAN RELATIONS OR HUMAN RESOURCES?

Recently school executives have been more cautious in using coercive and utilitarian compliance strategies and have adopted what appear to be normative patterns. Many of these executives complain, however, that the newer approaches have not lived up to promises. It is important to recognize that normative compliance strategies offer no panacea to the practice of school administration. Part of the failure of normative approaches rests with school executives who have misunderstood the focus of such patterns. Many have adopted an operational version of the human relations approach which emphasizes making subordinates feel important as individuals and as part of the school. This is considerably different from incorporating all members of the human organization as actual shareholders in the school and its activities. Others have attempted to take features of the human relations approach and incorporate them without altering previous assumptions about people, or concepts and ideas about administration and organization. Human relations administration may provide one kind of normative compliance strategy, but it is a relatively shallow strategy which lacks sufficient substance or honesty for dealing with professional teachers or with youngsters.[13] An alternative normative strategy is patterned after a human resources model proposed by Raymond Miles.[14] He contrasts human relations and human resources on three important levels: the attitudes of the administrator toward people, the kind and amount of participation permitted to subordinates, and the expectations which the administrator has as a result of management strategy he chooses. An altered version of Miles's comparisons appears in Table 3-1.

ADMINISTRATIVE ASSUMPTIONS

The influence of a school executive's philosophy on his administrative behavior cannot be overemphasized. Relationships between philosophy and behavior are often attributed to the self-fulfilling prophecy: This phenomenon suggests that individuals respond to the expectations that important others hold for their behavior. The self-fulfilling prophecy has been documented reasonably well in a number of instances relating to behavior and performance of school youngsters.[15]

Perhaps the most popular illustration of how the self-fulfilling prophecy works for administrators is the now classic McGregor comparison of traditional management theory, Theory X, with that of newer theories or approaches to management, which he labels

Theory Y. Fundamental to Theory X are certain widespread assumptions and beliefs:

1. The average man is by nature indolent—he works as little as possible.
2. He lacks ambition, dislikes responsibility, prefers to be led.
3. He is inherently self-centered, indifferent to organizational needs.
4. He is by nature resistant to change.
5. He is gullible, not very bright, the ready dupe of the charlatan and the demagogue.[16]

School executives and others who hold these Theory X assumptions view their jobs with respect to people as directing the efforts of subordinates, motivating subordinates, controlling them, and modifying their behavior to fit the needs of the school or organization. McGregor argues that Theory X administrators believe that without active intervention people would be passive, if not resistant, to organizational needs. The two most common approaches to Theory X are (1) the hard sell, where authoritarian and coercive leadership is exerted; and (2) the soft sell, where human relations or "democratic" and paternal administration prevails. *In practice, human relations is little more than a softer version of Theory X.* In each instance subordinates must be persuaded, rewarded, punished, and controlled. It is important that activities of subordinates be directed, for the task of management consists of getting things done through other people. McGregor

Table 3–1 NORMATIVE COMPLIANCE STRATEGIES

HUMAN RELATIONS MODEL	HUMAN RESOURCES MODEL
ATTITUDES TOWARD PEOPLE	
1. People in our culture, teachers and students among them, share a common set of needs—to belong, to be liked, to be respected.	1. In addition to sharing common needs for belonging and respect, most people in our culture, teachers and students among them, desire to contribute effectively and creatively to the accomplishment of worthwhile objectives.
2. Although teachers and students desire individual recognition, they more importantly want to feel useful to the school and to their own work group.	2. The majority of teachers and students are capable of exercising far more initiative, responsibility, and creativity than their present jobs or work circumstances require or allow.
3. They tend to cooperate willingly and comply with school goals if these important needs are fulfilled.	3. These capabilities represent untapped resources which are presently being wasted.

Table 3–1   *(Continued)*

HUMAN RELATIONS MODEL	HUMAN RESOURCES MODEL
KIND AND AMOUNT OF PARTICIPATION	
1. The school executive's basic task (or in reference to students, the teacher's basic task) is to make each subordinate believe that he is a useful and important part of the team.	1. The school executive's basic task (or in reference to students, the teacher's basic task) is to create an environment in which subordinates can contribute their full range of talents to the accomplishment of school goals. He works to uncover the creative resources of his subordinates.
2. The school executive is willing to explain his decisions and to discuss his subordinates' objections to his plans. On routine matters, he encourages his subordinates in planning and in decision-making.	2. The school executive allows and encourages subordinates to participate in important as well as routine decisions. In fact, the more important a decision is to the school, the greater the school executive's efforts to tap faculty resources.
3. Within narrow limits, the faculty or individual teachers who comprise the faculty should be allowed to exercise self-direction and self-control in carrying out plans.	3. School executives work continually to expand the areas over which subordinates exercise self-direction and self-control as they develop and demonstrate greater insight and ability.
EXPECTATIONS	
1. Sharing information with subordinates and involving them in school decision-making will help satisfy their basic needs for belonging and for individual recognition.	1. The overall quality of decision-making and performance will improve as school executives make use of the full range of experience, insight, and creative ability which exists in their schools.
2. Satisfying these needs will improve faculty morale and will reduce resistance to formal authority.	2. Subordinates will exercise responsible self-direction and self-control in the accomplishment of worthwhile objectives that they understand and have helped establish.
3. High faculty morale and reduced resistance to formal authority may lead to improved school performance. It will at least reduce friction and make the school executive's job easier.	3. Faculty satisfaction will increase as a by-product of improved performance and the opportunity to contribute creatively to this improvement.

SOURCE: This table is adapted from Raymond E. Miles, "Human Relations or Human Resources?" *Harvard Business Review*, July–August 1965, Copyright © 1965 by the President and Fellows of Harvard College; all rights reserved.

indicates that when management looks to people for justification of its actions, it finds that people do indeed live up to the beliefs which management has concerning them. The actions of Theory X are thus confirmed, which reinforces the original assumptions and the cycle tends to perpetuate itself. McGregor concludes that "the conventional approach of Theory X is based on mistaken notions of what is cause and what is effect."[17] The Theory X administrator believes that his behavior and assumptions are caused by the way subordinates react to him, to each other, and to their work.

By contrast, Theory Y administrators, according to the McGregor formulation, believe that people are not by nature passive, lazy, irresponsible, or resistant to organizational needs. Those who exhibit behavior of this sort have come to learn this work style as a result of experience in organizations. "The motivation, the potential for development, the capacity for assuming responsibility, the readiness to direct behavior toward organizational goals are all present in people. Management does not put them there. It is a responsibility of management ot make it possible for people to recognize and develop these human characteristics for themselves."[18] School executives and others who hold Theory Y assumptions see their jobs with respect to people as arranging organizational conditions and methods of operation in order to facilitate and support the efforts of subordinates. Subordinates, according to this view, are then better able to provide for their own needs and goals as well as those of the school.

McGregor suggests that in those cases where administrators operate in the realm of Theory Y, subordinates confirm administrative actions and beliefs and the cycle perpetuates itself. He concludes that "Theory X places exclusive reliance upon external control of human behavior, while Theory Y relies heavily on self-control and self-direction. It is worth noting that this difference is the difference between treating people as children and treating them as mature adults."[19] The Theory Y administrator believes that feelings, attitudes, and performance levels of subordinates are a direct reflection of his own attitudes and action.

Recalling the link between instrumental and substantive goals, it seems clear that school executives need to examine carefully what they believe about organization and administration and how they come to hold these beliefs. In our view, the unique role of the school as a humanizing and self-actualizing institution requires that school executives adopt the assumptions and behavior manifestations of Theory Y. Note, however, that Theories X and Y are general frames of reference for viewing administrative decision-making as it affects organizational members. Administrators who identify with Theory X often display behavior associated with Y (human relations practices, for example), and administrators who identify with Theory Y display X behavior from time to time in response to particular individuals or situations.

EUPSYCHIAN MANAGEMENT: MODEL ASSUMPTIONS FOR EDUCATIONAL ADMINISTRATION

This section proposes a philosophy of administration—partly based on faith, ethics, and humanistic concerns and partly based on theoretical and empirical foundations as a basis for an applied science of educational administration. This basis is generated from a contemporary movement in psychology which seeks a humanistic alternative to Freudian psychology and to the psychology behaviorists. The movement is sometimes referred to as "Third Force" psychology, and Abraham Maslow has historically been considered its preeminent spokesman.[20]

In 1962, the book *Eupsychian Management: A Journal* was published.[21] This book, which is an attempt to apply Third Force psychology to management, represents a record of experiences and observations penned by Maslow as a result of spending a period of time in residence at Non-Linear Systems, Incorporated, in California. "Eupsychia"[22] means moving toward psychological health or "healthward." Eupsychian management then is a manifest effort to bring optimum growth and development to all who are in contact with the school. This is an extraordinary task, and we have no illusion about its practicality. We do believe, however, that to shoot for anything less than this goal is inconsistent with statements of objectives for schools such as those which appeared earlier in this chapter. The assumptions which underlie Eupsychian management policy and which are proposed as the basis for a humanly oriented applied science of educational administration appear in Table 3-2.

Schools are far from operating under Eupsychian ideals, and teachers have not demonstrated convincingly that they are able to operate in Eupsychian ways. On the other hand, school executives have not worked diligently to foster, promote, and reward behavior of this sort. They can work to bring about this reality by (1) assuming that all school members are capable of operating under these principles and (2) making particular exceptions to these principles only as they find individuals who do not or cannot operate in accordance with them. Note that the assumptions are never abandoned but that some people are exempted from them. Three alternatives for dealing with these exceptions are: (1) work-

TABLE 3–2 EUPSYCHIAN MANAGEMENT ASSUMPTIONS

1. *Assume everyone is to be trusted.*
2. *Assume everyone is to be informed as completely as possible of as many facts and truths as possible.*
3. *Assume in all your people the impulse to achieve.* Assume that each is willing and able to give top performance if provided with the opportunity to do so.
4. *Assume that there is no dominance-subordination hierarchy in the jungle sense or authoritarian sense.* A feeling of brotherhood, sharing of goals, and identification with school objectives cannot be commanded. While legitimate and hierarchial authority is recognized, so is ability authority or functional authority.
5. *Assume that everyone will have the same ultimate managerial objectives and will identify with them no matter where they are in the organization or in the hierarchy.* If this is the case, then the school can become problem-solving oriented rather than self- or ego oriented. with full confidence that outcomes will be consistent with school goals. Self and ego are advanced through this effort.
6. *Eupsychian economics must assume good will among all the members of the organization rather than rivalry or jealousy.* A certain amount of rivalry among junior executives and other subordinates is only natural. In fact, rivalry can be used to advantage by devious school executives as they consolidate and secure their own positions. We must not forget the "motivational" aspects of cutthroat competition. If the school perceives of its staff as an interdependent group of professionals who exert team efforts toward common school goals, then win-lose rivalry and competition are dysfunctional. If, however, school executives view the work of the school as being best accomplished by individuals working independently (often against each other) in a rather random fashion—then this assumption should be ignored or reversed.
7. *Assume the "Ability to Admire."* Here Maslow refers to objective and detached judgment about capacities and skills of others as well as of self. Recognizing the limitations of human weakness, of prejudice, of favoritism, of defensiveness, and the like, he suggests that we need to adopt the custom of the Plains Indians, who freely but honestly boast of their strength and contributions but who also recognize their limitations. While acceptance and love are not contingent upon what one can do, status and responsibility are.
8. *We must assume that the people in Eupsychian plants [schools] are not fixated at the safety-need level.* They are relatively anxiety-free, are not obsessed with fear, and have the courage to face uncertainty in the future.
9. *Assume an active trend to self-actualization.*
10. *Assume that everyone can enjoy good team work, friendship, good group spirit, good group harmony, good belongingness, and group love.*
11. *Assume hostility to be primarily reactive rather than character-based.* If this is the case, then hostility and conflict are positive stimulants to school success. Reactive hostility is no more than simply honesty which will move the school and its people closer to authenticity. Maslow suggests, for example, that the better the manager the more

Table 3–2 (Continued)

freedom people will feel to express irritation and disagreement. The more accepting teachers are of each other as people, the more accepting they will be of criticism interchanges.

12. *Assume that people can take it.* People like to be reasonably stretched and challenged, particularly if they view their work as meaningful to them as people and to the school in terms of its goals.

13. *Eupsychian management assumes that people are improvable.* Growth and development personally or professionally are not fixed, nor do teachers wish them to be fixed.

14. *Assume that everyone prefers to feel important, needed, useful, successful, proud, respected, rather than unimportant, interchangeable, anonymous, wasted, unused, expendable, disrespected.* We do not confine "everyone" to the administrative and teaching staff, but include students, janitors, cooks, secretaries, groundskeepers, lunchroom supervisors, book salesmen, crossing guards, and bus drivers.

15. *Assume that everyone prefers or perhaps even needs to love his boss (rather than to hate him) and that everyone prefers to respect his boss (rather than to disrespect him).* Maslow feels that respect is probably prepotent over love. If one were to choose between respect or love for his superior, he would prefer to respect and not love than to love and not respect. This hypothesis has strong negative implications concerning human relations management.

16. *Eupsychian management assumes everyone prefers to be a prime mover rather than a passive helper.*

17. *Assume a tendency to improve things, . . . to put things right, make things better, to do things better.*

18. *Assume that growth occurs through delight and through boredom.* Eupsychian management flourishes on delight in novelty, change, new and varied activities. Maslow suggests that sooner or later things become easy and familiar—prerequisites to boredom. It is this boredom which moves people to search further for new ideas and for work at higher levels of skill.

19. *Assume preference for being a whole person and not a part, not a thing, or an implement, or tool, or "hand."* With specialization taking place rapidly in education, there is a tendency for school executives to view people only with respect to one or two specialized skills which they bring to the school. One becomes a data-processing man; another, a budget man; and a third, the primary-reading specialist.

20. *Assume the preference for working rather than being idle.* We refer here to meaningful work, for people do indeed prefer idleness to busy work, wasted work, or work perceived not to be related to organizational or individual goals.

21. *Assume the preference for personhood, uniqueness as a person, identity (in contrast to being anonymous or interchangeable).*

22. *We must assume the wisdom and the efficacy of self-choice.*

23. *We must assume that everyone likes to be justly and fairly appreciated, preferably in public.*

24. *Assume that everyone but especially the more developed person prefers responsibility to dependency and passivity most of the time.*

25. *The general assumption is that people will get more pleasure out of loving than they will out of hating.*

Table 3–2   *(Continued)*

26. *Assume that fairly well-developed people would rather be interested than destroy.*
27. *Assume that fairly well-developed people would rather be interested than be bored.*
28. *We must ultimately assume at the highest theoretical levels of Eupsychian theory, a preference or a tendency to identify with more and more of the world, moving toward the ultimate of mysticism, a fusion with the world, or peak experience, cosmic consciousness.* This assumption is a challenge to student alienation, to teacher-administration polarization, and to local school provincialism.
29. *We must assume the defense and growth dialectic for all these positive trends that we have already listed above.* There are positive and negative tendencies in each of us with respect to all of the principles of Eupsychian management. While each of us has a tendency to self-actualization, we also have a trend toward regression, fear of growth, avoidance of responsibility, and so on. Eupsychian management works to help people (teachers, administrators, and students) and the school to overcome such regressive tendencies.

SOURCE: Abraham S. Maslow, *Eupsychian Management* (Homewood, Ill.: Richard D. Irwin, Inc., © 1965), pp. 17–33.

ing to build and support people so that they are, as Maslow puts it, "converted"; (2) dismissing them and analyzing more thoroughly selection procedures so that the casualty rate decreases; or (3) assigning them to positions in which they will be least harmful to the school. We believe that the first alternative—converting them—is a viable one for the majority (but not all) of educational workers and discuss how this might be done in Part II of the book.

ADMINISTRATIVE EFFECTIVENESS MODEL

In Figure 3-2, our discussion of Part I, "The Belief System," is placed into perspective with other parts of the book in a model of administrative effectiveness for school executives. The chapters in Part I provide a basis for an evaluative screen which school executives need to develop. This screen enables them to sift and sort from science and intuition that which is most consistent with the school as a human organization and with school goals of intellectual, social, and emotional self-actualization for youngsters.

The following chapter, "Administrative Values and Decision-Making: A Contingency Approach," concludes Part I. Contingency theory is a construct and mechanism for resolving seemingly contradictory prescriptions and findings in the literature of educational administration and for selecting insights and prescriptions from a variety of sources for matching to unique value characteris-

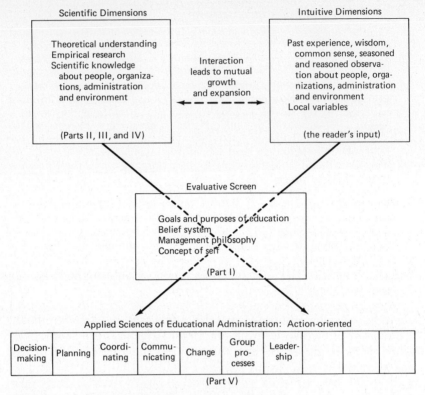

Figure 3-2 Administrative Effectiveness Model.

tics and problem situations. One's belief system is the energy which ultimately drives any contingency theory.

Notes

1. By "goals" we refer to general statements which define the direction of educational development, help select desirable learning activities, and define the scope of the educational program. By "objectives" we refer to more specific statements which are a translation of goals. See, for example, Virgil E. Herrick, "The Function of General Objectives," in *Strategies of Curriculum Development,* James B. Macdonald et al., eds. (Columbus, Ohio: Charles E. Merrill, 1965).
2. *Cardinal Principles of Secondary Education,* Bureau of Education Bulletin, no. 35 (Washington, D.C.: Department of the Interior, 1918), and *Cardinal Principles of Secondary Education* (Washington, D.C.: Office of Education, U.S. Department of Health, Education and Welfare, 1962).
3. Ibid.
4. Educational Policies Commission, *The Purposes of Education in*

American Democracy (Washington, D.C.: National Education Association, 1938).

5. AASA Commission of Imperatives of Education, *Imperatives in Education* (Washington, D.C.: American Association of School Administrators, 1966).

6. If disagreement exists, it usually centers on what proportions of each of these contributors to self-actualization is critical for effective education. The concept of self-actualization is generally attributed to the distinguished psychologist Abraham H. Maslow. Self-actualization means experiencing fully, vividly, selflessly, and with total absorption. This is accomplished by making growth choices rather than fear choices, developing a respect for and understanding of oneself, emphasizing honesty and authenticity rather than role playing, accepting responsibility, and developing and using one's potential. See, for example, Abraham Maslow, "Self-actualization and Beyond," in *Challenges of Humanistic Psychology,* James Bugental, ed. (New York: McGraw-Hill, 1967). pp. 279–86.

7. The references for Figure 3-1, in alphabetical order according to authors' last names, are: R. Barth, "So You Want to Change to an Open Classroom," *Phi Delta Kappan,* vol. 53, no. 2, 1971; W. G. Bennis, *Changing Organizations* (New York: McGraw-Hill, 1966); T. Burns and G. M. Stalker, *The Management of Innovation* (London: Tabistock Publications, 1961); A. Coombs, *Educational Accountability Beyond Behavioral Objectives* (Washington, D.C.: Association for Supervision and Curriculum Development, 1972); J. Hage, "An Axiomatic Theory of Organization," *Administrative Science Quarterly* 10, no. 3 (1975); A. Halpin, *Theory and Research in Administration* (New York: Macmillan, 1967); R. Likert, *The Human Organization: Its Management and Value* (New York: McGraw-Hill, 1967); J. McDonald, "An Image of Man: The Learner Himself," in *Individualizing Instruction* (Washington, D.C.: Association for Supervision and Curriculum Development, 1964); D. McGregor, *The Human Side of Enterprise* (New York: McGraw-Hill, 1960); A. Maslow, "Some Basic Propositions of a Growth and Self Actualizing Psychology," in *Perceiving, Behaving, Becoming* (Washington, D.C.: Association for Supervision and Curriculum Development, 1962); A. Maslow, *Motivation and Personality* (New York: Harper & Row, 1954); M. Miles, "Planned Change and Organizational Health: Figure and Ground," in Richard O. Carlson et al., *Change Processes in the Public Schools* (Eugene, Oreg.: Center for the Advanced Study of Educational Administration, 1965); E. Schein, *Organizational Psychology* (Englewood Cliffs, N.J.: Prentice-Hall, 1965); H. Thelen, "Secularizing the Classroom's Semisacred Culture," *School Review* 79, no. 1 (1970); D. Willower, T. Eidel, and W. Hoy, *The School and Pupil Control Ideology* (University Park, Pa.: Pennsylvania State University Studies Monograph, no. 24, 1967).

8. The concept of climate was popularized for educators by Andrew Halpin; see his *Theory and Research in Education* (New York: Macmillan, 1966), chap. 4. For an example of climate concerns in

business organizations, see R. Tagiuri and G. Litwin, eds., *Organizational Climate: Exploration of a Concept* (Boston: Division of Research, Graduate School of Business, Harvard University, 1968). For support of the hypothesis concerning interdependence between classroom learning and organizational climates, see Andrew Halpin, "Change and Organizational Climate," *Journal of Educational Administration* 5, no. 1 (May 1967):5–25. Rensis Likert views climate as an intervening variable with telling effects on organizational effectiveness. See Rensis Likert, *The Human Organization* (N.Y.: McGraw-Hill, 1967).

9. Alfred de Grazia, "The Science and Values of Administration—I," *Administrative Science Quarterly* 5 (December 1960):386.

10. Amitai Etzioni, *A Comparative Analysis of Complex Organizations* (New York: The Free Press, 1961). The components and characteristics of Etzioni's compliance theory are illustrated on pp. 12 and 74.

11. Three sets of goals are identified in the Etzioni formulation: order goals, economic goals, and cultural goals. Order goals focus on the control of actors or people in the organization. Economic goals focus on increasing or maintaining output at a favorable cost to the organization. Cultural goals focus on socializing, institutionalizing, preserving, extending, and applying value and life systems.

12. Thomas J. Sergiovanni and Robert J. Starratt, *Supervision Human Perspectives*, 2nd ed. (New York: McGraw-Hill, 1979), pp. 142–143.

13. The "democratic administration" movement, still popular in some educational administration circles, is a spin-off of the human relations movement. We prefer to describe the former movement as paternal administration which is hardly "democratic."

14. Raymond E. Miles, "Human Relations or Human Resources?" *Harvard Business Review* 43, no. 4 (1965):148–63.

15. Robert Rosenthal and Lenore Jacobson, *Pygmalion in the Classroom* (New York: Holt, Rinehart and Winston, 1968). Although this work and the study upon which it is based are criticized by Robert Thorndike (*American Educational Research Journal* 5, no. 4 [November 1968]: 708) and others, we believe that the findings cannot be dismissed. For application of the phenomenon to executives, see J. Sterling Livingston, "Pygmalion in Management," *Harvard Business Review* 47, no. 4 (July-August 1969):81–89. (Pygmalion is the sculptor in Greek mythology who carved a statue of a beautiful woman which subsequently came to life.)

16. Douglas McGregor, "The Human Side of Enterprise," *The Management Review* 46 (1957):22. See also McGregor's book, *The Human Side of Enterprise* (New York: McGraw-Hill, 1958).

17. Ibid., p. 24.

18. Ibid., p. 90.

19. Ibid.

20. The blossoming of Third Force psychology can be seen in Abraham Maslow's *Motivation and Personality* (New York: Harper & Row, 1954) and *Toward a Psychology of Being* (New York: Harper & Row,

1966). Note also Eric Fromm, *Man for Himself* (New York: Rinehart and Winston, 1947).

21. Abraham Maslow, *Eupsychian Management: A Journal* (Homewood, Ill.: Richard D. Irwin and Dorsey Press, 1965). This book is prepared in informal journal style and as such offers some challenges to readers conditioned to polished manuscripts arranged sequentially.

22. Maslow coined the word "Eupsychia" and defines it as "the culture that would be generated by 1,000 self-actualizing people on some sheltered island where they would not be interfered with" (ibid., p. xi).

Chapter 4
Administrative Values and Decision-Making:
A Contingency Approach

A basic premise of this book is that decision-making can best be understood from the perspectives of preference theory rather than rational theory. True, in an absolute sense school executives are not free to make any decision they prefer, and true, preferences are not drawn from a universe of possibilities; but within the many constraints that executives face choices are made, nevertheless, largely on the basis of one's perception of reality, values, beliefs, and ambitions. Educational and management platforms are key determiners of preference for an individual.

In this sense educational administration and supervision might more adequately be viewed as an artificial than a natural science, and, following Herbert Simon,[1] theories of educational administration might more adequately be viewed as theories of the artificial. Simon differentiates between the "natural" and "artificial" sciences as follows: "A natural science is a body of knowledge about some class of things—objects or phenomena—in the world: about the characteristics and properties that they have; about how they behave and interact with each other."[2] Sciences of the artificial, by contrast, are created by human convention and conditioned by human choice. Such sciences are concerned with how things ought to be and with designing artifacts to attain goals. As Simon suggests, "The thesis is that certain phenomena are 'artificial' in a very special sense: they are as they are only because of a system's being molded, by *goals and purposes,* to the environment in which it lives."[3] These goals and purposes are, in turn, limited and enhanced by an individual's or group's view of reality. From an individual perspective goals and purposes are a function of one's cultural and psychological self, and from a group perspective goals and purposes are arrived at through the political process.

Viewing educational administration from the perspectives of a preference theory of decision-making on the one hand and as a field of study and practice more artificial than natural on the other represents a radical departure from traditional organizational and management thought. Traditional views are now referred to in the literature of administration and organization as "closed systems." Max Weber's early writings on bureaucracy[4] and Frederick Taylor's principles of scientific management[5] are often cited as classic examples of closed-systems thinking.

Some have come to interpret murmurs of preference theory and artificiality as not only a wide departure from closed-system thinking but as a synonym for the other extreme—open-systems thinking. Open-systems theories generally view decision-making as hopelessly irrational and organizational environments as hopelessly turbulent and ambiguous. Organizations, it is suggested, achieve some sense of shape, character, and direction as a result of the interplay of various internal and external forces and pressures which are largely *beyond* the control of the administrator. In the extreme, the administrator's role is portrayed as that of accepting pieces of the puzzle that somehow appear before him or her and assembling them in a makeshift pattern in response to constantly changing internal and external requirements—responsive coalition-building some call it. As exclusive images of reality and exclusive bases for professional practice, both closed- and open-systems thinking are inadequate. In the remainder of this chapter examples of open- and closed-systems views of management and organization are discussed and a third view, based on contingency theory, is proposed. Contingency theory, like most other conceptualizations, has both expansive and limiting qualities. These qualities are discussed in the form of strengths and caveats in application to professional practice. Contingency theory responds to the particulars found in the environment at large, the unique work or technology of a particular organization, and the needs of individuals who are members of the organization. The chapter concludes with a review of these particulars as they apply to the unique characteristics of schools as a group of special organizations on the one hand and differences among schools on the other.

SCHOOLS AS ORGANIZATIONAL SYSTEMS

Following Talcott Parsons[6] the school is viewed as an organization concerned with three identifiably distinct levels of responsibility and control—technical, managerial, and institutional. Prominent at the technical level is the professional subsystem of the school. This subsystem is concerned with the actual provision of classroom and other instructional opportunities to students and includes concern for intents and objectives, curriculum materials, teacher and student roles, classroom organization, instructional strategies, clinical supervision, and other aspects of the school's educational program.

At the managerial level Parsons refers to the servicing, facilitating, and procuring functions which sustain, control, and administer the technical level. Prominent at this level is the school's organizational subsystem. This subsystem includes manifestations of structures such as the school's emphasis or lack of emphasis on formalization, specialization, reliability, centralization, integration, adaptiveness, efficiency, and productivity and the school's organizational climate as reflected in management assumptions, leadership processes, the distribution of power and authority, decision-making systems, and communications patterns.

The school, with its organizational and professional subsystems, is also part of a broader social system which Parsons refers to as the institutional level. It is this broader social system which legitimizes the school and provides it with support. State and local regulatory agencies, community pressure groups, and competing community organizations are examples of forces which comprise the institutional level. In exchange for legitimization and support the broader system makes demands upon the school's organizational and professional subsystems.

This distinction of organizational levels becomes important as one views patterns of interaction and interdependence which exist between and among levels. Further, the extent to which an organization such as a school is considered a relatively open system characterized by uncertainty or a closed system characterized by rationality, if viewed within the Parsonian conceptualization, can provide a useful analytical device for viewing differences and similarities among schools of thought in organizational and management theory.

The School as a Closed-Rational System

If an educational organization is viewed as a closed system, then the institutional level is viewed as providing a steady state of support to the school and as making fairly predictable and reliable demands in the form of expectations. Community expectations, state governmental requirements and other outside forces, for example, are fixed and predictable. These are norms of rationality characterized by a minimum of environmental uncertainty which in turn permits the organizational level to devote its attention to matters internal to the school. The system is closed in the sense that uncertainty, not being an issue, is largely ignored and attention is turned to norms of rationality.[7] By norms of rationality we mean the ability of the organization to operate in an environment of certainty or a determinate system[8] which permits the identification of clearly operational objectives and the development of plans, strategies, roles, and mechanisms which permit the maximizing of those objectives. Sometimes these objectives are implicit or take the form of cultural norms. They stand, nevertheless, as accepted patterns of expectations to which the school presumably responds in rational and predictable ways. Peshkin's study of school-community relations in Mansfield, as described in Chapter 2 of this book, would be an example.[9] Since the identification of objectives and the development of strategies are typically seen as a management function, the technical core of the organization (or in the case of schools, the professional subsystem) is subordinate to and programmed by the organizational subsystem. Community expectations are known and fixed, and the broader legal-political context of education is similarly predictable. These expectations govern organizational and administrative practices which are in turn designed to develop and maintain an appropriate educational program.

Closed-system thinking is perhaps best represented by the writings of Taylor,[10] Gulick and Urwick,[11] Mooney and Reilly,[12] Fayol,[13] and Weber.[14] In his *Principles of Scientific Management* Taylor, for example, offered four rational principles which were the foundation for his science of work and organization. The first is to replace intuitive, or idiosyncratic methods of doing the work of the organization with a scientific method based on observation and analysis to obtain the best cost-benefit ratio. For every task a *one best way* should be determined. The second is to select scientifically the best person for the job and train him thoroughly in the tasks and procedures he is to follow. Third, "heartily cooperate with the men" to ensure that the work is being done according to established standards and procedures. Fourth, divide the work of managers and workers so that managers assume responsibility for planning and preparing work and for supervising. In Taylor's words, "The management takes over the work for which they are better fitted than the work man."[15]

Writing in education at about the same time, Franklin Bobbit stated:

> In any organization, the directive and supervisory members must clearly define the ends toward which the organization strives. They must coordinate the labors of all so as to attain those ends. They must find the best methods of work, and they must enforce the use of these methods on the part of the workers. They must determine the qualifications necessary for the workers and see that each rises to the standard qualifications, if it is possible; and when impossible, see that he is separated from the organization. This requires direct or indirect responsibility for the preliminary training of workers before service and for keeping them up to standard qualifications during service. Directors and supervisors must keep the workers supplied with detailed instructions as to the work to be done, the standards to be reached, the methods to be employed, and the materials and appliances to be used. They must supply the workers with the necessary materials and appliances. They must place incentives before the worker in order to stimulate desirable effort. Whatever the nature or purpose of the organization, if it is an effective one, these are always the directive and supervisory tasks.[16]

Bureaucracy was a mechanism for refining the norms of rationality and certainty so characteristic of scientific management. It was assumed that all aspects of the organization from its mission, technical requirement, and work flow to the details of its organizational structure could be defined into a *permanent* grand design. All that remained was to find people who could be programmed into this design and to turn the key. According to Weber, "The fully developed bureaucratic mechanism compares with other organizations exactly as does the machine with the non-mechanical modes of production . . . precision, speed, unambiguity, continuity, discretion, unity, . . . these are raised to the optimum point in a strictly bureaucratic administration."[17]

The School as an Open-Uncertain System

At the other extreme is an open-systems view of organization characterized by a frequent but uncertain and unpredictable flow of interaction and press between the organization and its broader social system—the institutional level. This openness introduces demands and expectations into the system that are rapidly changing and often in conflict. Demands made by the array of community interest groups typically found in urban school-communities is an example. Further, the sheer volume of unpredictable input introduces more variables than can be handled by conventional rational strategies. Certainty does not exist in fixing goals and objectives, and planning is seen as unrealistic. Administrators in open-uncertain systems concede not only that rationality is beyond man and organization but that attempts at approximating rationality are not possible.

In open-systems thinking the organization is seen as constantly seeking a level of accommodation with its external environment. This accommodation requires adjustment at the institutional level and internally in the organizational and technical subsystems. Organizations attempt to insulate their technologies from institutional level forces by erecting buffers.[18] Aspects of the school code, school district standard operating procedures, the jargon of professional education, goals and objectives, academic requirements, the mystique associated with grade books, tests, I.Q., achievement scores, and other measurement and evaluation artifacts are examples of buffers. The extent to which they are successful in this effort depends upon the strength of the technical core in question and upon the ability of administrators to articulate this technology persuasively. In medical organizations, for example, the technical core interacts either directly or through the organizational subsystem with the institutional level as an equal or superior partner. In elementary and secondary education the technical core seems by comparison weak and typically is not understood and articulated persuasively by administrators, and therefore this core is more vulnerable to forces at other levels. The man in the street concedes medical expertise to doctors; he considers himself an expert on education.

As the organizational subsystem tries to mediate this institutional-technical core tension, the limits on rationality[19] are such that compromise is in order and "satisficing" rather than "maximizing"[20] goals and processes are developed. What is best is abandoned in favor of the first option which will work or what can be successfully exchanged in the marketplace of constant intra- and interorganizational adjustment. Thus in order to survive against strong and constantly shifting outside forces in an environment marked by uncertainty, the organizational system makes constant adjustments in its technical core. A modified junior high school is adopted to appease middle school and mini-high school advocates. An open-space building is constructed, but educational program and student control practices remain the same. A naturally integrated school is closed in favor of one artificially integrated because of dollar savings for the community, and so on. Open-systems thinking, much like that of closed-systems thinking, leads one to conclude that the professional subsystem of the educational organization is again subordinate to the organizational subsystem. In this case, however, subordination takes the form of being a source for organizational trade-offs and side payments as the organizational subsystem increases its ability to survive and perhaps even gain in power and status, by a strategy of appeasement at the institutional level.

In critiquing the open-system perspective Richard Hall notes:

> The open-system perspective suggests that rationality within organizations is, or can be, drastically impaired and also that events occur without organizational intent—that interaction patterns, norms, and structure show tendencies to grow in number and complexity beyond what is foreseen or intended for the "official" formal system. A total acceptance of the open-system approach . . . would make it appear that there is actually little need for organizations at all, since things just seem to happen. Rather obviously, this is too extreme a position. The very nature of organizations signifies that they do accomplish certain things. They do alter their inputs and produce outputs and make decisions; and these things are done on a relatively predictable and relatively stable basis.[21]

A CONTINGENCY PERSPECTIVE

Which of the images of organization and management, closed or open systems, best fits the school? Would some schools appropriately fit one image and other schools the other? Would one image be more appropriate for a school at time 1 and the other at time 2? Are certain aspects of school organization and management more likely to fit one image than another? Can some school goals and activities be more effectively pursued through one image than the other? Indeed, can features of open systems be effectively combined with those of closed systems in the same school? These are the sorts of questions which interest those who seek to apply contingency theory to educational administration. Contingency theory is concerned with organizational and situational differences. Rather than specifying one best way to operate, for example consistent with either open- or closed-system thinking, this approach assumes that appropriate organizational structure, leadership, planning, staffing, decision-making, and controlling are *contingent* upon the unique nature of a given organization's *external environment, task or technology, and organizational member characteristics.*

Organizational environments and member characteristics are examined in detail in Parts II, III, and IV of this book as we consider the school's human, organizational, and political systems. By way of example, Burns and Stalker[22] found that highly programmed "mechanistic" organizational structures were more effective for organizations with relatively stable and predictable environments and that highly flexible "organic" organizational structures were more effective for organizations whose environments were characterized by uncertainty and rapid changes in technology. And Victor Vroom[23] found that participative leadership styles of administrators had positive effects on employees who had a high need for independence and strong nonauthoritarian values, but employees with a high desire for structure and low needs for independence *did not* react favorably to participative leadership styles. In the first example contingency theorists would suggest that effective organizational structure depends in part upon the characteristics of that organization's environment and in the second example that effective leadership style depends in part on the needs and dispositions of organizational members.

In addition to organizational environment and member disposition, contingency theorists have also examined the tasks and dominant technologies of organizations. Jane Woodward's work stands out as a classical example of studying the relationship between technology and organizational-management structure.[24] Her studies, which began in 1953 and involved 100 diverse industrial firms in South Essex, England, revealed that effective organizational and management systems were dependent upon characteristics of the organization's production or technical subsystem. This revelation contributed to the founding of the sociotechnical theory of organizations. The Woodward researchers were able to divide the organizations under study into three distinct groups. One group was comprised of unit and small-batch organizations involved in production according to customer requirements. Organizations of this type custom-tailored products to client specifications and possessed craftlike characteristics. Another group consisted of large batch-mass production organizations which were concerned with producing large quantities of standard products. The third group were long-run complex-process-oriented organizations which required highly specialized technical functions.

The organizational types could be conceived as being on a continuum of technical sophistication with the small-batch custom-product organizations at one end being more craft than technical; the mass-production organizations requiring a moderate amount of technical sophistication, and the complex-process organizations requiring a sophisticated technology. Woodward observed that *successful* organizations *at either end of this continuum* (the craftlike and the complex process) were characterized by flexible and organic structures and *successful* organizations in the middle range (mass production) displayed the characteristics of the highly programmed mechanistic model. Woodward noted that though the small-batch and the complex-process organizations differed in technical sophistication, they were similar in the need to be adaptive and in the importance placed upon ability (in a craft or technical sense) and authority. Further, both were geared toward problem solving whereas, by contrast, the mass-production organizations were geared toward production.

In examining the interaction between technology and organizational structure James Thompson proposed a slightly different typology.[25] His categories included long-linked technology, mediating technology, and intensive technology. An organization with a long-linked technology is characterized by fixed demands in product, certainty in goals, and programmed activities or in Thompson's words, "serial interdependence in the sense that act Z can be performed only after successful completion of act Y, which in turn rests on X, and so on."[26] Scientific management in one or another of its forms seems compatible with organizations of this type. Education program formats which rely heavily on specifying detailed objectives or competency levels linked to continuous-progress instructional packages are examples of the long-linked technology.

An organization with a mediating technology has as its primary function "the linking of clients or customers who are or wish to be interdependent. Banks, post offices, insurance companies, and telephone utilities are examples of organizations with mediating technologies. In each case the organization is faced with the challenge of handling diverse inputs in standard ways. Borrowers' needs may vary, but standard rules typically govern the loan. Organizations of this type find needed comfort within the bureaucratic model. Consider here a high school with a standard curriculum or with standard curriculum options which are applied similarly to all students. Once a student opts for English 101 or Vocational Education 101, he or she is expected to cover the standard course material and is evaluated accordingly.

Organizations with intensive technologies bring to bear a variety of resources in order to bring about a change in a particular object. The selection, combination, and order of application of these resources, however, are determined on the basis of interaction with this object. In Thompson's words, "the intensive technology is a custom technology. Its successful employment rests in part on the availability of all the capacities potentially needed, but equally on the appropriate custom combination of selected capacities as required by the individual case or project."[27] The flexible, organic model of organizations seems most suited to intensive technologies. The middle school interdisciplinary teaching team which exercises a great deal of autonomy in deciding curriculum and scheduling formats for particular groups of students displays characteristics of the intensive technology.

Consider, for example, one important professional property of the school's technical subsystem—the nature of goals and objectives. To the extent that it is appropriate for objectives to be predetermined and stated precisely, then the educational program and instructional system together with its organizational features should take on long-linked characteristics in accordance with closed-system management principles. In instances where it is desirable to leave the discovery of objectives entirely to students, then a more laissez-faire instructional system might be suitable. And where it is desirable for teachers and students to interact together to establish or discover objectives, then still a third approach might be suitable.

SOME CAVEATS IN APPLYING CONTINGENCY THEORY

We began this chapter by stating that exclusive images of schools which result in "one best way prescriptions" or singular interpretations are faulty. Open- and closed-system views of organization and management were used as examples. Contingency theory was offered as an alternative way for school executives to view organizational and management phenomena. Specifically, it was suggested that features of both open- and closed-systems thinking might be appropriate or not depending upon the unique circumstances which define an organization or situation. With respect to organization, it was suggested that school executives give attention to three classes of contingency variables—the nature of the organizational environment, the characteristics of that organization's task or technology, and the unique needs and dispositions of organizational members.

Contingency theory offers irresistible possibilities which enhance its attractiveness to both the theoretician and the practitioner. But lurking beneath this attractiveness are some dangers which need attention. Taken literally this approach suggests an "anything goes" approach to organization and management. Effectiveness becomes equated with efficient congruence between and among situational characteristics. Though this ideology represents the epitomy of efficiency, it is devoid of ethical and value considerations. Back to the basics cannot be justified simply because it appeases an important pressure group, criminal activity by students in schools cannot be overlooked because of permissive parental pressure, laissez-faire supervision cannot be practiced because it meets the expectations of teachers, and embarrassing youngsters cannot be justified merely because it is an effective means of student control.

A strength of contingency theory as it relates to an organization's technical system is that it emphasizes the principle "form should follow function." But functions are subject to evaluation—not all are equal or acceptable. Contingency theory cannot be applied in the abstract but must take into account the unique qualities and value inclinations of educational organizations.

DIFFERENTIATING BETWEEN PUBLIC AND PRIVATE MANAGEMENT

We have suggested that applying values of efficiency to schools as the effectiveness criterion for contingency theory is both common and faulty. Private organizations, particularly business firms, have traditionally been the focus of attention for organizational and management theorists, and the literature is richest in its application to this sector. Further, school executives are under pressure by local boards and paradoxically governmental agencies to be more businesslike and efficiency-minded. The result is often willy-nilly application of management and organizational principles appropriate for the business firm but ill suited to public organizations such as schools.

One cannot deny that at one level of analysis management is management but though public and private organizations share many features, the differences are significant. Wallace Sayre, a well-known management professor, has suggested that "business and government administration are alike in all unimportant respects,"[28] and Joseph Bower of the Harvard Business School notes that "American business is an inappropriate analogy for discussing and evaluating public management. In the public sector, *purpose, organization* and *people* do not have the same meaning and significance that they have in business."[29]

Some important differences between schools, as one kind of public organization, and private organizations are contrasted as follows. School executives face the task of managing in an environment where:

1. Power over money, organization and personnel rests in the hands of the legislature, school code, and local school board rather than in the hands of management.
2. Measures of progress toward goals are difficult to devise. What are the school measures of good citizenship, intellectual enrichment, problem-solving ability, independent thinking, a desire to learn, economic sufficiency, and effective family living, for example? These are contrasted with the readily understood and quantifiable economic objectives of private organizations.
3. Public accounting to which the school is subjected is designed to *control* current expenditures as contrasted with business accounting, which tends to support future planning, research, and development.
4. Tenure laws and civil service laws tend to protect educational workers from the control of administrators and supervisors.
5. School purposes and organizational processes designed to achieve these purposes are influenced indirectly by administrators through individuals and groups (a political process) rather than directly by administrators (a management process).
6. Goals and objectives are often unclear and contradictory. The latent custodial functions of schools, for example, contradict the manifest self-actualization functions.
7. No market exists to determine effectiveness. Expensive special educational programs, for example, are maintained for political and legal reasons though, if subjected to a market economy, general consumer interest would not likely be sufficient to sustain them. By comparison, product lines of firms are thinned out by a market economy.
8. Resources are distributed on the basis of formula and other approximations of "equity" rather than on "merit." Allocating greater resources to "high producing" schools, for example, would be considered fraudulent.
9. Administrators work with an array of people whose careers are outside of management control.
10. Administrators are expected to accomplish goals in less time than normally allowed to managers of business firms.
11. A tight coupling exists between means and ends or products and processes. Schooling is a human activity with human ends.
12. Many objectives are pursued with scarce resources as contrasted with the firm, which allocates more resources to fewer, indeed more focused, objectives.

These differences clearly overshadow management similarities between public and private organizations and must be taken into account as organizational and management theory is translated to practice in education.

HUMAN AND ECONOMIC RATIONALITY

The application of organizational and management theory to education is characterized by a dichotomy which places human rationality and economic rationality at odds. Decision-making, on the one hand, is viewed as a rigorous kind of economic rationality, but human behavior, on the other hand, is viewed as human rationality. In this dichotomy Crozier notes:

> As a consequence, considerations of human relations have always been subordinated to economic considerations. What we have learned in studying human relations has been used not to reform structures, but in an ancillary way to help people adjust. This procedure may be convenient so long as the general pressure of the environment and of competition makes it difficult to manipulate people and obliges management to bargain, but it is basically unsound and leads to the routinization of whole sectors of otherwise efficient enterprises.
>
> Such an uneasy compromise disintegrates in fields like education, welfare, and rehabilitation, where human relations are the substance of the performance and not one of its means.[30]

Crozier also observes that though business firms are able to balance off human and economic rationality, attention to human rationality is receiving unprecedented attention. Curiously, as business firms shift their emphasis toward human rationality, educational organizations seem headed in the opposite direction.

OPEN SYSTEMS AND NORMS OF RATIONALITY

In the first edition of *The New School Executive* we made the case against viewing the school exclusively as a rigidly structured closed system and against widespread adoption of mechanistic organizational and management practices. But viewing the school exclusively as a flexible-open system is a flawed alternative. Schools are better viewed as open systems faced with uncertainty *but* subject to norms of rationality and needing some certainty.[31] The norms of rationality depend upon strength of commitment of the organization's human system. *Though it is not realistic to see goals as unduly fixed and operational and to develop stepwise plans and strategies, persons, though quite complex and difficult to label, are capable of valuing, agreements are possible, goals can be determined, and persons as individuals and the human system of an organization as a whole are capable of intrinsic, goal-seeking behavior.*

In Pondy's view, "The vast majority of organizational theorists have downplayed man's higher capacities, including his ability to use language, his awareness of his own awareness, and his capacity to attribute meaning to events, to make sense of things."[32] Pondy continues, "what we need to do is to 'bring mind back in' to organizational theory."[33] And on the same theme Philip Runkel argues:

> When we treat schools as open systems, but no more than open systems, we recognize the fact that they depend on their environments for their existence. We recognize their interdependence with parents and community. We recognize that their functioning depends on the family backgrounds of their students, we recognize that citizens' groups can help or hinder their functioning, and we recognize their adequacy or lack of it in matching their curricula to the economic and cultural community into which their graduates will go.
>
> But if we treat schools as no more than systems at level 4, we ignore the capacity the school may have (or lack of capacity) for codifying the nature of their functioning, for specifying the similarities and differences between their manner of functioning and the manner of functioning of other schools, and for making adaptive alterations of ideas they get from elsewhere; we ignore the norms that hold in place its manner of doing things and the norms that may prevent other schools from learning its manner of doing things; we ignore the ability (or lack of ability) members have to understand their school and their environment and ascribe them to others; most of all, we ignore the fact that every human member of a school will perceive its human components, the school as a whole, and the environment differently from every other human component.[34]

The school is not a passive receiver of inputs as we are led to believe by open-systems models. As an organization, the school's collective psychology twists and turns inputs to its own image and modifies the nomenclature and meaning of inputs to fit its own culture. *Organizations are not objective but normative, and organizational cultures distort inputs accordingly.* For these reasons educational administration is best viewed as an artificial rather than natural science.

ARTIFICIAL INTELLIGENCE IN ORGANIZATIONS

We have described schools as essentially cultural-bound normative organizations dominated by preference theories of decision-

Table 4-1 ARTIFICIAL INTELLIGENCE AND ORGANIZATIONAL VARIABLES

	ORGANIZATIONAL VARIABLES			
ARTIFICIAL INTELLIGENCE	SPAN OF CONTROL	RATIO OF ADMINISTRATIVE TO PRODUCTION PERSONNEL	TIME SPAN OVER WHICH EMPLOYEE CAN COMMIT RESOURCES	DEGREE OF CENTRALIZATION IN DECISION MAKING
ORGANIZA- TIONAL PERCEPTION	A large span of control enlarges a supervisor's breadth of view and thereby increases his perception.	A high ratio increases the number of personnel responsible for overseeing the work of others and thereby augments perception.		Decentralized decision making causes personnel throughout the organization to involve themselves in decision problems and thereby encourages perception among these personnel.
ORGANIZA- TIONAL MEMORY	A wide span of control enlarges a supervisor's scope of concern and thereby involves him in a larger body of data and increases his memory.	A high ratio increases the number of personnel entrusted with broad data and thereby enlarges memory.		Decentralized decision making forces personnel throughout organization to store data for future decision problems and thereby enlarges memory.
ORGANIZA- TIONAL REASON		A high ratio increases the number of personnel concerned with decision making and thereby augments reason.		Decentralized decision making brings more minds into decision-making processes and thereby augments reasoning capacity in the organization.
ORGANIZA- TIONAL IMAGINATION		A high ratio increases the number of personnel employed to generate new ideas and thereby enlarges imagination.	A long time span allows employees to ponder problems and purposes at length, which permits imaginative ideas to arise in the mind.	Decentralized decision making causes more minds to be engaged in problem solving and thereby increases the use of imagination among personnel.
ORGANIZA- TIONAL MOTIVATION		A high ratio increases the number of personnel with a career interest in the organization and thereby augments motivation.	A long time span enables the employee to accomplish major tasks of great importance and thereby furthers motivation.	Decentralized decision making accords greater responsibilities for important work to more personnel and thereby increases motivation.

SOURCE: Reprinted by permission of the publisher, from *Organizational Evolution* by Gerald Skibbens, © 1974 by AMACOM, a division of American Management Associations. All rights reserved.

PROPORTION OF PERSONS IN ONE UNIT HAVING OPPORTUNITY TO INTERACT WITH PERSONS IN OTHER UNITS	QUANTITY OF FORMAL RULES	SPECIFICITY OF JOB GOALS (LOCAL VS. GLOBAL)	ADVISORY CONTENT OF COMMUNICATIONS (VS. ORDERS)	KNOWLEDGE-BASED AUTHORITY (VS. POSITION-BASED)
A high proportion enlarges the exposure of personnel to activities throughout the organization and thereby increases perception.	A small quantity of rules makes personnel receptive to innovative ideas and thereby encourages perception.	A low specificity of goals causes personnel to relate to overall aims of the organization and thereby promotes a greater breadth of perception among personnel.	A high advisory content leaves more personnel with the responsibility of managing their own activities and thereby encourages greater perception.	A high knowledge orientation places a premium on awareness among personnel and thereby promotes perception in the organization.
	A small quantity of rules broadens the scope of potentially relevant data and thereby enlarges the memory in the organization.	A low specificity of goals widens the base of data relevant to individual personnel and thereby increases memory.		A high knowledge orientation forces personnel to amass data in order to advance and thereby enlarges memory.
A high proportion encourages the pooling of minds in response to problems to be solved and thereby augments reason.	A small quantity of rules exposes more procedures and practices to critical evaluation and thereby increases reason.	A low specificity of goals causes personnel to concentrate their thoughts on the ultimate objectives of the organization and thereby augments effective reason.	A high advisory content leaves more personnel with problem-solving responsibilities of their own and thereby enlarges the exercise of reason.	A high knowledge orientation furthers logical thought activity among personnel in their effort to expand their knowledge and thereby increases reason.
A high proportion tends to draw many minds into problem-solving processes and thereby enlarges the exercise of imagination.	A small quantity of rules frees the minds of personnel for creative thinking and thereby encourages imagination.		A high advisory content allows greater freedom of action among personnel and thereby encourages the use of imagination.	A high knowledge orientation encourages growth in the data base as a stimulant to new ideas and thereby promotes imagination.
A high proportion makes personnel aware of their own places in the overall functions of the organization and thereby increases motivation.	A small quantity of rules permits personnel to exercise individual preferences and thereby increases motivation.	A low specificity of goals involves personnel in the ultimate, major aims of the organization and thereby encourages higher identification and motivation.	A high advisory content promotes participatory management in the organization and thereby increases motivation.	

making. The school contains several governing platforms which form the basis for decision-making. Individual educational and management platforms are examples.[35] These platforms are often implicit and usually latent but nevertheless profoundly influence individual decision-making. The curious and typically competing mixture of these individual platforms over time and the interaction of these platforms with factors and forces from the school's institutional level define for that school certain norms which constitute its unique organizational platform. Theories of educational effectiveness which fail to account for these governing platforms are inadequate.

Governing platforms bring to the school a sense of normative rationality as contrasted with the objective rationality of closed-system models and the nonrationality of open-system models. This normative rationality can be thought of as comprising a set of intervening variables which helps mediate the effects of organizational inputs or outputs. Rensis Likert,[36] for example, views the quality of an organization's human system as comprising intervening variables which largely account for organizational effectiveness. This quality is defined by Likert as favorable attitudes toward superiors, high levels of confidence and trust, reciprocal influence, peer-group loyalty, communications adequacy, and high peer-performance goals. In Likert's view, measures of effectiveness for a school executive would be his ability to influence positively these intervening variables. In turn, this effect would result in high performance and quality output from students and teachers.[37] The Likert formulation is important and significant but narrow. Sufficient attention is not given to the full array of intervening variables which influence effectiveness.

A more complete and promising conceptualization of intervening variables is to view schools and other organizations as possessing intellectual capacities similar to individual humans. The faculties of reason, imagination, memory, perception, and motivation are generally attributed to a human's capacity to adapt to changes in his or her environment—an important characteristic of human intelligence. The more developed these faculties, the more intelligent the person and the greater his or her adaptive capacities.

Is it possible to simulate these human faculties of intelligence in organizations? Can organizations increase their perceptions, reasoning, motivations, memory, and imagination? The answer, we suggest, is yes, and further, the extent to which these qualities of artificial intelligence are developed (or retarded) determines to a great extent the organization's adaptive potential.

In Table 4-1 the effects of certain standard organizational

variables on the faculties of artificial intelligence are suggested by Gerald Skibbens.[38] With respect to the organizational variable "Specificity of Job Goals," for example, Skibbens hypothesizes that low specification increases organizational *perception* by requiring individuals to focus more broadly on overall aims; enhances organizational *meaning* by widening the data base for decision-making (inputs and search behavior are not limited, for example, by narrowly defined objectives); enhances organizational *reason* by linking activities to broader purpose, rather than means objectives which often become ends in themselves; and enhances organizational *motivation* by providing more discretion to individuals and thus increasing levels of commitment.

Skibbens's conceptualization of artificial intelligence and its link to organizational variables is admittedly speculative, but the basic concept of simulating human intelligence in organization and viewing the nurturing of this intelligence as a key intervening variable leading to increased organizational effectiveness is intriguing nevertheless and worthy of further speculation and investigation.

One can hypothesize, for example, that a direct relationship exists between the development and growth of a school organization's perception, memory, reasoning, imagination and motivation and similar characteristics in a classroom's organization. These classroom characteristics, in turn, have a direct and telling effect on student perception, memory, reasoning, imagination and motivation—the building blocks of one's intellectual development. If this is the case, then organizational factors are more important than most realize.

In this chapter we have suggested that organization and management in education is far more complex than suggested by the highly rational and structured closed-system models. Open-system thinking, however, does not provide an adequate alternative conceptualization of the school as an organization. What the school lacks in objective rationality, for example, is overshadowed by its cultural-normative rationality characterized by its collective valuing capacity. This normative rationality and valuing capacity of schools, underestimated by open-system models of organizations and management, suggests that educational decision-making can best be understood from the perspective of preference theory rather than rational theory. The importance of preference theory is highlighted by the differences which exist between public and private administration. These differences, in turn, are important building blocks for establishing a unique applied science of educational administration.

Notes

1. Herbert A. Simon, *The Sciences of the Artificial* (Cambridge, Mass.: The MIT Press, 1969).
2. Ibid., p. 16.
3. Ibid.
4. See, for example, Max Weber, "Bureaucracy," from Max Weber, *Essays in Sociology,* H. H. Gerth and C. W. Mills, trans. and ed. (New York: Oxford University Press, 1946). Reprinted in Joseph Litterer, *Organizations: Structure and Behavior* (New York: John Wiley and Sons, 1969). See also Max Weber, *The Theory of Social and Economic Organization,* A. M. Henderson, T. Parsons, trans., T. Parsons, ed. (New York: The Free Press of Glencoe, 1947).
5. Frederick Taylor, *The Principles of Scientific Management* (New York: Harper & Row, 1911). Reprinted by Harter & Row in 1945.
6. Talcott Parsons, *Structure and Process in Modern Societies* (New York: The Free Press of Glencoe, 1960).
7. James D. Thompson, *Organizations in Action* (New York: McGraw-Hill, 1967).
8. W. Ross Ashby, *An Introduction to Cybernetics* (London: Chapman and Hall Ltd., 1956).
9. Alan Peshkin, "Whom Shall the Schools Serve? Some Dilemmas of Local Control in a Rural School District," *Curriculum Inquiry* 6, no. 3 (1977):187–189.
10. Taylor, *Principles of Scientific Management.*
11. Luther Gulick and L. Urwick, eds., *Papers on the Science of Administration* (New York: Institute of Public Administration, 1937).
12. James D. Mooney and Allen C. Reilly, *Onward Industry* (New York: Harper and Bros., 1939).
13. Henri Fayol, *General and Industrial Management,* Constance Storrs (trans.) (London: Sir Isaac Pitman and Sons, 1949).
14. Weber, "Bureaucracy" and *Theory of Social and Economic Organization.*
15. Taylor, *Principles of Scientific Management.*
16. Franklin Bobbitt, "The Supervision of City Schools: Some General Principles of Management Applied to the Problems of City-School Systems," *Twelfth Yearbook of the National Society for the Study of Education* (Bloomington, Ill., 1913).
17. Weber, "Bureaucracy."
18. Thompson, *Organizations in Action.*
19. Herbert Simon, *Administrative Behavior: A Study of Decision-Making Processes in Administrative Organizations* (New York: Macmillan Co., 1945).
20. John March and Herbert Simon, *Organizations* (New York: John Wiley, Inc., 1958).
21. Richard H. Hall, *Organization's Structure and Processes,* 2nd ed. (Englewood Cliffs, N.J.: Prentice-Hall, 1977), p. 59.
22. Tom Burns and G. M. Stalker, *The Management of Innovation* (London: Tavistock Publications, 1961). See also F. E. Emery and E. L. Trist, "The Causal Texture of Organizational Environments," *Human*

Relations 18, no. 2 (1963):268–281; Shirley Terreberry, "The Evolution of Organizational Environments," *Administrative Science Quarterly* 12, no. 4 (1968):590–613.

23. Victor Vroom, "Some Personality Determinants of the Effects of Participation." *Journal of Abnormal and Social Psychology* 59, no. 3 (1959):322–327.

24. Joan Woodward, *Industrial Organization: Theory and Practice* (London: Oxford University Press, 1965).

25. Thompson, *Organizations in Action.*

26. Ibid., p. 16.

27. Ibid., p. 18.

28. As mentioned in Joseph Bower, "Effective Public Management; It Isn't the Same as Effective Business Management," *Harvard Business Review* 55, no. 2 (March–April 1977):131–140.

29. Ibid., p. 140. Bower further notes, "Often we seem to assume that effective management in the public sector has the same basic qualities as effective management in the private sector. Yet, several years after Watergate, Americans are still chafing at the acts of a president who claimed to have taken considerable care to keep his office businesslike. To him, that meant no leaks, absolute loyalty to the organization, tight hierarchy in structure and operations, and a single coordinated voice in relation with other organizations and the public. Some observers have taken the consequences of the Nixon White House to be evidence not merely of the personal failure involved but also of the inherent weakness of applying a business model to government activity" (p. 131).

30. Michel Crozier, "A New Rationale for American Business," *Daedalus* 98 (1969):154.

31. Thompson, *Organizations in Action.*

32. Louis R. Pondy, "Beyond Open Systems Models of Organization," paper presented at the annual meeting of the Academy of Management, Kansas City, Mo., August 12, 1976.

33. Pondy, "Beyond Open Systems Models."

34. Philip J. Runkel, "The Capacity of Human Systems for Solving Problems," unpublished paper, Center for Educational Policy and Management, University of Oregon, December 1976.

35. For a discussion of educational platform, see Decker Walker, "A Naturalistic Model for Curriculum Development," *The School Review* 80 (1971):51–65 and Thomas J. Sergiovanni, "Toward a Theory of Clinical Supervision," *Journal of Research and Development in Education* 9, no. 2 (1976):20–29.

36. Rensis Likert, *The Human Organization* (New York: McGraw-Hill, 1967), p. 137.

37. For an application of Likert's ideas to education, see Thomas J. Sergiovanni and Robert J. Starratt, *Supervision: Human Perspectives,* 2nd ed. (New York: McGraw-Hill, 1978).

38. Gerald Skibbens, *Organizational Evolution* (New York: AMACOM, 1974).

Part II
THE HUMAN SYSTEM

Chapter 5
The Problem of Adult Motivation

Motivation is an important word to educators. As it applies to students, motivation has received considerable attention in the preparation programs of teachers and has also received attention as an integral component of curriculum development. Yet with all of this emphasis on motivation for students, educators have tended to overlook the topic of motivation as it relates to professional workers. This chapter proposes, discusses, and critiques a theory of adult motivation which seems particularly compatible with the unique characteristics of work in schools. Schools are human organizations in the sense that they have human purposes and pursue these purposes by working directly with students as both processes and products. Further, the technology of schools is labor intensive as opposed to being dominated by machinery or other technical processes and devices.

Intensive human qualities of work in schools require that not only should student and adult motivation receive significant attention in any theory of administration but that strategies of motivation should possess humanistic characteristics. The theory of adult motivation proposed in this chapter is consistent with the Eupsychian management principles discussed in Chapter 3. Further, this theory provides a basis for further consideration of the schools' human system, which follows in other chapters of Part II.

Throughout Part II the authors sift through the evidence in establishing a theoretical and empirical link between motivational strategies, improved performance of teachers, and more effective schools. Providing teachers with opportunities for experiencing intrinsic satisfaction through more enriched work is the means advocated. Though the theoretical and empirical case for our prescriptions for professional practice is made, it is a moot case, for we believe that workers—teachers and students among them—are entitled to more satisfying and enriching jobs. The chapters in Part II are concerned with the human dimension in administration and are critical in understanding the school's sociological, organizational, and political characteristics, which are concerns of Parts III and IV. Further, this human dimension provides the criteria for developing the action strategies which comprise the process of administration discussed in Part V of the book.

THIRD FORCE PSYCHOLOGY

Psychology has been dominated by two schools of thought—that of the behaviorists and that of the Freudians.[1] The schools differ in many dimensions but share a common view of the person as a spectator who reacts to forces outside of himself (behaviorists) or to forces within (Freudians). Humans, according to these points of view, are perceived largely in a negative sense as passive and reactive animals.

Third Force psychology, an alternative and indeed more usable field of psychology for school practitioners, does not deny the negative and reactive aspects of humankind but does not accept this view alone. Combined with a person's reactive tendency is a proactive tendency based on the need to grow and develop—to behave in a positive way and indeed to shape *the very forces which require one to react.* Third Force psychology argues that humankind is not entirely motivated by that which is past (Freud) or by the conditions of one's present environment (Skinner) but is also, perhaps primarily, motivated by the attraction of what is ahead. According to this view, one's visions and goals, hopes and aspirations are the prime motivators—not one's fears, doubts, and hates—or what one can get for the moment in a stimulus-response interchange. This movement in psychology, in other words, does not reject the negative and reactive side of humankind, but rather places it properly in relation to one's positive side.

It is not the intent of this chapter to give a short course in psychology, but, at great risk of oversimplification, the chapter does provide samples of thinking characteristic of Third Force psychology, deriving from such thinking an operational theory of human motivation which can be applied to teachers and other professionals at work.

A THEORY OF HUMAN MOTIVATION

It can be argued that people express their needs in two ways—reactive and proactive. Herzberg[2] finds it useful to describe these expressions as two independent drives—avoidance and approach. People, for example, tend to avoid certain things like hunger, fear, the cold, the loss of a job, embarrassment, psychological exposure, ridicule, hostility, shame, and other things that suggest pain, discomfort, and failure. In order to provide for these very real and important avoidance needs, one reacts by avoiding a hostile environment. For example, a school executive responding to pressure from a board member may react to avoid interpersonal conflict, or perhaps the loss of a job, or the loss of benefits which one can obtain by being in the board member's good graces.

When people are motivated by approach drives, they act not to avoid the unpleasant but rather to seek benefits and satisfactions at a higher level. A person acts because actions are good, are meaningful, make the person feel good, or make others feel good about the person. It is assumed that people have a desire to be considered by others as worthy and important, and to have control over their destinies, for these improve a person's self-image.

The Needs Hierarchy

Abraham Maslow[3] has developed an interesting and useful framework which takes expressions of needs at the commonsense level—such as air, water, food, protection, love, control, sex, respect, doing good, having influence, and so on—and incorporates them into a five-level taxonomy arranged in hierarchical order of prepotency. The prepotency feature of this formulation is of importance, for it specifies that the most basic needs must be reasonably satisfied or "programmed" before one is interested in needs at the next highest level. Further, the theory suggests that as long as a lower-order need is satisfied, it is not a motivation of behavior.

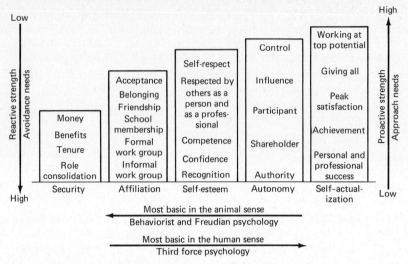

Figure 5-1   The needs hierarchy.

Needs at the highest level of this hierarchy are really the most basic in the human sense, although they have low priority in prepotency. This suggests the foremost challenge for school executives— facilitating the emergence of basic needs in the human sense.

The five need levels according to the Maslow formulation are physiological, security, social, esteem, and self-actualization. Figure 5-1 presents a slightly altered needs hierarchy developed by Lyman Porter,[4] an adaptation which deletes physiological needs and adds autonomy needs (physiological needs seem reasonably well met for school professionals in our society and the need for autonomy—the desire for control over one's environment or destiny—seems particularly important for school professionals). Figure 5-2 illustrates the prepotency feature of Maslow's theory with affiliation dominating. According to the theory, one is not apt to be too concerned with self-esteem, autonomy, or self-actualization while seeking acceptance. A person will abandon affiliation gains, however, if they threaten security. By the same token, one cannot begin to approach satisfaction of autonomy and self-actualization needs until he or she feels reasonably safe, loved, and competent (self-esteem).

The Needs Hierarchy and Teachers

Of concern to school executives is to find out at what levels teachers are with respect to the hierarchy. Knowing the levels of prepotency of teachers is important because it does not make sense to motivate

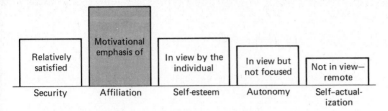

Relatively satisfied	Motivational emphasis of	In view by the individual	In view but not focused	Not in view—remote
Security	Affiliation	Self-esteem	Autonomy	Self-actualization

Figure 5-2   Prepotency ordering when affiliation dominates.

at the autonomy level if teachers are insecure or to motivate at the security level when they seek autonomy. Inexperienced school executives often overestimate the operating-need level of teachers and "scare them off" with ultraparticipatory "self-actualizing" administration. This is as ineffective as denying teachers meaningful satisfaction by underestimating operating-need levels. The intent of this discussion is not to abandon our goal or self-actualizing administration, but to suggest that people are likely to retreat if they are not ready for additional growth opportunities. The goal for school executives should be growth from whatever level teachers are at present.

In Figures 5-3 and 5-4 prepotency levels of need operation for educators are shown. The figures were originally constructed from data collected in 1966 from 233 educators in a suburban Rochester, New York, school district.[5] The shaded bars in Figures 5-3 and 5-4 represent the 1966 Rochester data. Superimposed on the bars are 1977 data collected by Richard Birarda.[6] Birarda studied 330 educators employed by the Calgary, Alberta, public school system.[7]

Figure 5-5 was originally constructed from 1969 data collected from 1593 secondary school teachers in 36 Illinois high schools.[8] Superimposed on the original bars are data collected in 1978. Surveyed were 585 teachers from 7 of the same Illinois high schools used in 1969.[9]

Let us examine perceptions of need deficiency in Figures 5-3 and 5-4 first, keeping in mind the cautions described in note 7. For educators who responded in 1966, esteem seemed to be the level of need showing the greatest deficiency. Large deficiencies were also reported for autonomy and self-actualization. Security deficiencies, by comparison, were lower for this group though still somewhat high for all but the youngest age group. In every case, the social need category accounted for the smallest perceived need deficiencies for the 1966 teachers.

Perceived need deficiencies reported by the teachers surveyed by Birarda in 1977 differ somewhat from those of the earlier survey. Esteem still appears as a dominant area of perceived need defi-

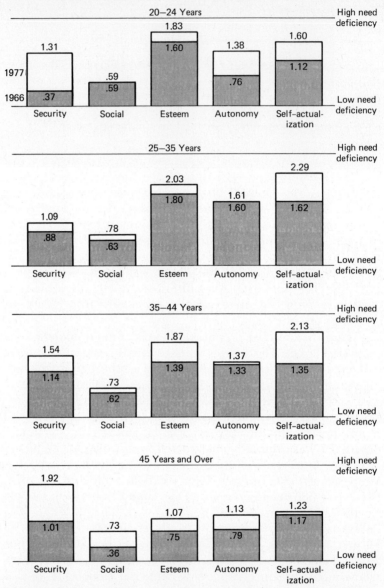

Figure 5-3   1966 prepotency levels of need operation for suburban Rochester, New York, educators grouped by age as compared with 1977 data from Calgary, Alberta, educators.
Note: The shaded bars represent the 1966 data.

ciency, actually increasing for all but the oldest age group. But esteem is rivaled in 1977 by important increases in perceived need deficiencies for all groups at the self-actualization level on the one hand and (except for the 25-to-34 age group) security on the other.

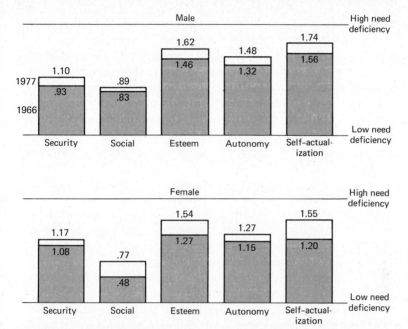

Figure 5-4   1966 prepotency levels of need operation for suburban Rochester, New York, educators grouped by sex as compared with 1977 data from Calgary, Alberta, educators.
Note: The shaded bars represent the 1966 data.

Changes in the work demands of educators and in the work environment may well be contributors to these increases in security. One can reasonably speculate that accountability, increased lay participation, state- and provincial-mandated competency testing, and general increases in the political nature of education influence feelings of security. These pressures, combined with the prospect of older educators facing retirement in an age of economic uncertainty, can take obvious tolls.

As compared with perceptions of educators surveyed in 1966, the 1977 educators in the youngest age group (20 to 24) show the largest increases in nearly all need categories. A 250 percent increase in perceived deficiencies at the security level, for example, may reflect the tightening job market and pressures of reduction in force.

By contrast, the 1977, 25-to-30 age group shows a small decline in perceived need deficiencies at the security level—perhaps suggesting a sigh of relief as this group accumulates enough service to afford job protection. But this same age group reports the largest need deficiencies in esteem, autonomy, and self-actualization categories—a distinction shared with their 1966 counterparts but only more so. The years from 25 to 34 seem to represent a period of hope and despair for the educators. Expectations are high at this stage of one's career. Teachers are moving into supervisory and administrative posts at an earlier age—it is now or never for many of these people. This is also the age for most rapid career development in other occupations. Although teachers hold their own with other occupationsl groups (in terms of promotion and salary) in the early years, people in other occupations move ahead at this time. The engineer next door (same age) has moved to a "better" neighborhood and the accountant across the street (same age) has had his fourth promotion—junior partner is next.

It seems clear that educators in this group want more satisfaction from their work at the esteem, autonomy, and self-actualization levels than at other stages of their careers. Further, dissatisfaction is high, reflecting the school's inability to respond to these desires.

In 1966 and 1977, smallest need deficiencies are reported by the older teachers, particularly those 45 and over. One is tempted to interpret this as a positive sign, indicating that perseverance pays off or that things go better with age. Out data in the Illinois study, however, reveal a tendency quite to the contrary. *These teachers are not getting more in terms of need fulfillment as the years go by but, rather, are expecting less.* Levels of aspiration seem to drop considerably with age. Perhaps teachers become more "realistic" or resigned to things as they are.

The relative unimportance of social needs reflected in the low perceived need deficiency scores for this category of both 1966 and 1977 respondents should cast conclusive doubts on the utility of human relations strategies for educational administrators and supervisors. Indeed, the findings from both surveys suggest that schools overstress this dimension. Educators, it seems, do not seek additional job satisfaction from the school's social climate itself. Deficiencies perceived at the esteem and other higher levels suggest the personal attention they seek is that derived from the work itself (recognition for achievement, participating in decisions about work, responsibility for achieving outcomes, and challenging assignments) rather than its context (pleasant surroundings, nice administrators and supervisors, and close friends with whom to work).

Figure 5-4 depicts comparisons of educators by sex. The data suggest that women are becoming more "liberated" by expecting more from work in 1977 than 1966 and indeed expecting as much as men. As a result of this increase in expectations, women enjoy the liberated privilege of increased dissatisfaction with present levels

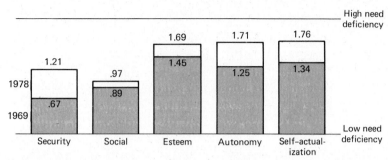

Figure 5-5   1969 prepotency levels of need operation for 1593 secondary school teachers in Illinois as compared with 585 teachers from several of the same schools collected in 1978.
Note: The shaded bars represent the 1969 data.

of need fulfillment. The women surveyed in 1977 report higher levels of need deficiency than their 1966 counterparts in all categories. Despite these increases, they remain relatively satisfied when compared with men. Indeed, the men surveyed in 1977 as compared with those surveyed in 1966 show a decline in perceived need deficiencies in the esteem and autonomy categories.

JOB SATISFACTION OF TEACHERS: THE BRIGHT AND DARK SIDES

The findings illustrated in Figure 5-5 are highly supportive of those illustrated in Figures 5-3 and 5-4. Figure 5-5 is constructed from better data in the statistical sense; therefore, this support is reassuring. Again the findings suggest that while comparatively teachers are generally well satisfied with the two lower-order needs, they are appreciably less satisfied with need fulfillment for the three higher-order needs. It does appear, therefore, that higher-order need satisfaction opportunities are not as available to teachers as those associated with lower need satisfaction. This suggests that much work still needs to be done to enrich the job of teaching in efforts to increase opportunities for higher need satisfaction. But one development which cannot be ignored in comparing the 1969 and 1978 responses is the large, indeed 55 percent increase in perceived need deficiencies at the security level. We are further behind in providing opportunities for higher-level satisfaction, and the high security deficiencies suggest that if Maslow's prepotency hypothesis is true, improvement will be slow.

Table 5-1 compares need prepotency levels of need operation for secondary school teachers in 1969 and 1978 with those reported by Birarda in his 1977 study of Calgary education. The trends

Table 5-1 COMPARISON OF MEAN PREPOTENCY LEVELS OF NEED OPERATION FOR SECONDARY SCHOOL TEACHERS IN ILLINOIS IN 1969 AND 1978 AND CALGARY EDUCATORS IN 1977

NEED CATEGORY	PERCEIVED NEED DEFICIENCY		
	ILLINOIS TEACHERS (1969)	ILLINOIS TEACHERS (1978)	CALGARY EDUCATORS (1977)
Security	0.67	1.21	1.14
Social	0.89	0.97	0.78
Esteem	1.45	1.69	1.50
Autonomy	1.25	1.71	1.28
Self-actualization	1.34	1.76	1.63

suggested in Figure 5-5 are enhanced by this comparison. Perceived need deficiencies increases are reported in all categories in both later samples when compared with the 1969 data. Of particular note are the large increases reported at the security and self-actualization levels.

Nevertheless, the most pressing need of teachers seems to us to be at the esteem level. True, this need is now confounded by large security deficiencies, and serious attention needs to be given to how school executives can best deal with this problem. Unfortunately, many of the forces (mandated accountability pressures, taxpayer revolts, declining student enrollments, for example) contributing to security deficiencies are outside of the direct control of school executives. One strategy might be clearly to separate these forces from others which contribute to higher-order need fulfillment. This assumes that teachers are able to respond to need fulfillment more ambiguously than suggested by Maslow. The strength and attractiveness of other need-level opportunities would probably be an important factor in one's ability to respond to need levels more ambiguously.[10]

The recent need deficiency studies by Birarda[11] and by Goldsberry[12] and his colleagues paint a dark portrait of teacher job satisfaction. The Illinois study, for example, shows substantial across-the-board increases in all areas of perceived need deficiency except security. But there is a bright side to this practice. In the 1978 Illinois study, Goldsberry and his colleagues asked teachers three general satisfaction questions: How satisfied are you with your present job, would you advise a good friend to become a teacher, and would you advise a friend to teach in your school? The responses to these questions are summarized in Table 5-2.

The first question, satisfaction with present job, was designed to assess general satisfaction from the respondent's personal per-

Table 5-2   THREE QUESTIONS ON GENERAL JOB SATISFACTION

I. HOW SATISFIED ARE YOU WITH YOUR PRESENT JOB?

VALUE	NUMBER ($n = 584$)	PERCENT
1. Highly satisfied	184	31
2. Moderately satisfied	204	35
3. Slightly satisfied	47	8
4. Slightly dissatisfied	43	7
5. Moderately dissatisfied	59	10
6. Highly dissatisfied	47	8
Value categories 1 and 2	388	66
Value categories 3 and 4	90	15
Value categories 5 and 6	106	18

II. WOULD YOU ADVISE A GOOD FRIEND TO BECOME A TEACHER?

VALUE	NUMBER ($n = 578$)	PERCENT
1. Strongly recommend	196	34
2. Have doubts	283	49
3. Advise against	99	17

III. WOULD YOU ADVISE A FRIEND TO TEACH IN YOUR SCHOOL?

VALUE	NUMBER ($n = 582$)	PERCENT
1. Strongly recommend	339	58
2. Have doubts	161	27
3. Advise against	82	14

SOURCE: Lee Goldsberry, Robbie Henderson, and Thomas J. Sergiovanni, "Perceived Need Deficiencies of Teachers in 1978 as Compared with 1968." Educational Administrator and Supervision, University of Illinois, Urbana-Champaign, 1978.

spective. Of the secondary school teachers who responded, 66 percent indicated that they were either highly or moderately satisfied, 18 percent that they were highly or moderately dissatisfied, and 15 percent were in the middle categories. This response pattern is fairly hopeful particularly when it is generally recognized that elementary school teachers tend to be more satisfied with jobs than secondary school teachers.[13] The third question was designed to assess the potential respondents perceived their present job afforded newcomers for experiencing job satisfaction. Of the teachers who responded, 58 percent strongly recommended their school for newcomers and 14 percent advised against it. This response pattern, though less hopeful, still suggests that overall conditions in the particular schools of respondents are not too bad. The second question—Would you advise a good friend to become a teacher?—was designed to assess feelings of respondents toward job satisfaction potential and job conditions in education generally. This response pattern is more bleak. About half of the teachers who responded, for example, had doubts and another 17 percent advised against becoming a teacher. The bright side of the picture, as we see it, is that in the face of increases in perceived need deficiencies, teachers remain fairly hopeful. Further, they are able to differentiate between conditions they face in their own particular jobs and the general climate facing the teaching professions as a whole with the former apparently being better than the latter.

CRITIQUE OF MASLOW'S THEORY

Maslow's theory of human motivation and particularly the prepotency feature of his theory has been subjected to numerous tests by researchers, with mixed results.[14] Basically, when the theory is *operationalized into practice,* it tends to underestimate individual differences among workers, overestimate the prepotency feature which suggests that a person is not motivated at a higher level unless satisfied at lower levels, and oversimply the concept of need satisfaction.

On the question of individual needs, it is more useful to assume that hierarchies of needs are individually determined and that variations exist from teacher to teacher. The Maslow hierarchy and other features of the theory should be considered as a means for understanding these individual differences rather than a template to impose uniformly on teachers.

On the question of prepotency, the evidence suggests that when the theory is operationalized into practice, it is better to think of two levels of need then five: a higher-order and a lower-order level. As Coffer and Appley suggest:

> Maslow's formulation that needs or drives are arranged in a sort of dominance heirarchy does, we think, receive at least partial support from various kinds of evidence. That the support is partial is because the evidence concerns only the needs at the two lower levels of his heirarchy, the physiological and anxiety (social) needs . . . while there is some evidence that intense physiological and safety needs can dominate behavior, evidence for the hierarchical relationship of other needs is wanting.[15]

It appears that though the prepotency aspect of Maslow's theory operates to some extent, this aspect is strongest when viewed simply as lower- or higher-order needs. For most people expressions of higher-order needs will be muted if fulfilling lower-order needs is seriously deficient. It is possible, nevertheless, for various needs to be present and attended to simultaneously. Following this level of reasoning, a better representation

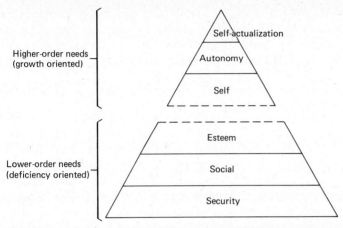

Figure 5-6   Maslow's hierarchy of needs in two categories.

of the theory is suggested by a truncated pyramid as illustrated in Figure 5-6.

On the question of oversimplifying the concept of need satisfaction, perhaps the word "satisfaction" itself is too strong to capture adequately the intent of the theory. Satisfaction has a certain finality to it and implies repletion of a need to the point that interest and desire are eliminated. *No need is ever satisfied in this sense.* Lower-order needs, for example, never get satisfied. Consider, for example, the constant demand by teachers for more security guarantees. No matter how wonderful a bargain is struck on the negotiating table this year, back they come with hands out the next year.

Witness also the seemingly never-ending search for status and the aquisition of its symbols. The new coat, the latest fashion, and an up-to-date car are part of our life-style. *Appeasement* is perhaps a better word to use than satisfaction. *Need appeasement would suggest pacifying a need or causing a need to subside thus allowing attention to other needs and concerns, but knowing that the appeased need will likely surface again.*

In fairness to Maslow, deficiencies in the theory stem from its articulation into management practice. Maslow did not intend to propose a motivational recipe for administrative use, but rather a general framework for analysis perhaps more akin to philosophy than psychology. Maslow was speaking of needs as a whole and humankind in general. His framework emerged from a lifetime of studying major theories of personality on the one hand and religions of the world on the other. Clearly, the managerial context was not in his mind. But his framework does have utility for management if it is viewed as a "thinking" theory—one which helps a school executive frame his or her thoughts about the problems of motivating teachers.

BUILDING ESTEEM

Our findings from the need deficiency studies suggest that esteem remains a powerful motivator for today's teachers. This simply means that most of today's teachers will work harder for rewards at the esteem level than for other rewards. Our findings also suggest that providing social rewards will not have much payoff in terms of increased or improved professional performance from teachers. Our discussion of esteem needs should be tempered by the importance of tending to the security needs of teachers as well. To the extent that the prepotency feature is valid, then needs evoked by severe deprivation in the security area will supersede esteem needs.

Esteem needs are particularly important, for they involve the concept of self. Teachers need to feel important as persons (self-concept) and as recognized, respected, and competent professionals (professional concept). The esteem stage in motivational development is an important one for education in that as gains are made in this stage, teachers will be able to seek satisfaction at higher levels. In other words, it is the springboard from esteem to autonomy to self-actualization which promises so much to education. Once this progression is completed, teachers will operate as self-motivated, responsible, dedicated professionals, requiring little or no supervision or regulation. Two important dimensions of esteem are examined next—the professional need for feelings of competence and the concept of self.

The Competence Motive

The psychologist Robert White[16] believes that one important thrust of human motivation is getting to know what the world is like, shaping that world, and getting that which one wants from it. He refers to this motivational thrust as a desire for competence—control over social and physical environmental factors. This desire for control is readily observable in young children as they probe, seek, and explore all that they encounter. The early successes or early failures that youngsters have, as the case may be, suggest the strength of the competence motive in later life. However, while the competence motive is cumulative—that is, it gets stronger or weaker depending upon past experience—it is not fixed in a person for life. A person whose past experience favors more failures than successes is not irrecoverable as far as competencies are concerned—his or her competence needs can be restored with repeated successes. Although it is possible, therefore, to recover from early failures, White and others believe that the power of the self-fulfilling prophecy usually takes over, and the competent get better while their counterparts get worse.

The competence motive is expressed by teachers as a desire for job mastery and professional growth. Teachers so motivated work to apply—indeed to match—their skills, abilities, and competencies against the problems of the job. Each success reinforces their image of being personally and professionally worthy.

In describing the competence motive, Gellerman states:

> The job can be one of the few remaining arenas in which man can match his skills against environment in a contest which is neither absurdly easy nor prohibitively difficult. Where such a contest is possible, the competence motive may be exercised and considerable rewards may be enjoyed. But, where it is impossible, as in most routinized or oversupervised jobs, a strong competence motive leads only to frustration, while a weak one merely encourages resignation and dependency. Further, the sense of competence probably plays a key role in effecting job success, especially in those jobs where initiative or innovation is essential. A man who trusts his own ability to influence his environment will actually try to influence it more often and more boldly than someone who is inclined to let the environment influence him.[17]

School executives need to be continually alert to manifest and latent expressions of the competence motive in teachers. The manifest expressions come early in a person's career and depend upon reinforcement, encouragement, and facilitation if they are to be encouraged to form a pattern for the person's career. The person with latent potential to express this need but who holds back for fear or other reasons needs reassurance and encouragement. Thus teachers, administrators, staff, and nonprofessional school workers who are new to the school need early success if they are to adopt the competence pattern. We do not refer here to small successes but, rather, to large ones which point the way for a career pattern which is enjoyable and beneficial to the individual and enjoyable and profitable to the school and its students.

Teachers who are midcareer and who have not expressed this need may not be completely lost regarding the competency dimension either. Many such people will respond later if success becomes a habit. Some psychologists have expressed a concern over competency loss in employees as they get older.[18] A widespread belief is that advancing age brings with it a decline in physical and mental abilities; therefore, it is more difficult to maintain and increase professional competency. This decline renders the person unable to compete with younger and more vigorous co-workers. If such declines are real rather than myth, surely they are gradual ones which are more than offset by wisdom and maturity. Gellerman notes, "There is more variability in productivity *within* any age group than there is *between* any two age groups. The latter is perhaps the hardest fact we have to guide us. It strongly suggests that increasing age, in itself, has only a minor tendency to bring about competence loss. Other causes . . . are surely more important."[19]

Competence loss is a problem to older school professionals, but it is probably so in terms of self-perception rather than objective fact. If one believes that he or she is becoming less competent professionally with age, then he or she is. Certain generalizations can be made about the competence motive:

1. People motivated by the competence need have much to bring to the school and its clients in the form of extraordinary performance. They do not fulfill this need in the faculty lounge.
2. School executives should provide all school participants opportunities to express this competence need and should reward those who express it. For many, the need must be instilled. No progress can be made until lower-order needs (security and affiliation or social) are reasonably taken care of and until teachers experience what competence has to offer to esteem building.
3. Robert White's research suggests that the years six to nine are crucial in the *initial* development of the competence motive. This suggests that we need to rid the school of manifestations of failure if we prize competence development in youngsters.
4. If teachers and others become bored with our efforts to reward and to facilitate expression of the competence motive, this is a sign of our success, for it suggests that they are better able to work more deliberately at the autonomy and self-actualization levels of the Maslow needs hierarchy. A note of caution may be in order, however. The "rules" of motivation do not permit taking away rewards, but rather building upon those already offered even as raising the

stakes in poker does not eliminate the maintenance of the cumulative pot.

Usually, whatever a person does makes self-sense. One's concept of self is an image that one builds over the years. At best, this image is a gross approximation, but each of us displays and demonstrates amazing loyalty to it nonetheless. By and large we accept things, ideas, and cues which are consistent with our self-image and reject those which are not. If someone forces an inconsistency upon us, we panic and seek defense mechanisms which will protect us or which will explain away the inconsistencies. As we get older or as we move to positions of responsibility, we often become even more resistant to self-image alterations—indeed, to change itself. We simply have too much invested in building and protecting our self-concept to accept change readily and, therefore, risk alteration.

One's concepts of self can be changed, altered, or modified if one perceives that he or she will gain from such change. Change comes about by adding new and broadening dimensions which expand one's image so that it is richer. By broadening the concept of self, through increased self-awareness, more and more changes are acceptable and compatible to this image.

Why do some educational workers have relatively low, protective self-concepts whereas others have higher, more open self-concepts? Those with low self-concepts are sometimes labeled "failure avoiders," for they devote their energies (indeed are motivated) to self-protection and ego defense. They are not likely to seek responsibility, to call attention to themselves, to take risks, to be innovative, to overcommit themselves, to show independence, or to work for autonomy. Rather, they seek and work for a relatively safe environment, free of risks, tension, and change. They prefer being told what to do and largely avoid opportunities for independent responsibility. Success seekers, on the other hand, seek all of the action that failure avoiders avoid. Although they too are interested in a resonably safe, secure environment which offers some protection, they are not satisfied with this alone as they continually seek reinforcement for their competence needs, as well as expressions of autonomy and self-actualization. The key differentiator between success seekers and failure avoiders is found in the development of the competence motive (see Figure 5-7).

Conceptual understanding of human need and its relationship to adult motivation, while extremely useful, is still removed somewhat from a prescription for administrative action. We move closer

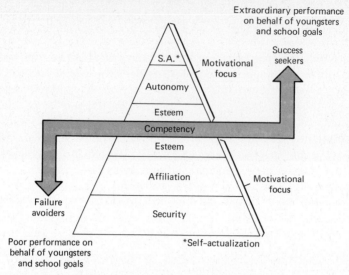

Figure 5-7   Development of the competence motive: differentiation between success seekers and failure avoiders.

to practical prescription in the next chapter as we examine the concept of job satisfaction and the motivation-hygiene theory.

Notes

1. See, for example, B. F. Skinner, *Science and Human Behavior* (New York: Macmillan, 1953); and Sigmund Freud, *Civilization and Its Discontents: The Future of an Illusion*, 3rd ed. (London: Hogarth Press, 1946), or *The Collected Papers of Sigmund Freud* (New York: International Psychoanalytic Press, 1950).
2. Frederick Herzberg, *Work and the Nature of Man* (New York: World, 1966).
3. Abraham Maslow, *Motivation and Personality* (New York: Harper & Row, 1954).
4. Lyman Porter, "Job Attitudes in Management I. Perceived Deficiencies in Need Fulfillment as a Function of Job Level," *Journal of Applied Psychology* 47 (December 1963):386–397.
5. Francis M. Trusty and Thomas J. Sergiovanni, "Perceived Need Deficiencies of Teachers and Administrators: A Proposal for Restructuring Teacher Roles," *Educational Administration Quarterly* 2 (Autumn 1966):168–180.
6. Richard W. Birarda, "Educator Aspirations, Perceived Need Deficiencies, and Response to Organizational Rewards." Master's Thesis, Department of Educational Administration, University of Calgary, Calgary, Alberta, 1978.

7. Comparing need deficiencies of educators from suburban Rochester, New York, at time one with those of educators from Calgary, Alberta, at time two has its risks, and caution is urged in interpreting findings. Nevertheless, though important differences exist, our personal experience with educators in Alberta and in the Rochester area suggests that similarities in economic conditions, values, cultures, work setting, life-style, and work expectations make these comparisons useful. See, for example, Edward A. Holdaway, "Facet and Overall Satisfaction of Teachers," *Educational Administration Quarterly* 14, no. 1 (1978): 30–47, for another study of Alberta teachers with a "familiar ring." Our discussion however, should be viewed as speculative generations of hypotheses rather than the rendering of facts.

8. Fred D. Carver and Thomas J. Sergiovanni, "The School as a Complex Organization: An Analysis of Three Structural Elements," Department of Educational Administration, University of Illinois, Urbana-Champaign, June 1968 (mimeographed). See also Carver and Sergiovanni, "Complexity, Adaptability and Job Satisfaction in High Schools: An Axiomatic Theory Applied," *Journal of Educational Administrators* 9, no. 1 (May 1971): 16, Table 2. Questionnaire items appear in note 15. Figure 5-5 was constructed from data collected as part of the larger study cited previously and reported in Thomas J. Sergiovanni and Robert J. Starratt, *Supervision: Human Perspectives,* 2nd ed. (New York: McGraw-Hill, 1979), chap. 8. In each instance (notes 5, 6, 9, and here) respondents completed a 13-item need deficiency questionnaire modeled after each of five categories of a modified version of Abraham Maslow's need heirarchy. The instrument assessed on a seven-point scale the amount of need fulfillment available for each of the five categories as well as the amount each respondent felt he or she needed. The difference between actual and desired need fulfillment was computed and labeled a "perceived need deficiency." Mean differences between actual and desired need fulfillment were used to construct Figures 5-3, 5-4, and 5-5. In the Trusty-Sergiovanni study and in the Birarda study, data were grouped by age, sex, experience, and professional role. In the Carver-Sergiovanni study and in the Goldsberry, Henderson, and Sergiovanni study (note 9), adjusted school mean scores were computed by controlling, through the use of analysis of covariance techniques, the effects of age, sex, and teaching experience.

9. Lee Goldsberry, Robbie Henderson, and Thomas J. Sergiovanni, "Perceived Need Deficiencies of Teachers in 1978 as Compared with 1968," Department of Educational Administration and Supervision, University of Illinois, Urbana-Champaign, 1978.

10. Consider many persons throughout the world who live in constant threat to their security but are able nevertheless to obtain satisfaction at higher levels.

11. Birarda, "Educator Aspirations."

12. Goldsberry et al., "Perceived Need Deficiencies of Teachers in 1978."

13. See, for example, David G. Ryans, *Characteristics of Teachers* (Washington D.C.: American Council on Education, 1960), p. 385, and Trusty and Sergiovanni, "Perceived Need Deficiencies of Teachers and Administrators," p. 175.
14. See, for example, Benjamin Schneider and Clayton Alderfer, "Three Studies of Need Satisfaction in Organizations," *Administrative Science Quarterly* 18, no. 4 (1973):489–505.
15. C. N. Cofer and M. H. Appley, *Motivation: Theory and Research* (New York: John Wiley & Sons, 1964), pp. 684, 691.
16. Robert W. White, "Motivation Reconsidered: The Concept of Competence," *Psychological Review* 66, no. 5 (1959):297–329. White's position is that Freudian theory with its reliance on reaction from within is too simple to account for the broad spectrum of human behavior. White argues that man is also an active observer and shaper of his life and his environment, and attributes this positive tendency to "the competence motive."
17. Saul Gellerman, *Motivation and Productivity*, (New York: The American Management Association, 1963), p. 114.
18. Saul Gellerman, *Management by Motivation* (New York: The American Management Association, 1968), chapter 8.
19. Ibid., p. 138.

Chapter 6
Job Satisfaction:
Motivation in Practice

Have we misjudged what really makes a difference to teachers on the job in terms of stimulating their performance? Have we assumed that factors which attract and keep teachers on the job are the same as those which motivate them to work in extraordinary ways? Have we confused the absence of job dissatisfaction in teachers with the presence of job satisfaction? Are we overestimating the importance of extrinsic factors in dealing with teachers? Are we underestimating the importance of intrinsic factors? Are we confusing symptoms of unrest among teachers with causes of unrest? Indeed, are we confusing satisfaction factors which contribute to fulfilling our basic needs with those which contribute to fulfilling our growth needs?

A growing body of literature seems to suggest that the answer to each of these questions is yes. Most of this literature is based on the work of Fredrick Herzberg, a motivational psychologist, whose provocative and important work requires that we critically evaluate present practices which characterize personnel administration. In this chapter the work of Herzberg and of others is examined with regard to the nature of satisfaction in work for teachers, and the meaning of this satisfaction both in attracting and keeping competent staff and in stimulating extraordinary performance on behalf of school goals.

JOB SATISFACTION RESEARCH

Over the years a number of studies have been made of teacher satisfaction and morale. Chase,[1] for example, found that an important factor relating to satisfaction for teachers was the dynamic and stimulating leadership of the principal. Teachers also emphasized helpfulness, opportunities for professional growth, respect, and friendliness as administrative qualities which contributed to job satisfaction. Bidwell, in a related study,[2] found that teacher satisfaction depends upon teacher expectations of how administrators should behave and the extent to which these expectations were fulfilled. Other investigators find that large classes are a source of dissatisfaction, that higher morale exists when teachers have more free time away from pupils, and that satisfaction is directly related to the extent that teachers participate in decision-making.

Findings of this sort are interesting and useful, but many are largely descriptive, unrelated, and divorced from theory. This is a serious handicap, for such findings, not being linked to theoretical constructs, have limited potential for guiding the development of personnel practices.

One significant problem with job satisfaction research in education has been the assumption that factors which contribute to job satisfaction and those which contribute to job dissatisfaction are the same. For example, if teachers are dissatisfied with large classes, it has been assumed that providing them with smaller classes will produce satisfaction. Second, it has been assumed that manipulating or changing job variables relating to satisfaction has relatively single-track effects. We know that teachers like friendly principals as well as principals who help them grow professionally, but what effects do each of these behaviors of principals have on teacher performance? New evidence seems to suggest that friendliness, although a contributor to attracting and keeping staff, has little influence on stimulating performance for most teachers. Professional growth opportunities, on the other hand, seem not to have much effect on attracting and keeping most teachers but do indeed stimulate them to perform in extraordinary ways. Further, although friendliness does not motivate teachers to perform better, lack of friendliness is a distractor from performance. In other words,

teachers are not likely to perform well in an unfriendly environment, *but* teachers, by and large, are not necessarily motivated
simply because the school and the principal are friendly either. By
the same token, professional growth opportunities motivate
teachers to perform well, but the absence of these opportunities
seldom produces enough dissatisfaction to cause teachers to change
jobs. Although explaining this relationship sounds somewhat like a
semantic ruse, it is the core of the motivation-hygiene theory which
is discussed next.

THE MOTIVATION-HYGIENE THEORY

The work of Herzberg and his associates[3] suggests an alternative to
the continuum hypothesis which for so long has dominated job
satisfaction research and writing in education. Herzberg proposes
that factors which contribute to job satisfaction and factors which
contribute to job dissatisfaction form two separate sets. His hypothesis is that factors from one set (e.g., opportunities for professional
growth) contribute to satisfaction if present but not dissatisfaction if
absent, whereas factors from the other set (e.g., friendly expressions
from the principal) lead to dissatisfaction if not present, but their
presence does not contribute very much to satisfaction. The factors
which comprise the first set, called *satisfiers*, are directly related to
intrinsic matters derived from the work itself. The factors which
comprise the second set, called *dissatisfiers*, are directly related to
extrinsic matters derived from the conditions of work.

Before the nature of the factors which comprise each of these
sets is examined, it is important to make one more distinction
between them. The dissatisfiers are factors which take care of one's
avoidance needs—those basic in an animalistic sense—while the
satisfiers are factors which take care of one's approach needs—
those basic in a humanistic sense. Satisfiers and dissatisfiers are
illustrated in Figure 6-1.

Since the dissatisfiers are related to the conditions of work
rather than the work itself, they have little motivational potential
for most people. The satisfiers, which are directly related to the
work itself and are indeed derived from the work itself, are
motivators by definition. The importance of the dissatisfiers cannot
be overlooked, however, for they provide the necessary preparation
for facilitating the satisfiers. Herzberg refers to these as "hygienic"
in nature because they help to prevent on-the-job trouble. Of course,
salary, working conditions, good supervision, teaching materials,
small classes, preparation periods, overtime pay, and other

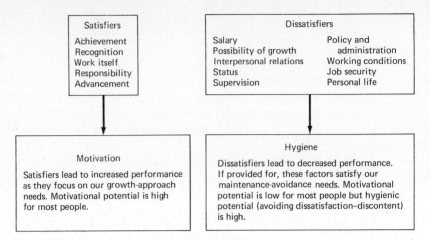

Satisfiers	Dissatisfiers	
Achievement	Salary	Policy and
Recognition	Possibility of growth	administration
Work itself	Interpersonal relations	Working conditions
Responsibility	Status	Job security
Advancement	Supervision	Personal life

Motivation	Hygiene
Satisfiers lead to increased performance as they focus on our growth-approach needs. Motivational potential is high for most people.	Dissatisfiers lead to decreased performance. If provided for, these factors satisfy our maintenance-avoidance needs. Motivational potential is low for most people but hygienic potential (avoiding dissatisfaction–discontent) is high.

Figure 6-1   Satisfiers and dissatisfiers.

hygienic factors must be provided to teachers if we are to prevent dissatisfaction. It must be remembered however, that in general, providing for hygienic needs prevents decreases in performance but will not increase performance. The motivation to work beyond what is necessary to meet minimum requirements comes from the satisfier set—achievement and recognition, for example. According to the theory, these are the motivators. This concept is of fundamental importance, for the theory suggests that it is a mistaken notion to assume that school executives can buy teacher motivation through concessions across the collective-bargaining table or in similar ways. The bargaining process as we presently know it is largely limited to hygienic concerns.

EVIDENCE SUPPORTING THE MOTIVATION-HYGIENE THEORY

The original research upon which Herzberg's motivation-hygiene theory is based was conducted with accountants and engineers from the greater Pittsburgh area. Using interview techniques, Herzberg asked respondents to identify high and low feelings about their jobs and collected stories from the respondents which accounted for these feelings. By means of content analysis and factor techniques, the stories were examined and sorted into 16 job factors. These factors were then examined to see which accounted for high feelings (the satisfier set) and which accounted for low feelings (the dissatisfier set). The researchers also investigated the effects that these feelings and factors had on performance. Further, data on the duration of feelings for each of the factors were also collected. Herzberg's findings are summarized in Figure 6-2.

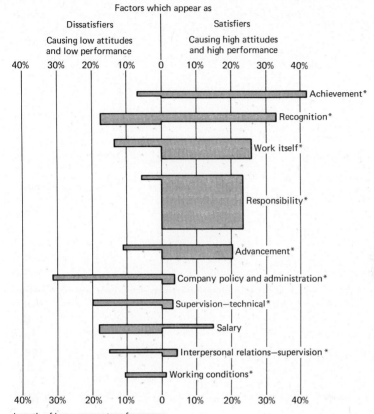

Factors which appear as

Dissatisfiers | Satisfiers

Causing low attitudes and low performance | Causing high attitudes and high performance

40% 30% 20% 10% 0 10% 20% 30% 40%

Achievement*
Recognition*
Work itself*
Responsibility*
Advancement*
Company policy and administration*
Supervision—technical*
Salary
Interpersonal relations—supervision *
Working conditions*

40% 30% 20% 10% 0 10% 20% 30% 40%

Length of bar = percentage frequency
Depth of bar = duration of attitude change

* Significant relationship

Figure 6-2 Comparison of satisfiers and dissatisfiers. (Source: Adapted from Frederick Herzberg, Bernard Mausner, Barbara Snyderman, *The Motivation to Work* [New York: John Wiley, 1959], p. 81.)

Achievement, which appeared in 40 percent of the high-attitude stories but only 7 percent of the low-attitude stories, was the most frequently mentioned motivator. Feelings derived from *achievement,* however, were of short duration. Contrast this with *responsibility,* which accounted for 22 percent of the high-attitude stories and 6 percent of the low-attitude stories.[4] High feelings derived from this factor had long-lasting effects. *Company policy and administration* and *technical supervision* were most often mentioned as dissatisfiers. *Salary* seemed to be mentioned as often as satisfier as it was as dissatisfier. (There will be more about salary later.)

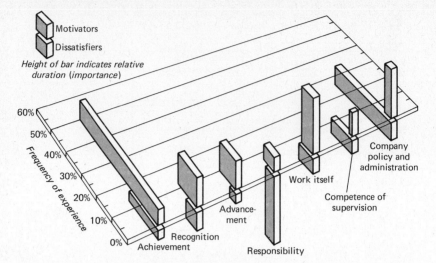

Figure 6-3 Factors affecting motivation of scientists. (Source: M. Scott Myers, "Who Are Your Motivated Workers?" *Harvard Business Review*, January–February 1964, Copyright © 1963 by the President and Fellows of Harvard College; all rights reserved.)

M. Scott Myers,[5] using methods similar to Herzberg's, has conducted extensive research testing the satisfaction-dissatisfaction (motivation-hygiene) hypothesis at Texas Instruments Corporation. Myers's respondents included scientists, supervisors, engineers, hourly male technicians, and female assembly workers. In Figures 6-3 and 6-4, we show his results for scientists and for supervisors, respondents reasonably similar to high school and elementary school teachers.

The length of the shaded bars appearing above the horizontal planes shows the percentage of high feelings associated with each factor. Similarly, the length of the bars below the planes shows the percentage of low feelings for each factor. (Remember, duration reflects relative importance of the factor to respondents.) Scientists at Texas Instruments Corporation reported achievement recognition and advancement as the most frequent motivators, and poor policy and administration and competence of supervision as the greatest sources of dissatisfaction.

Though work itself did not appear often as a satisfier nor lack of responsibility as a dissatisfier, when they did appear—in high- or low-attitude stories as the case may be—feelings and effects lasted a long time.

In general, supervisors at Texas Instruments Corporation responded similarly to scientists, but important differences existed.

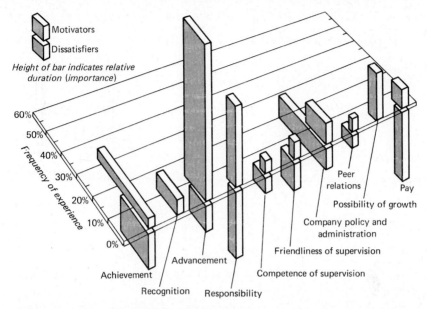

Figure 6-4   Factors affecting motivation of supervisors. (Source: M. Scott Myers, "Who Are Your Motivated Workers?" *Harvard Business Review,* January–February 1964, Copyright © 1963 by the President and Fellows of Harvard College; all rights reserved.)

Pay, for example, which did not appear often as a dissatisfier, had a lasting effect when it did appear. Similarly, advancement, although not a frequent motivator, was a lasting one. Achievement was again most often cited as a motivator although it had short-term effects.

There is an important question concerning the use of theory which relies heavily on research from areas other than education for support: Are the theoretical propositions and supporting findings applicable? We believe the motivation-hygiene theory to be applicable to educational organizations and, indeed, to teachers and students for two reasons: (1) the theory is consistent with the humanistic belief pattern which forms one dimension of our applied science of educational administration; and (2) when the Herzberg hypothesis is tested using teachers and other educators as respondents, results similar to those found for other groups are obtained.[6] The findings from one such study, a replication of Herzberg's work, are illustrated in Figure 6-5.

Shaded areas in each of the circles indicate the job factors which were significant sources of high feelings or low feelings for teachers. Two factors, achievement and recognition, were sources of 58 percent of the high-attitude stories contributed by teachers.

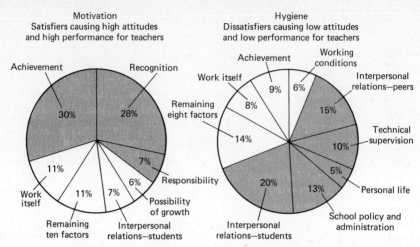

Figure 6-5   Comparison of satisfiers and dissatisfiers for teachers.
(Source: Constructed from data which appear in Thomas J. Sergiovanni,
"Factors Which Affect Satisfaction and Dissatisfaction in Teaching,"
Journal of Educational Administration 5 (May 1967): 66–82.)
Note: Shaded areas indicate that a factor appeared more significantly
as high than low on the circle to the left, and more low than high on
the circle to the right. Frequency of appearance is given in percentages.

These were found to be powerful motivators. Responsibility, although a significant contributor to high feelings, appeared in only 7
percent of the high-attitude stories. This finding suggests that we
do not take advantage of the motivational possibilities of responsibility in education—this factor is relatively standardized for
teachers in that responsibility does not vary very much from one
teacher to another. Work itself accounted for 11 percent of the
high-attitude stories for teachers, but did not appear significantly
more often as a contributor to high feelings. This factor also
accounted for 8 percent of the low-attitude stories. Apparently,
elements of the job of teaching as we presently know it are
inherently less than satisfying. Among these are routine house-
keeping, attendance, milk money, paper work, study hall, lunch
duty, and the like. The negative aspects of clerk, cop, and custodial
roles seem to neutralize the positive aspects of teaching and
guidance roles. Poor interpersonal relations with students; inadequate, incompetent, insensitive, and close styles of supervision;
unfair, rigid, and inflexible school policies and administrative
practices; poor interpersonal relations with other teachers and with
parents; and incidents in one's personal life[7] were the job factors
found to contribute significantly to low attitudes for teachers.

This study suggests that factors which contribute to teacher motivation (that stimulate extraordinary performance) form a cluster characterized by achievement, recognition, and responsibility. The absence of these factors, however, does not contribute to work dissatisfaction. Dissatisfaction for teachers seems to result from three clusters: (1) poor interpersonal relations; (2) incompetent, inadequate, or unfair administrative and supervisory practices; and (3) matters external to the school which comprise one's personal life. These factors have the potential to lower one's performance, but neutralizing them or improving them does not motivate teachers to perform in extraordinary ways.

One important omission from the data on teachers is the advancement factor. This factor was an important motivator for Herzberg's accountants and engineers and for Myers's supervisors and scientists. Advancement was simply not mentioned by teachers because teaching as an occupation offers so little opportunity for advancement. If one wishes to advance in teaching, he must leave teaching for a related education profession such as administration, supervision, and counseling. Much can be done in increasing motivation for teachers by expanding the reward system. This can be done by:

1. providing opportunities for teachers to advance within the ranks of teaching.
2. altering responsibilities among the various teaching roles and keying advancement to responsibility.
3. eliminating aspects of the work itself which are sources of dissatisfaction for teachers, thereby salvaging this factor as a motivator. Use of para-professionals would be helpful in this effort.

In summary, teaching roles and reward systems need to vary according to responsibility and levels of achievement.

The Meaning of Money

Conspicuously absent from this discussion is the role of money as a satisfier or dissatisfier. In the study discussed previously, teachers rarely mentioned money as a contributor to high or low feelings. When money was mentioned, it was explained away by other factors.[8] The problem in discussing money as a factor is that money means different things to different people. For some it is a powerful motivator, for it can buy status and security. For those who are top achievers at work, money is a legitimate form of recognition. The status and recognition that money brings is universally understood by everyone. In a sense, money communicates to others that one is a success. We should understand, however, that money is a secondary factor, which is used to purchase, legitimize, or communicate other rewards. Indeed, using money to motivate is often wasteful, and economies can be obtained if other rewards were provided in sufficient quantities.[9] Many well-paid assembly-line workers, for example, would gladly swap their jobs for those which paid less money, but which permitted them to enjoy more status, responsibility, and autonomy. Can money motivate directly? Yes, but large sums will probably be needed. Teachers would probably be motivated to work by a $5,000 salary increase, but not by a $500 salary increase. Motivating by such means is an expensive proposition, however, since the following year a larger increase will be demanded. It should be noted that although large sums make a difference in motivation, small—even paltry—sums make a difference in dissatisfaction. It is not uncommon for people to change jobs or to revise performance downward upon discovering they earn $100 less than someone whom they believe they outperform.

How much money is enough? Two characteristics about people and money are clear: (1) people always feel entitled to more money; and (2) regardless of what is paid, satisfaction with wages is short-lived and dissatisfaction waits around the corner. Within these constraints of intermittent but perpetual dissatisfaction with money, we believe that successful wage administration is possible if it is perceived as fair by teachers. Feeling underpaid but *fairly* paid may be the best that we can hope for. The basis upon which one decides if he or she is being paid fairly is comparison. Thus teachers as individuals and as groups continually compare their earnings with others in the same district, in other schools districts, and in other occupations. If teachers feel, for example, that supervisors, principals, counselors, and custodians are paid too much as compared with them, they will be dissatisfied. A pay hike in a neighboring district also produces dissatisfaction with wages. Similarly, financial gains made in occupations other than education cause teacher salary dissatisfaction regardless of the fact that such gains are beyond the school's control. Gellerman states the case well:

> . . . the main motivational significance of money is undoubtedly its role as an indicator of equitability. Money is primarily a means of dispensing justice, and this is why a continual process of internal and external wage comparisons is essential. It is also why wage settlements that

change the traditional relationships between jobs should be made only when there is clear proof that the job in question is being underpaid relative to its comparative importance.

The only motivational value of equitability, despite all the difficulties of attaining it, is that it motivates people *not* to leave, complain, strike, restrict production, or waste material. Thus for most people, effective motivation is primarily a matter of nonfinancial rewards.[10]

Wage administration remains an important aspect of personnel administration; but its focus must change as we begin to understand the varied meanings of money to people, as well as the potentials and limitations of money as a motivator.

As a summarizing device, Figure 6-6 illustrates the distribution of job factors from several studies conducted by Herzberg and his associates and from the teacher study discussed earlier. The teacher study is illustrated by the shaded bars.

CRITIQUE OF THE MOTIVATION-HYGIENE THEORY

Motivation-hygiene theory has had a great impact on the field of job attitudes and motivation both in affecting the practice of administrators and the thinking of scholars. In many respects the theory represents a radical departure from conventional wisdom about the issue of motivation to work. Whereas traditionally, satisfaction and dissatisfaction have been viewed as opposite poles of the same continuum, motivation-hygiene theory proposes that two separate and distinct sets of job factors (motivation and hygiene) exist which account for two separate and distinct sets of feelings (satisfaction and dissatisfaction) in people at work. Further, one of these sets of feelings (satisfaction) accounts for the presence and absence of extraordinary effort at work, and the other (dissatisfaction) for the presence and absence of ordinary effort at work. Motivation factors, being intrinsic, are associated with the work itself and provide people with opportunities for psychological success. Hygiene factors, being extrinsic, are associated with the conditions of work and provide people with relief from physical and psychological discomfort. This thinking represents a significant departure from traditional satisfaction and motivation theories which assume that job factors, and feeling and effects associated with them, are linearly related to the same continuum.

Methodologically, motivation-hygiene theory research relies heavily on the critical-incident method and on in-depth interview methods as contrasted with the heavy, and indeed almost exclusive,

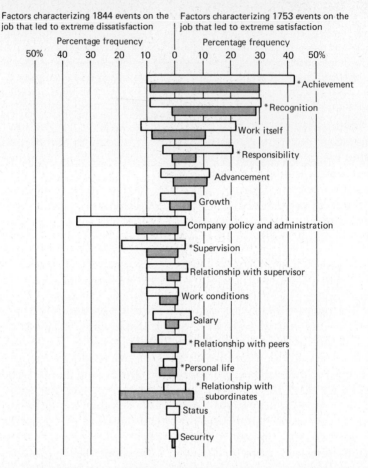

Figure 6-6   Herzberg: factors affecting job attitudes. (Source: Frederick Herzberg "One More Time: How Do You Motivate Employees?" *Harvard Business Review,* January–February 1968, Copyright © 1967 by the President and Fellows of Harvard College; all rights reserved; and Thomas J. Sergiovanni and David Elliott, *Educational and Organizational Leadership in Elementary Schools* [Englewood Cliffs, N.J.: Prentice-Hall, 1975], p. 146.) *Note:* The shaded bars included with the Herzberg data are the results of a study conducted with the teachers in 1966. The teacher study included 142 dissatisfaction events and 142 satisfaction events. Asterisks identify those factors in the teacher study found to contribute significantly to either satisfaction or dissatisfaction.

use of rating scales and other questionnaire schemata which are normally considered tools of the trade by organizational psychologists. Radical departures in method and findings have understandably resulted in controversy about the theory among scholars *despite wide acceptance of the theory among practitioners.*[11]

It is often noted by critics of motivation-hygiene theory that the hundreds of studies which tend to support the theory rely on critical-incident and interview methods but when rating scales and other questionnaire schemata are used, results are uneven at best, and typically do not sustain the two-factor hypothesis so critical to the theory. Many scholars feel that acceptance of this theory requires confirmation by alternative (namely, questionnaire) methods. But this principle of alternative confirmation is not a universal scientific standard, and not all agree therefore that the theory is invalid on this basis.

Herzberg and his associates feel that questionnaire methodologies are not appropriate to test the hypotheses suggested by motivation-hygiene theory. Herzberg, for example, comments:

> The rating-scale procedure is not appropriate for testing Motivation-Hygiene Theory because it has several serious limitations. First, since in this procedure employees are forced to rate job factors that have been determined by the researchers and not by themselves, *ratings* of attitudes and feelings may be obtained when none in *reality* may exist. This, of course, produces irrelevant, artificial, and invalid data. Second, cultural-noise responses, value systems, and socially expected responses are too often the product of the rating-scale procedure. Such responses prevent the investigation of basic psychological processes, since they almost always reflect only the influences of a given situation and not the operation of more universal and fundamental processes. Third, the rating-scale procedure has been acknowledged in most textbooks of industrial psychology to suffer from a large array of additional disadvantages: it is easy to fake; it is global and undifferentiating in its assessment; and it is quite unreliable.[12]

Herzberg and his associates also note that many of the nonconfirming studies, in addition to relying on questionnaire data, do not test hypotheses derived from the theory. One often quoted study conducted by Hindricks and Mischkind,[13] for example, assumes that motivation-hygiene theory proposes two sets of factors which account for *overall satisfaction* rather than *two distinct kinds of satisfaction*. This is a common replication error among those who seek questionnaire confirmation of the theory. This same deficiency appears in the well-known Hulin and Smith[14] studies. In both studies *overall* job satisfaction was determined in part by the General Motor Faces Scale. Respondents were asked to check 1 of 11 faces which varied from a large smile to a large frown, choosing the face which best represented their *overall* job feelings.[15] The middle face, being neutral, was assumed to be the dividing point between satisfaction and dissatisfaction though one could argue persuasively that the faces represent a *unidimensial* scale broken into two parts. These well-known critics of motivation-hygiene theory can in turn be criticized for reaching conclusions about the theory from tests of hypotheses not logically derived from the theory. As a result of the controversy, one conclusion which can be reached to date is that researchers have not been successful in developing alternative techniques to the critical-incident and interview methods for testing the theory.[16]

Our purpose in this section is not to confirm or deny the motivation-hygiene theory but to suggest that though many questions have been raised, answers are not sufficiently strong or convincing to warrant rejection of the theory. Further, though motivation-hygiene theory is argued by Herzberg as universally appropriate to the workplace, it seems particularly appropriate to professional and normative occupations such as education, where professional commitment, the Protestant work ethic, and client service still play fairly important roles. And, finally, the theory is consistent with the basic tenets of other and similar theories proposed by Maslow, Likert, Arygris and McClelland, and thus its general features are sustained on the basis of corroborative evidence.

AN INDIVIDUAL APPROACH TO MOTIVATION

In many respects, the motivation-hygiene theory provides simple answers to complex questions. It is a bold theory which provides broad and general guidelines to school executives interested in administrative effectiveness. However, its boldness and its broad propositions—although extremely useful—require intelligent caution as one applies the theory to practice. For example, although the theory suggests that by and large only the satisfiers motivate, it would be wrong to conclude that some people are not motivated by the dissatisfiers. Herzberg and others[17] concede that some individuals are "motivated" by the dissatisfiers but combine this concession with the suggestion that under ordinary circumstances it is not natural to be so motivated. The implication is that healthy individuals respond to the motivation-hygiene theory, whereas less than healthy individuals do not. Furthermore, healthy individuals who are deprived of work satisfactions which come from the motivator set seek these satisfactions elsewhere—for instance through family membership, hobbies, community activity, sports, and the like. Attention to these aspects of one's life are important to all of us, but the world of work seems the more natural place for professional workers to find satisfaction for their needs of esteem, competence, achievement, autonomy, and self-actualization.

As part of a leadership study in which one of the authors was involved, the extent to which teachers displayed motivation-seeking tendencies as opposed to hygiene-seeking tendencies was measured. One of the findings was that two-thirds of the respondents were motivation seekers, one-fourth were hygiene seekers, and the remaining 8 percent were at a point midway between the two orientations.[18] This ratio remained about the same when the sample was examined by sex and by teaching level, and when Catholic teaching sisters were compared with public school teachers. There are large numbers of hygiene seekers teaching in the schools, and they require motivational strategies and opportunities different from teachers who are motivation seekers.

Hygiene Seekers

Teachers who tend toward hygiene seeking can be classified into three groups: (1) those who have the potential for motivation seeking but are frustrated by insensitive and closed administrative, supervisory, and organizational policies and practices; (2) those who have the potential for motivation seeking but who elect to channel this potential into other (nonprofessional or nonschool) areas of their lives; and (3) those who do not have the potential for motivation seeking on or off the job. Those in the second and third groups are classified as instrumentalists[19] who use their jobs as a means to gain or achieve goals not related to the school.

The second group includes many teachers whose goals are a second car, a vacation house, supplementing husband's or wife's income in order to achieve a reasonable standard of living, putting husband, wife or children through college, and so on. Further, teachers in this group often use the teaching occupation as a means to step to another job. Physical education people, for example, often use teaching as a means to find employment as coaches; junior high teachers as a means to qualify for high school positions; aspiring school executives use teaching as a means to administration, and so on.

The third group includes individuals who could be considered fixated at lower need levels. Indeed, they may be so obsessed with "avoiding" that they have not developed the ability to seek satisfaction through the motivators and at higher need levels. Many psychologists and social psychologists regard this obsession as a symptom of poor mental health. Selection procedures should be devised which will identify and filter out this type of teacher. Those already tenured in the school need to be heavily supervised and should be given assignments which reduce their contact with students.

Instrumentalists who have the potential for motivation but who elect to seek satisfactions outside of the school (group 2) provide a fair day's work for a fair day's pay. Many are good teachers who give honest labor in exchange for that which they hope to gain from the school. Extraordinary performance is lacking, however, for full commitment to the school and its purposes are lacking. Instrumentalists of this kind will be with us for a long time, but they cannot be depended upon to upgrade substantially the nation's schools or to display much interest in becoming full partners in the school enterprise. They are interested in participating in decision-making and are supportive of collective-bargaining efforts, but this interest is usually in the hygienic areas rather than in the professional work of the school. Instrumentalists with motivation potential are less interested, for example, in curriculum development committee work than they are in serving on welfare and salary committees. They can make significant contributions to the school's work if competently supervised or combined with the motivation seekers in schools with differentiated roles and responsibilities for teachers.

Hygiene seekers in the first group—those who have the potential for motivation seeking but who are frustrated by the school and its administration—are unfortunate casualties. When teachers are denied opportunities for motivation expression, not only are valuable human resources wasted but students are denied important opportunities for self-actualization. Hygiene seekers think of their jobs primarily (perhaps "excessively" is a better word, for all of us are reasonably concerned with hygienic factors) in terms of salary, working conditions, supervision, status, job security, school policies, and administrative and social relationships.

Motivation Seekers

In reexamining and extending Herzberg's work, Hackman[20] identifies clusters of feelings which are tied to three motivational channels and also identifies the job factor which supports those feelings. One of the clusters of feelings describes the instrumentalists (hygiene seekers) whom we have already discussed. The remaining clusters of feelings, derived from the satisfiers, describe two types of motivation seekers—those who focus on closure and

The accomplishment pattern looke like this:

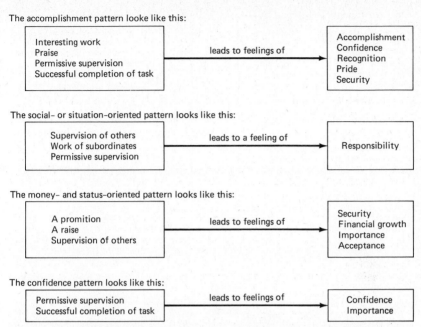

Figure 6-7 Relationship between job factors and employee feelings. (Source: Reprinted by permission of the publisher from *The Motivated Working Adult,* by Ray Hackman. © 1969 by the American Management Association Inc.)

those who focus on responsibility. *Closure seekers* are primarily interested in accomplishment, confidence, pride, and recognition. Job factors which support these feelings are interesting and challenging work, permissive supervision, successful completion of task, and praise. *Responsibility seekers* are primarily interested in responsibility and personal growth. Job factors which support these feelings are supervision of others and good work by subordinates. Responsibility seekers and closure seekers view their jobs as direct means to satisfaction, as opposed to instrumentalists, who use the job to accrue nonrelated satisfaction.

Closure seekers are largely task oriented and usually have relatively specialized professional competencies and skills. They are well trained and find great joy in promoting, extending, and developing their own areas of competence or specialization. Nothing is more important to a math teacher (or special education, early childhood, or whatever) who is a closure seeker than math. In the extreme, he may feel that other subjects, curriculum experiences, and teachers are there (or ought to be there) to support his particular program specialization.

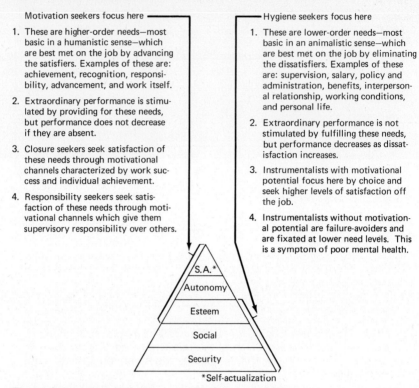

Motivation seekers focus here ●————— ┐   ┌————● Hygiene seekers focus here

1. These are higher-order needs—most basic in a humanistic sense—which are best met on the job by advancing the satisfiers. Examples of these are: achievement, recognition, responsibility, advancement, and work itself.

2. Extraordinary performance is stimulated by providing for these needs, but performance does not decrease if they are absent.

3. Closure seekers seek satisfaction of these needs through motivational channels characterized by work success and individual achievement.

4. Responsibility seekers seek satisfaction of these needs through motivational channels which give them supervisory responsibility over others.

1. These are lower-order needs—most basic in an animalistic sense—which are best met on the job by eliminating the dissatisfiers. Examples of these are: supervision, salary, policy and administration, benefits, interpersonal relationship, working conditions, and personal life.

2. Extraordinary performance is not stimulated by fulfilling these needs, but performance decreases as dissatisfaction increases.

3. Instrumentalists with motivational potential focus here by choice and seek higher levels of satisfaction off the job.

4. Instrumentalists without motivational potential are failure-avoiders and are fixated at lower need levels. This is a symptom of poor mental health.

S.A.*
Autonomy
Esteem
Social
Security

*Self-actualization

Figure 6-8   Job satisfaction: motivation in practice.

Responsibility seekers, on the other hand, although professionally trained and competent, are more interested in professional people than in professional content. Whereas closure seekers work very hard to keep up in their areas of specialization, responsibility seekers are willing to spend less time in keeping up but more time in developing interpersonal and organizational skills. They work for supervisory responsibility. Once given this responsibility, they derive satisfaction from the professional successes of subordinates. The responsibility seeker is thus more social or situation oriented than his closure counterpart. He is interested in accomplishment, and as is the closure seeker, but derives satisfaction from helping the closure seeker succeed. Teachers are provided with very few opportunities for expression of responsibility-seeking needs. Further, students should not be considered as supervisory charges under this framework. *Responsibility seekers are interested in supervising other adults.* Outlets that do exist for this expression (for instance, serving as special subject consultants or moving into administration) usually require that the responsibility seeker leave the classroom. Unfortunately, present school structures and

Table 6-1   DIFFERENTIATING HYGIENE SEEKERS FROM MOTIVATION SEEKERS

MOTIVATION SEEKERS	HYGIENE SEEKERS
1. Emphasize the nature of the task.	Emphasize the nature of the environment.
2. Are primarily committed to the goals of the school or profession and work to pursue these goals.	Are primarily committed to private goals or extraschool goals and work for rewards from the school which help to pursue or purchase these nonschool or nonprofessional goals.
3. Show higher, *but not unlimited,* tolerance for poor hygiene factors.	Intermittent but chronic dissatisfaction with aspects of the work environment such as salary, supervision, working conditions, status, security, administrative policy, and fellow workers.
4. Show less reaction to improvement of hygiene factors.	Tend to overreact in satisfaction to hygiene factors.
5. Satisfaction is short-lived when hygiene factors are improved.	Satisfaction is short-lived when hygiene factors are improved.
6. Milder discontent when hygiene factors need improvement.	Tend to overreact with dissatisfaction when hygiene factors are not improved.
7. Realize great satisfaction from accomplishments.	Realize little satisfaction from accomplishments.
8. Genuinely enjoy the kind of work they do.	Show little interest in the kind or quality of work they do.
9. Profit personally and professionally from experience.	Do not profit personally or professionally from experience.
10. Have positive feelings toward work and life.	Generally cynical toward work and life.
11. Belief systems are sincere.	Prone to cultural noises—i.e., take extreme positions that are fashionable, superficially espouse management philosophy, act more like top management than top management does.

SOURCE: Adapted from Table II, p. 90 from *Work and the Nature of Man* by Frederick Herzberg (World Publishing Company). Copyright © 1966 by Frederick Herzberg. Reprinted by permission of Harper & Row, Publishers, Inc.

methods of organization place unreasonable restrictions on altering reward systems for teachers.

Hackman also identifies four reward patterns which link job factors with employee feelings.[21] These are illustrated in Figure 6-7.

This discussion of job satisfaction is intended to operationalize for school practice the concept of need fulfillment. Indeed, job satisfaction is motivation in practice. Through providing proper motivation opportunities, one provides for satisfaction at work and therefore enables oneself and others to fulfill basic and growth needs. This relationship is illuminated in Figure 6-8. Here the concept of job satisfaction and the motivation-hygiene theory are linked to the concept of human needs and the problems of adult motivation (discussed in Chapter 5). As a summary, some clues for telling motivation-seeking teachers from those who focus on hygiene are provided in Table 6-1.

Notes

1. Francis S. Chase, "Professional Leadership and Teacher Morale," *Administrator's Notebook* 1 (March 1953):1–4; see also his "Factors for Satisfaction in Teaching," *Phi Delta Kappan* 33 (November 1951): 127–32. For years these have been widely quoted in the literature. Chase's studies involved over 1800 teachers, representing 216 school districts in 43 states.
2. Charles E. Bidwell, "The Administrative Role and Satisfaction in Teaching," *Journal of Educational Sociology* 29 (September 1955): 41–47.
3. Frederick Herzberg, Bernard Mausner, and Barbara Snyderman, *The Motivation to Work* (New York: John Wiley, 1959). For an extension of the theory and additional supporting evidence, see Herzberg's *Work and the Nature of Man* (New York: World, 1966).
4. The percentages of highs and lows in Herzberg's work do not equal 100, for more than one factor could appear in each story.
5. M. Scott Myers, "Who Are Your Motivated Workers?" *Harvard Business Review* 42, no. 1 (January–February 1964):73–89.
6. Thomas J. Sergiovanni, "Factors Which Affect Satisfaction and Dissatisfaction of Teachers," *Journal of Educational Administration* 5 (May 1967):66–82.
7. Personal life stories were contributed entirely by female teachers and contained two themes: (1) romance and premarriage anxiety or disappointment and (2) role conflict of the wife-teacher and mother-teacher variety.
8. Money accounted for 2 percent of the high-attitude stories and 3 percent of the low-attitude ones.
9. We are assuming, of course, that enough money is provided to take care of one's hygienic or avoidance needs reasonably well.
10. Saul Gellerman, *Management by Motivation* (New York: American Management Association, 1968), pp. 217–18. The author states parenthetically that the use of coercive bargaining power by a group is not proof of underpayment.
11. In commenting on this controversy Herzberg notes: "Even among my critics it has been acknowledged that the theory is controversial

because it upset all previous thinking related to job attitudes. It is the nature of the game that a theory that comes along and cannot be incorporated into everybody else's work will be controversial, not only at the professional level but also, obviously, at the ego level." He also says: "The theory not only upset a lot of theoretical and experimental work, it also questioned the tools of the psychologist and behavioral scientist." He further comments, "I suspect that much of the criticism of Motivation-Hygiene Theory stems from its questioning of the behavioral scientist's tools." See Frederick Herzberg, *The Managerial Choice: To Be Efficient and to Be Human* (Homewood, Ill.: Dow Jones-Irwin, 1976), p. 321.

12. Ibid., p. 246.
13. J. R. Hinricks and L. A. Mischkind, "Empirical and Theoretical Limitations of the Two-Factor Hypothesis of Job Satisfaction," *Journal of Applied Psychology* 51 (1967):191–200.
14. C. L. Hulin and P. A. Smith, "An Empirical Investigation of Two Implications of the Two-Factor Theory of Job Satisfaction," *Journal of Applied Psychology* 51 (1967):396–402.
15. See also G. B. Graen and C. L. Hulin, "Addendum to 'An Empirical Investigation of Two Implications of the Two-Factor Theory of Job Satisfaction,'" *Journal of Applied Psychology* 52 (1968):341–342.
16. For examples of articles which deal further with the controversy see: D. A. Whitsett and E. K. Winslow, "An Analysis of Studies Critical of the Motivation-Hygiene Theory," *Personnel Psychology* 20 (1967): 121–32; N. King, "A Clarification and Evaluation of the Two-Factor Theory of Job Satisfaction," *Psychological Bulletin* 74 (1970): 18–31; J. Schneider and E. A. Locke, "A Critique of Herzberg's Incident Classification System and a Suggested Revision," *Organizational Behavior and Human Performance* 6 (1971):441–457; and B. Grigaliunas and Yoash Wiener, "Has the Research Challenge to Motivation-Hygiene Theory Been Conclusive? An Analysis of Critical Studies," *Human Relations* 27, no. 9:839–871.
17. Herzberg, *Work and the Nature of Man*, op. cit. See also Roy Hamlin and Robert Nemo, "Self Actualization in Choice Scores of Improved Schizophrenics," *Journal of Clinical Psychology* 18 (January 1962): 51–57. The theme here is that "hygienic motivation" is associated with poor mental health. For a study linking approach drives to students with motivation orientation and avoidance drives to students with hygienic orientation, see Carl Haywood and Virginia Dobbs, "Motivation and Anxiety in High School Boys," *Journal of Personality* 32, no. 3 (September 1964):371–379. Again, the theme is that fixation at the avoidance level (hygienic factors) is less than healthy.
18. Thomas J. Sergiovanni, Richard Metzcus, and Larry Burden, "Toward a Particularistic Approach to Leadership Style: Some Findings," *American Educational Research Journal* 6, no. 1 (January 1969):62–79. Motivation-seeking and hygiene-seeking tendencies were determined by responses to The Choice-Motivator Scale. The sample consisted of 227 elementary and secondary school teachers enrolled in sections of a

required graduate course in educational psychology at the University of Illinois.

19. Ray Hackman, *The Motivational Working Adult* (New York: American Management Association, 1969). Hackman's work is an extension of Frederick Herzberg's. Hackman identifies three motivational channels and labels individuals who pursue one or another as (1) instrumentalists (hygiene seekers), (2) closure seekers, and (3) responsibility seekers.

20. Ibid., p. 129.

21. Ibid., p. 40.

Chapter 7
Job Enrichment as a Motivational Strategy

One important mechanism for enhancing teacher motivation which is within the province of administrators and supervisors is the structure of the teacher's job. Jobs can be altered in a fashion which increases opportunities for teachers and others to experience intrinsic satisfaction. That is, administrators and supervisors can deliberately plan to build into the teacher's job increased opportunities for experiencing achievement, recognition, advancement, growth opportunities, and increased competence. Teaching jobs can be deliberately upgraded in responsibility, scope, importance, and challenge. Changing the job of teaching to improve opportunities for experiencing intrinsic satisfaction is called job enrichment. The concept is similar to providing "enrichment" activities to students. In both cases job enrichment is attractive to many and can be a powerful stimulus to increased motivation. Motivation-hygiene theory is a useful and effective conceptual framework for thinking about and developing job enrichment strategies. Not everyone, however, seeks more enriching jobs, and indeed some enrichment possibilities may be attractive to some but not others. In the section which follows, a contingency approach to motivation is suggested to help us deal with these individual expectations.

A CONTINGENCY APPROACH TO TEACHER MOTIVATION

Motivation-hygiene theory provides school executives with a broad framework for understanding the problem of adult motivation and from which to develop motivation policies for the school district. Specific application of this or any theory, however, is particularistic, and the best practices are those that are contingent upon or take into account unique characteristics of the administrator's situation. Viewing particular teachers as motivation and hygiene seekers of various types, for example, and taking these differences into account as practices are prescribed are examples of using a contingency approach to management and motivation.

Vroom's expectancy theory of motivation is one such contingency approach which has received attention.[1] Vroom's is a contingency theory in that he views motivation as a response in a person's needs to a specific goal he seeks. Performance on the job, according to the theory, is a means by which the person can achieve his personal goals. Basically, individual motivation is viewed as a function of a person's perception that his increased performance will result in certain rewards which will help him attain personal goals. If a teacher's goal is to be promoted to an administrative position, then motivation will depend upon his or her perception that increased performance (volunteering for difficult curriculum work and doing a good job of it) will lead to appropriate rewards (winning the professional respect and attention of administrators) which will in turn enable him or her to achieve the aspired goal (get promoted). By the same token, another individual with personal goals of group acceptance may not be motivated to volunteer for additional work and if assigned such work, not likely to perform in an extraordinary way if these behaviors are not associated with group acceptance.

Since personal goals are likely to differ, rewards which appeal to some teachers may not appeal to others. The theory suggests, therefore, that it is necessary, on the one hand, to individualize rewards to match personal goals which are consistent with those of the school and, on the other hand, to help build better congruency between personal and school goals. Further, the relationship among individual performance, organizational rewards, and personal goals is not always clear to teachers, and clarification of this relationship by administrators may be necessary.

Expectancy theory helps school executives think about teacher motivation as follows:

1. Motivation will take place if the incentives available to teachers are consistent with their personal goals and work values. Theorists such as Maslow, McClelland, Herzberg, and White would suggest that needs such as recognition, esteem, and achievement are likely to be important to most individuals. But variation in personal goals and work values of teachers can be expected and must be taken into account. If incentives are not important to a particular person, motivation and increased performance will not occur.

2. If incentives available are important to a person, does the person feel that extra effort on his or her part will result in obtaining these incentives? Does the person feel, for example, that on the basis of previous experience he or she can do the job? Does the amount of effort needed represent an equitable exchange for the devised incentive? Does the person have the necessary materials and administrative support to function adequately? Is the organizational climate supportive? In essence, can the person expect success?

3. If the answers to the foregoing questions are generally yes, then behavior is likely to be motivated, personal goals are likely to be achieved successfully, and job satisfaction will result.

Note that in expectancy theory, job satisfaction is derived from performance. Similarly in motivation-hygiene theory, *intrinsic* satisfaction is derived from performing the work itself. Satisfaction from achievement, recognition, and responsibility, for example, are earned as a result of accomplishing work. This thinking (improved performance leads to satisfaction) is an improvement over human relation theories which tend to assume that job satisfaction itself is linked to improved performance.

THE RELATIONSHIP BETWEEN INTRINSIC AND EXTRINSIC SATISFACTION

Though motivation-hygiene theory suggests that intrinsic satisfaction is related to increased performance and extrinsic satisfaction is not, the relationships are more complex. There is good evidence which suggests that in schools, and in voluntary organizations such as the Red Cross, United Way, and church groups, extrinsic rewards (grades, salaries) have a negative effect on performance. Lepper, Greene, and Nisbett[2] note, for example, that many educational tasks are inherently interesting to students and would likely be performed without extrinsic rewards and indeed such rewards convert interesting activity into "work." Further, extrinsic rewards are likely to convert learning activities into behavior which will not be performed in the future (when students leave school, for example) without some extrinsic force. Similarly, Staw suggests "if for some reason extrinsic rewards were to be offered to voluntary workers for performing their services, we would expect to find, as in the educational setting, a decrease in intrinsic motivation."[3] The effect would be that volunteers probably would not be willing to perform other tasks without pay or other extrinsic inducements.

In the traditional work organization such as the industrial plant or the school, it is expected that extrinsic rewards be provided for services and indeed these conditions provide the material essentials for an employee's existence. As motivation-hygiene theory suggests, not providing for the hygiene factors is likely to result in worker dissatisfaction. But it is the intrinsic factors which provide the cutting edge from ordinary to extraordinary performance.

A Job Enrichment Model

There are a number of ways in which the work of teachers can be changed to increase intrinsic motivation including increasing task variety, task complexity, opportunities for social interaction, task identity, work significance, teacher responsibility for results and providing knowledge of results.[4] In each case these characteristics enrich the job in a manner which increases opportunities for greater intrinsic satisfaction. Following is a brief description of these job enrichment characteristics:

> *Task variety* implies building into the teaching job a greater assortment of tasks. It is assumed that varied work increases interest. This is in contrast to curriculum-building strategies, for example, which emphasize breaking down teaching episodes into small parts and assigning them to "specialists."
>
> *Task uncertainty* refers to tasks which involve information processing and cognitive stimulation. Teaching tasks are viewed as problems to be solved rather than details to be conveyed to students. Tasks arranged in a mechanical way may not be very satisfying to many teachers. Detailed curricular formats which, by following directions, can be implemented as well by the substitute teacher do not comprise very meaty or challenging work for most teachers.

Social interaction recognizes that individuals at work generally derive satisfaction from interacting with others and for many, this source of satisfaction can be an inducement for working[5] or at the least a stimulus to building commitment and loyalty to the work group and school.[6] Despite the wide acceptance of importance of social interaction among workers, and recognizing that significant gains are being made in schools in using teaching teams, teaching is still a relatively private activity.

Task significance refers to the perceived importance by teachers of the work to be done. It is often assumed that providing teachers with detailed objectives increases task significance when indeed the opposite may be the case. Task significance requires an understanding and appreciation of what the educational program as a whole tries to accomplish and how one's individual efforts fit into the larger view.

Task identity, related to task significance, requires that one have a larger view of what the school is about and that one sees how his or her part contributes to this larger purpose. Fragmented curriculum formats, narrow departmentalization, and detailed teaching assignments tend to work against task identity.

Responsibility for results requires that teachers be given a great deal of discretion over task activities but held more accountable for obtaining results. A caveat is in order here. To many, results only imply learning objectives achieved. But in education process and product, means and ends, are so indistinguishable that both should be included in results. Therefore, characteristics such as classroom learning climate and general ambience, energy levels of teachers and students, and patterns of verbal interaction should be considered, along with reading achievement, as results.

Knowledge of results refers to feedback as to the quality of one's performance. Clearly, without feedback it is difficult to derive satisfaction from accomplishment.

Staw suggests that task variety, task uncertainty, and social interaction are characteristics associated with task behaviors which lead to greater intrinsic satisfaction, more voluntary participation on tasks, and greater persistence in pursuing tasks. Satisfaction, persistence, and participation, in turn, are related to the quality of task performance. He further suggests that task identity, task significance, and being responsible for results are also directly related to task accomplishment and the quality of performance.

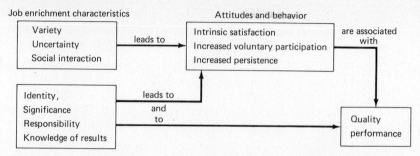

Figure 7-1   Job enrichment and quality performance. (Source: Adapted from Barry Staw, "Intrinsic and Extrinsic Motivation," faculty working paper no. 213 [Urbana: College of Commerce and Business Administration, University of Illinois, 1974], p. 68.)

Knowledge of results provides the person with a perceived probability estimate that his efforts lead to accomplishment, and this too is related to quality performance.[7] These relationships are summarized in Figure 7-1.

In a similar vein Hackman and Oldham propose a job characteristics model which enjoys a more direct research base.[8] Their model is depicted in Figure 7-2. Their research suggests that personal and work outcomes such as intrinsic motivation, high-quality work performance, high satisfaction with work, and low absenteeism are a function of the presence in individuals of three psychological states: *experienced meaningfulness of the work, experienced responsibility for work outcomes, and knowledge of results.* Further, five job characteristics which evoke these psychological states are identified. Three of the characteristics—skill variety, task identity, and task significance—combine additively to determine meaningfulness. Autonomy, a fourth job characteristic, is associated with feelings of responsibility and feedback, a final job characteristic proposed by these researchers, and is associated with knowledge of results.

The job characteristics model suggests that in teaching, jobs which (1) require different activities in carrying out the work and the use of a variety of teacher talents and skills (skill variety), (2) require that teachers engage in holistic or complete and identifiable tasks (task identity), (3) are viewed by teachers as having a substantial and significant impact on the lives or work of other people (task significance), (4) provide substantial freedom, independence, and direction to individual teachers in scheduling work and in deciding on classroom organizational and instructional procedures (autonomy), and (5) provide teachers with direct and clear information about the effects of their performance (feedback),

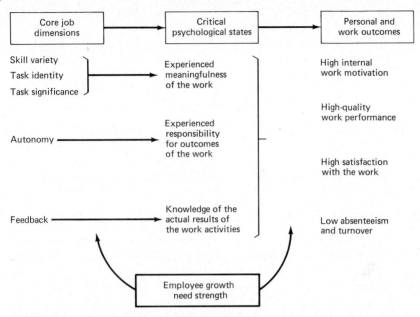

Figure 7-2   The job characteristics model of work motivation. (Source: J. R. Hackman and G. Oldham, "Motivation Through the Design of Work: Test of a Theory," *Organizational Behavior and Human Performance* 16 [1976]:256.)

are likely to evoke the psychological states in teachers of meaningfulness, responsibility, and knowledge of results. These in turn, Hackman and Oldham suggest, result in high work motivation, high-quality performance, high job satisfaction, and low absenteeism among teachers.[9]

Of particular importance to the Hackman and Oldham model is the *growth need strength* feature. Growth need strength is a measure of the extent to which a person is alienated from or identified with middle-class work norms. A number of investigators have found that individuals who do not identify with or who are alienated from middle-class work norms typically react negatively to enriched jobs, and reject the motivation functions.[10] Hackman and Oldham's research found no evidence to support this contention. They note, for example, "while individuals with strong growth needs do react more positively to complex jobs than do individuals with weak needs for growth, the signs of the relationship between the job characteristics and the outcome measurers are positive even for people in the bottom quartile of the growth need measure."[11] Their finding suggests that one's work needs can and do adjust to work environments. Growth needs increase as one is confronted with a complex job which demands self-development and the exercise of independent thought and action in his work. Similarly, one would suspect, growth needs decrease in more deprived work environments.

KEEPING TEACHERS IN EFFECTIVE SERVICE

The seventies and eighties mark a new era in understanding job satisfaction and the motivation of teachers. We are experiencing a period of entrenchment in education characterized by declining student enrollments on the one hand and a surplus of teachers in many academic areas and in many parts of the country on the other. In 1982, for example, it is estimated that the supply of teachers will exceed demand by about 200,000.[12] New teaching positions are not easy to find, and once teachers obtain employment they are likely to stay in that job. Teachers presently employed in a particular school are likely to stay in that school or district for a career. With the average age of teachers estimated at 33, this observation is particularly significant.[13]

A decade or so ago one could think of change and improvements in education resulting from the infusion of "new blood" into the system, but today, school executives realize that one must rely on the teachers presently employed. Thus keeping teachers in effective service as interested, growing, and highly motivated individuals becomes a prime focus of administration and supervision. One way to examine the problems and challenges of keeping people in effective service as compared with those associated with merely getting and keeping people in minimum service is by differentiating the kinds of decisions people make in relation to their jobs and their work. In the next section two levels of decisions which face teachers as they enter, remain, and participate in the school are discussed.

First-Level and Second-Level Decisions

When a teacher decides to take a job with a particular school district, he commits himself to fulfilling minimum requirements as specified and implied by that school and by the profession at large. The decision to join a school district and to do all that is necessary to maintain membership in the school is a decision at the *first level*. School executives are understandably interested in enticing people to enter, remain, and participate in the school and its activities in a satisfactory manner. This interest is expressed by school personnel practices which are geared almost exclusively toward stimulating and continuing the first-level decision among teachers. It should be obvious that such efforts are important, for one needs to make the first-level decision before he opts for a decision at the second level.

Second-level decisions are characterized by performance and commitment over and above that which is necessary for meeting minimum requirements for membership. Excellence, professional growth, creative effort, and extraordinary commitment and performance are characteristic of the second-level decision. Teachers who make this decision are concerned with developing their skills, are absorbed in their work, and are focusing on achievement of personal and professional maturity as a means toward self-actualization.

The Focus of Practice: Current and Future

What are the circumstances which teachers take into account as they are faced with the first-level decision? What entices them to seek and accept employment in the district and consistently to maintain satisfactory membership in the district? Teachers seek jobs and stay on the job if physical, social, status, economic, and security dimensions associated with the conditions of work are satisfactory. If work conditions are not perceived as satisfactory, then turnover can be expected for teachers able to move and *psychological withdrawal can be expected for those unable to move.* Of crucial importance in understanding this relationship is accepting the proposition that, even though personnel administrators and others work to provide generously for those making the first-level decision, they cannot automatically expect the second-level decision to be made. This decision is a new game, so to speak, and therefore is evoked in accordance with a new set of rules. The relationship between decision levels is not unlike that which exists for the satisfaction and need factors which comprise the motivation-hygiene theory. Indeed, the hygiene factors are those which contribute to first-level decision-making, whereas their absence results in turnover or withdrawal. The motivation factors, on the other hand, contribute to and sustain the second-level decision. The decision levels, their relationship to needs, and the personnel practices which contribute to each are illustrated in Table 7-1.

Implementing the optimistic practices suggested in this chapter will not be easy. Alex Inkeles, for example, notes that the traditional American values exemplified in Ben Franklin's writing (hard work and frugality) may be slipping.[14] He cites a Detroit area study conducted between 1958 and 1971 which shows the number of people who consider the most important part of their jobs to be

Table 7-1   PERSONNEL PRACTICES IN SCHOOLS

THE PRESENT FOCUS IS ON HYGIENE NEEDS[a]		THE NEEDED FOCUS IS ON MOTIVATIONAL NEEDS[b]
SECURITY	SOCIAL	ACHIEVEMENT,
Fairness	Work groups	RESPONSIBILITY
Grievance procedure	Coffee groups	Delegation of
Protection from	Social contacts	authority
parents	Feelings of belonging	Participation
Protection from	and acceptance	Involvement
students	Professional groups	Planning
Support from ad-		Goal setting
ministration	STATUS	Freedom to act
Seniority and tenure	Job definition	Visibility
Union or association	Job title	Accountability
membership	Classroom size and	Creative expression
	location	Promotion
MONETARY	Equipment	
Salary schedules	Student type	RECOGNITION,
Retirement	Class load	PERSONAL AND
Sabbatical	Grade level	PROFESSIONAL
Sick leave	Privileges	GROWTH
Hospitalization		Merit increases
Insurance	SUPERVISION	Differentiated
Credit union	Recruitment	responsibility
Social security	Selection	Leadership role
Annuity	Assignment	Committee
Mutual fund	Orientation	responsibility
	In-service program	Publications
WORKING CONDITIONS	Evaluation programs	Innovations
Condition of the	Work rules	Supervisory
school	Communication	responsibility
Office and room space	channels	Problem solving
Lounge space	Committee work	Aptitudes utilized
Length of workday		
Number of students		
Hall duty		
Study hall assignments		
Parking facilities		
Lunch and rest periods		
Equipment		
Teaching schedule		

[a] These evoke the first-level decision. One is attracted to and stays on the job if these conditions are present in quantity and quality. Absence, turnover, and psychological withdrawal can be expected if these are not sufficiently provided.

[b] These evoke the second-level decision. One is stimulated to extraordinary performance and commitment if these opportunities are available. Their absence encourages focusing excessively on hygiene needs and results in mediocre performance.

School executives should not expect all school personnel to avail themselves of opportunities described under motivation needs (that is, to make the second-level decision), but opportunities should exist for those who wish to seek rewards of this kind. Those most likely to make this choice are responsibility seekers, closure seekers, and instrumentalists with proper motivational potential.

either intrinsic importance or promise of advancement fell steadily, whereas the importance of higher income and shorter hours grew more attractive. He further cites a national poll conducted by James Morgan and his associates which indicates that one-third of his respondents felt getting ahead in their line of work depended upon seniority and experience. Only 18 percent mentioned hard work and 1 percent cited taking on tough tasks, being aggressive, or showing initiative and enterprise. This tone of pessimism is reinforced somewhat by the findings in Chapter 5 on changes in patterns of need deficiencies of teachers from 1966 to 1978. Perhaps now more than ever hygienic factors are important to more and more teachers. But one principle remains clear—their necessity does not make the hygienic factors sufficient to bring about the kind of intrinsic satisfaction, increased participation and persistence at work, and increased quality of performance needed from teachers in order to build excellence in schools. For most teachers these characteristics will depend upon the presence of the motivation factors.

Notes

1. Victor H. Vroom, *Work and Motivation* (New York: John Wiley and Sons, 1964). See also Vroom, "Organizational Choice: A Study of Pre and Post Decision Processes," *Organizational Behavior and Human Performance* 1 (1966):212–225, and J. Galbraith and L. Cummings, "An Empirical Investigation of the Motivational Determinants of Task Performance: Interactive Effects Between Instrumentality—Valence and Motivation—Ability," *Organizational Behavior and Human Performance* 2 (1967):237–257, for studies which substantiate aspects of Vroom's theory. Other well-known expectancy theories are those proposed by Lewin, Rotter, and Atkinson. See, for example, Kurt Lewin, T. Dembo, L. Festinger, and P. W. Sears, "Level of Aspiration," in J. Mc V. Hunt, ed., *Personality and the Behavior Disorders,* vol. 1 (New York: Ronald Press, 1944), J. B. Rotter, "Generalized Expectancies for Internal Versus External Control of Reinforcement," *Psychological Monographs* 80, no. 1 (1966), and J. W. Atkinson, *An Introduction to Motivation* (New York: Van Nostrand Reinhold, 1964).
2. Mark Lepper, D. Greene, and R. E. Nisbett, "Undermining Children's Intrinsic Interest with Extrinsic Rewards. A Test of the 'Overjustification' Hypothesis," *Journal of Personality and Social Psychology* 28 (1973):129–137. See also David Greene and M. Lepper, "How to Turn Play into Work," *Psychology Today* (September 1974):49–52.
3. Barry M. Staw, "Intrinsic and Extrinsic Motivation," faculty working paper no. 213, College of Commerce and Business Administration, University of Illinois, Urbana, 1974, p. 49.
4. Ibid., pp. 16–19. See also J. R. Hackman and G. Oldham, "Motivation

Through the Design of Work: Test of a Theory," *Organizational Behavior and Human Performance* 16, no. 2 (1976):250–279 and "Human Resources Supervision," in T. J. Sergiovanni, ed., *Professional Supervision for Professional Teachers* (Washington D.C.: Association for Supervision and Curriculum Development, 1975), pp. 9–31.

5. See, for example, Hackman and Oldham, "Motivation Through the Design of Work."

6. See, for example, Rensis Likert, *New Patterns of Management* (New York: McGraw-Hill, 1961).

7. Staw, "Intrinsic and Extrinsic Motivation," p. 68.

8. Hackman and Oldham, "Motivation Through the Design of Work."

9. With some modification, the model should have general applicability to students as well. Factors such as peer-group pressure, the normative aspects of the student subculture, and maturity would probably result in modifying the job characteristics model somewhat.

10. See, for example, Charles Hulin and M. Blood, "Job Enlargement, Individual Differences, and Work Responses," *Psychological Bulletin* 69, (1968):41–55.

11. Hackman and Oldham, "Motivation Through the Design of Work," p. 274.

12. *The Condition of Education: A Statistical Report on the Condition of American Education, 1975.* National Center for Educational Statistics. United States Office of Education, p. 177.

13. "Status of the American Public School Teacher, 1975–76." National Education Association, Washington, D.C., 1977.

14. Alex Inkeles, "American Perceptions," *Change* 9, no. 8 (August 1977): 25–32.

Chapter 8
Patterns of Adjustment to Work

This chapter is concerned with how teachers, students, and school executives who find their lives in school less than enriching make the necessary adjustment.[1] Some sort of adjustment is required if they are to function adequately as members in schools as they are now constituted. Implicit in this discussion is the assumption that certain kinds of adjustment usually result in wasted human resources for both the individual and the school. Often, for example, human qualities such as creativity are compromised as being impractical, and the individual, instead, seeks to fit his ideas, need expression, hopes, and expectations into the organizational character of a given school.

It is important to emphasize that some adjustment is necessary in any job, particularly in relation to hygienic aspects of the work environment. Limitations with respect to schedules, supplies, space, equipment, and money, for example, require certain amounts of conformity and place obvious constraints on people. Those who can readily accept and live with a reasonable amount of inadequate hygiene are, indeed, described often as "well adjusted." Hygienic factors in schools are at best reasonably adequate and require some adjustment from all who wish to maintain school membership. Therefore, when we speak of adjustment, we are referring to *overadjustment*—behavior which involves compromising one's beliefs, values, abilities, skills, creative potential, and professional growth and in terms of organizational energy, drive, and creativity. Both the individual and the school are losers.

Adjustment of a person to his organization takes place at two levels: (1) at the individual level, through psychological adjustment; and (2) at the collective level, through informal and formal group membership. Each of these levels is examined in the sections which follow.

HOW TEACHERS ADJUST AS INDIVIDUALS

Several assumptions about adjustment to work have been suggested previously and are made explicit here:

1. A certain amount of adjustment and tolerance is necessary in any job, and successful adjustment of this kind is a sign of good mental health.
2. Hygienic work factors and conditions which are unreasonably or continuously poor set limits on one's tolerance. Such limits vary with individuals. Creative and challenging teaching can occur under the most adverse conditions but for the most part, long-term adjustment to these conditions is unnatural for healthy people. Motivation seekers as well as hygiene seekers need to have hygienic needs reasonably satisfied.
3. Adjustment to poor motivation conditions usually requires leveling one's hopes, aspirations, and performance downward.
4. It is unnatural—indeed unhealthy—therefore for one who has the potential to express his growth needs through creative, energetic, and professionally competent work to revise or abandon this expression. This is a serious problem in highly bureaucratic organizations which emphasize centralized decision-making, extensive and rigid policies and rules, strong organizational membership (unions, militant professional groups), authoritarian management systems, and closed school climates.

Many work adjustment problems are caused by poor management and organization. Other adjustment problems are brought to the school by teachers, students, and other school workers. In the second instance, we are referring to those individuals who are not able to make at least minimal adjustment to the job or work. Individuals of this type display symptoms which characterize five general and overlapping categories of work psychopathology.[2]

The first category of work psychopathology includes those individuals who have serious deficiencies in all aspects of work motivation. They come to the job with a negative conception of work which is manifested by extreme alienation or general indifference. Such persons, if they are to work at all, require powerful social coercion and can be expected to meet only minimal standards—and then only under close supervision.

A second category includes individuals whose predominant response to the job is fear and anxiety. This is a common form of work psychopathology. It describes those who believe that they are incapable of adequate performance. Ordinary supervision and general interpersonal contacts with other teachers and with superiors is perceived as being threatening to individuals of this type. Such feelings often result in gradual withdrawal from work and people.

A third category includes individuals who are openly hostile and continuously aggressive. Anger waits in ambush close to the surface and is easily aroused. Obsessed with protecting themselves and hypersensitive to threat, criticism, and supervision, individuals of this type defend themselves by attacking others. This form of work psychopathology is not readily noticeable at the selection stage, and such individuals are able to work reasonably well if left alone. Professional activities which require cooperation, teamwork, and coordination, however, place individuals who exhibit such manifestations in intolerable, threatening, and uncompromising situations.

A fourth category includes individuals who show symptoms of marked dependency. Their dependence is often expressed in strong identification with and reliance on superiors. Individuals of this type are able to work hard to please superiors, little substantial internal motivation is present, and independent work, individual initiative, and self-reliance are likely to be absent. Such individuals require close and continuous supervision, characterized by indulgent personal reinforcement. As flattering as this type of work psychopathology may be to administrators, it is a sign of poor mental health on the part of teachers and, moreover, places severe constraints on building a self-actualizing school.

A final category of work psychopathology is comprised of individuals who display a marked degree of social naïveté. Problems for this group stem from unrealistic images of work or from ignorance, rather than from fear, anger, rejection, or resistance. Individuals of this type often come from sheltered home and school settings. Unprepared for reasonable discomfort, detail, interpersonal tension, anger, respecting the needs of others, and reasonable frustration, they view work in a pastoral and naïve rather than realistic sense. The five common manifestations of work psychopathology characterize those unable to adjust to the minimal hygienic constraints present in any job and/or those unable to respond to motivation conditions.

What of teachers and other educational workers who *are* able to adjust to normal work constraints and, moreover, are able to contribute loyalty, spirit, energy, and skill to their professional work? How do these people react to (1) unreasonable absence of hygienic concerns and (2) lack of opportunities for expression of their growth needs on the job? Ray Hackman, in extending Frederick Herzberg's work (see Chapter 7), has empirically identified several clear-cut factors which are related to patterns of feelings healthy teachers and school executives, salesmen, professional women, bank officers, hourly workers, registered nurses, and other occupational groups exhibit as a result of poor work hygiene. These categories of feelings are frustration-aggression, anxiety, personal inadequacy, and social rejection. The relationship among sources of dissatisfaction, patterns of feelings, and intensity of feelings (as indicated by X's) are presented in Table 8-1.

Several observations are apparent from examining Hackman's data. Each of the negative feelings is produced by a variety of job conditions, and, indeed, some of these conditions—no praise and poor organization of work, for example—can produce all of the feelings in healthy people. Leadership styles of school executives are often described in accordance with the emphasis one gives to person and to task aspect of the job. One who emphasizes primarily person is considered person oriented, and one who emphasizes primarily task is considered task oriented. Praise is associated with the former and organization of work with the latter. The widespread negative feelings associated with *both* no praise and poor organization of work suggests that *both* task- and person-oriented leadership are required.[3] Some conditions (such as no promotion) produce only certain negative feelings, whereas other conditions (poor relationships with and poor work of subordinates) do not account for any of *these* negative feelings.

Table 8–1   RELATIONSHIPS BETWEEN SPECIFIC SOURCES OF DISSATISFACTION AND FEELING PATTERNS ACCOMPANYING THEM

SOURCE OF DISSATISFACTION	NEGATIVE FEELING PATTERN			
	FRUSTRATION-AGGRESSION	ANXIETY	PERSONAL INADEQUACY	SOCIAL REJECTION
No promotion	X			X
No raise			X	X
Loss of face	XX	XX		XX
Dull work			X	X
Failure to complete a task		X	X	
No praise	XX	XXX	XX	XXX
Close supervision	XX	XX	X	X
Critical supervision	X	XX	X	X
Unfriendly supervision	XX	XXX	X	XX
Incompetent supervision	XX	XXX	X	XX
Poor organization of work	XXX	XXX	XXX	XXX
Poor personnel policies	XX	X		XX
Disagreement with company or school goals	X	X		
Poor relations with subordinates				X
Poor work by subordinates				

SOURCE: Reprinted by permission of the publisher from *The Motivated Working Adult*, by Ray Hackman. © 1969 by the American Management Association, Inc.

NOTE: X's represent intensity of feelings.

TEACHERS AS COSMOPOLITANS AND LOCALS

Much can be gained by studying individual needs and satisfactions on a one-to-one basis, but certain combinations of needs, need patterns, and resultant behavior patterns emerge repeatedly. As the reliability of these combinations becomes established, they permit one to categorize and stereotype groups of people. Categorizing teachers and other educational workers is a shortcut method of showing the relationship between and among human and organizational variables, and of using this relationship to predict behavior. Stereotyping, then, is not unlike an ideal type framework and suffers from some of its faults—that is, although a general class of phenomena is described, the framework fails to describe any one specific case. However, despite the risks of stereotyping (including the dangers of inaccuracy, prejudice, disapproval, and the like), this technique is useful in explaining behavior if interpreted properly by the reader.

A particularly useful framework for stereotyping, one which seems to have a considerable amount of theoretical and empirical support, is that which distinguishes between two major latent role identities found in formal organizations: the cosmopolitan orientation and the local orientation.[4] In educational terms, three variables are used to distinguish between individuals with one orientation or the other: (1) loyalty to the school, (2) commitment to one's specialization or to one's professional skills, and (3) reference-group orientation. *Cosmopolitans* are described as those low in loyalty to the employing school, high on commitment to specialized professional skills, and likely to identify with an outside reference group. *Locals,* on the other hand, are those high in loyalty to the employing school, low in commitment to specialized professional skills, and likely to identify with an inner reference group. Of course, many teachers and administrators exhibit combinations of these traits but most, nevertheless, lean toward one or the other orientation.

Alvin Gouldner (see note 4) identifies four types of locals—those whom he calls the dedicated, the true bureaucrats, the homeguard, and the elders—and two types of cosmopolitans—the outsiders and the empire builders. Each of these types is described next. It is difficult to examine ideal types in a nonevaluative way, but it should be readily apparent that each of these types, in its own way, contributes to school success. Surely, management has prejudices which favor some types over others, but these are preferences of emphasis and focus rather than of exclusiveness. (This question is considered again later.) Adaptations of Gouldner's six types described in teacher terms are also considered next.

Locals: The Dedicated

Teachers with this orientation are the "true believers" who identify with and support the distinctive ideology—the belief system—of their school. They are deeply committed to this ideology and are concerned that those within the school support it, believing that community agreement is more important than the acceptance of individual differences. They would prefer that the school hire teachers with similar value systems over teachers with varied value systems but with superior technical competencies.

Organizationally, teachers and administrators of this type have strong commitments to their school rather than distinctive professional roles within the school. They support core-type programs rather than those that are more discipline oriented and are willing to accept transfers from one assignment or position to another within the school or school district. Their approach is one of maintenance of internal organizational consensus rather than one of pursuing professional specializations. Educators of this type are thought of as loyal and reliable members of the school.

Locals: The True Bureaucrats

Teachers of this type are inclined to oppose chapters of the American Federation of Teachers or National Education Association affiliates on the grounds that they are "outside" organizations or are controlled by "outsiders." True bureaucrats are distinguished from the dedicated locals in that they are oriented to the community and its people rather than to the school itself. They are not advocates of internal consensus and are willing to engage in conflict in order to bring about organizational adjustment. They seek, for example, more control over student behavior (or, if administrators, over teacher behavior) and call for tighter supervision over students. They are quick to remind others that curriculum changes will not be accepted by the community, that school integration plans need to reflect community opinion, and the like.

Gouldner suggests that generally, locals of this type do *not* regard salaries as too low, believe that teachers should *not* have more influence in the school as a whole, and would *not* favor lighter teaching loads to allow more time for professional development, research, project work, and similar activity. In Gouldner's words: "If the dedicated locals can be said to be concerned about the integrity of the organizational values, the true bureaucrat locals are concerned about the security of the organization. This they seek to accomplish by installing more authoritarian and *formal* regulations to control the behavior of others. It is because of this last propensity that we term them 'true bureaucrats.' "[5]

Locals: The Homeguard

Teachers of this type have the least amount of professional specialization, little or no advanced college work, attend few if any professional meetings, and typically are not involved in curriculum development and other professional activities. Many are high school graduates of the school district or of neighboring districts. This group is predominantly female and often includes wives whose husbands are "prominent" contributors to the school district. They occupy generalized teaching positions and readily assume responsibility for rather low-level administrative positions. Attendance responsibilities, record keeping, calendaring time, space, and events, assisting in the library, and the like, represent administrative jobs open to the homeguard local. They generally have personal reasons for sticking with and expressing loyalty to the school.

Locals: The Elders

This group of teachers owns the largest share of tenure in the school and is now committed to stay indefinitely. Some arrive at this commitment willingly; others find that as the years slip by, employment visibility to other institutions diminishes. Gouldner suggests that "senior citizenship" in the school influences reference orientation two ways:

1. It is likely that they are oriented to an informal peer group, those as old as themselves and those who came into the organization at about the same time as they did.
2. Having been with the group for a longer time than most, they are likely to evaluate its present in terms of its past. In other words, their reference orientation may be distinguished not by a special reference group, other elders, but by a concern about a special or earlier time period.[6]

Cosmopolitans: The Outsiders

Outsiders are teachers who have little loyalty to the school and normally do not intend to stay with the school permanently. They are willing to leave the school for more money, better position, or more prestige. Cosmopolitans of this type are not particularly close to students on a social basis although they are interested in student contact as it relates to their specialty. They are relatively infrequent or low-intensity participants in terms of faculty friendships and group interaction. Moreover, they wield little influence in the school and show no overt interest in increasing influence efforts.

As cosmopolitans, outsiders are highly committed to their specialized areas and their professional skills rather than to the school. As such, they are oriented toward an outside reference group and look outside of the school to colleagues elsewhere for intellectual and professional stimulation.

In times of expansion and mobility cosmopolitans of this type are likely to be very happy. But during periods of decline with its characteristic staff stability the outsider can feel trapped in a particular school or district. One can speculate that in time the outsider is likely to seek refuge in local teacher association activity.

Cosmopolitans: The Empire Builders

Teachers of this type enjoy high professional visibility outside of the school and thus feel less dependent upon the school for economic reasons and for replenishment of other lower-order needs. Although relatively satisfied with his present school, the empire builder remains on the lookout for a better position elsewhere. Like the outsider, he is committed to specialized areas and professional skills and often complains that maintenance demands (extracurricular activities and the like) are too heavy and indeed distract from his professional work.

Gouldner suggests that empire builders are cosmopolitans of a distinctive type: "Above all, they are committed to their specific academic departments, particularly in the physical sciences and the creative arts. . . . They seem to have a strong pull toward increased departmental autonomy. For example, they tend to resent the student rating system and to feel that power is too concentrated in the administration's hands."[7] Gouldner further suggests that, unlike the outsiders, empire builders are somewhat integrated into the school's formal structure.

Cosmopolitans are generally more difficult to accommodate within present school structures than locals. Nevertheless, providing meaningful outlets for their need expressions can harvest unique school benefits which are derived from the expertness and professional know-how that they offer. Schools have tended to seek, encourage, and reward local orientations in teachers primarily because locals are more easily pleased and more malleable in terms of administrative directions. Cosmopolitans, on the other hand, are often vocal, resentful, demanding, and self-exerting and often bring conflict to the school. Not surprisingly, cosmopolitan teachers are more likely to become locals as the years go by than are locals to become cosmopolitans.

Schools which are dominated by locals are perhaps more typical in America than those dominated by cosmopolitans. Well-known schools (those with reputations for quality or innovation or both, for example), on the other hand, tend to be influenced strongly by the cosmopolitan orientation. It should be readily apparent that schools which have an *exclusive* local or cosmopolitan orientation are likely to have problems. The local orientation provides the necessary cohesiveness and maintenance which constitutes the foundation for any school enterprise. The cosmopolitan orientation, however, offers the school the needed transfusion which keeps it in the mainstream of "what's happening" in American education and in society in general. Indeed, both orientations contribute to school success. Those who seek administrative effectiveness will need to concern themselves with a proper balance between the two by providing sufficient opportunity for expressing both these orientations as well as meaningful rewards for the expression of each. It seems that schools too easily reward the local orientation at the expense of the cosmopolitan. This trend works against administrative effectiveness and the school, for both need the professionalism, the expertness, and the dedication to education which the cosmopolitan has to offer. A better strategy is to use all of the human resources available, both local and cosmopolitan, on behalf of the school's goals. During periods of decline and stability, the local orientation is strongly favored in schools. Preserving a healthy cosmopolitan presence in the school, therefore, becomes a priority of great importance. Under these conditions if cosmopolitanism is not intentionally rewarded and nurtured, it will simply become an expression of intended teacher militancy. Interestingly, though many militant teachers identify primarily with national or statewide teacher associations, and therefore expressed cosmopolitan characteristics, entrenched teacher militancy can be a local orientation of another kind.

ADAPTING TO THE SCHOOL BUREAUCRACY

The sociologist Robert Presthus identifies three distinct patterns of accommodation which individuals use to comfort and assimilate their respective organizations or perhaps to submit to and be assimilated by them. He labels those who adopt the three patterns as *upward mobiles*, *ambivalents*, and *indifferents*.[8] Each of the patterns of accommodation is determined by a complex and interrelated system of personality variables which develops as a result of a multitude of factors, such as one's early life, previous experiences with organizations and with those in authority, patterns of successes and failures, belief-value systems, and need orientation.

Upward mobiles identify strongly with their school, its goals, value system, authority system, tradition, or simply its way of doing things. Added to this identification is a desire and indeed a need to be part of the system—to express loyalty, to provide support, and of course to partake of the generous rewards available to those who express these sentiments. Upward mobiles typically exhibit high job satisfaction and see a future for themselves in the school or district. Strong identification with the school qualifies them for generous organizational rewards, including acceptance to the "in" group, promotion, and status, as well as benefits which accrue outside of the school in terms of social and political rewards from the community. School executives and supervisors are flattered by subordinates who will follow them and their policies. Thus they reward heavily those who offer such unqualified confidence and support.

Upward mobiles are typically locals—individuals who find themselves accepted by the school as they accept the school, embraced by the school as they embrace it, and indeed promoted by the school as they promote it. They accommodate the school by permitting themselves to be co-opted by the school; and as they progress up the ladder of success, they ultimately co-opt the school and renew the pattern for others who are to follow. This pattern of accommodation often results in many benefits to the school, since upward mobiles can be relied on to perform diligently the school's expectations for them. However, since this pattern is that of accommodating to what is, little creativity can be expected from upward mobiles. They are not interested in rocking the boat, in conflict, or in any other situation which may place them at odds with superiors or with the school district.

The upward-mobile pattern is a frequent means of accommodation to bureaucratically oriented schools and is the organizational stype typically advocated (usually unintentionally) in administration-supervision university preparation programs and in administration-supervision textbooks.

The second pattern of accommodation described by Presthus is that of indifference or withdrawal. Indifferents simply refuse to compete, to play the game, for organizational success. Indifferents have resolved personal-organizational differences by withdrawing from the school environment and by redirecting interests and talents to off-the-job sources of satisfaction. The club, family, hobby, and team receive emphasis beyond that which is typically expected from most individuals, whereas the place of work is virtually ignored except as a source of security and salary which permits indifferents to buy the extra-job satisfactions they need. They reject status, success, and power. They seek, instead, security from the school and are attracted to circumstances which require them to contribute minimally to gain this security.

Indifferents offer little to school success. Usually quiet, stay-out-of-the-way types who will do all that they can to avoid calling attention to themselves, indifferents will do all that is necessary to perform at least satisfactorily. In other words, they hope to avoid higher performance expectations and additional responsibility. Although indifferents are easy to manage and supervise, they simply cannot contribute the required effort needed to change a complacent school into an extraordinary school.

Increasingly, educational workers seem to fall into a third pattern of accommodation to organizational life—one which Presthus describes as the ambivalent pattern. Ambivalents cannot reject the rewards of power and success their organization offers them, nor can they perform the necessary roles—in particular, adopt the perspective of upward mobiles—in order to obtain them.

> Despite his inability to meet bureaucratic demands, the ambivalent type plays a critical social role, namely, that of providing the insight, motivation, and the dialectic that inspire change. The upward mobile honors the status quo and the indifferent accepts it, but the ambivalent is always sensitive to the need for change. His innovating role is often obscured because the authority, leadership, and money needed to institutionalize change remain in the hands of organizational elites. Nevertheless, few ideals or institutions escape his critical scrutiny. In his view custom is no guarantee of either rationality or legitimacy. This perception is sharpened by his inability to accept charismatic and traditional bases of authority; rationality alone provides a compelling standard.[9]

Ambivalents are described as being introverts and as having deep intellectual interests, specialized knowledge, high aspirations, skilled professional know-how, idealistic perspectives, and a high tolerance for ambiguity. They often have limited interpersonal facility; are doubtful and fearful of authority systems other than merit; lose sight of practical realism; are doubtful of absolutism and "pet" solutions; are self-conscious and anxious; are critical of the establishment; and, finally, are demanding of others and themselves.

If one accepts existing school structures and traditional modes of operation as normal, then ambivalents, by not being able to adjust to the status quo, are misfit and presumably suffer from poor mental health. It may also be that the existing school structure accommodates only those who are less than mature and that symptoms of "poor" mental health are the responses that should be expected of the mature personality. An element of truth exists in each of these positions, and choosing between them seems less important than providing a variety of means for self-expression which will accommodate all who comprise the human organization of the school.

Ambivalents have much to offer the school in terms of professional talent and intellectual commitment, yet they frequently have difficulty with their organization as they work to make their commitment. A major problem facing modern school administration is allowing and encouraging ambivalents to function adequately within organizational structures, for function they must if schools are to meet their expanded commitments. Essentially, this includes legalizing the expert authority ambivalents typically possess and backing it up with appropriate resources.

FORMAL ADJUSTMENT THROUGH GROUP AND ORGANIZATIONAL MEMBERSHIP

Increasingly, teachers are turning to group membership and to collective alliances as a source of support and strength. Informal group membership has always been of interest to teachers and others in schools, and most educators accept the informal group as a normal part of school life. The current interest in collective alliances, however, is a relatively new phenomenon for educators. In many instances collective alliances are simply attempts to formalize informal groups and relationships. Some instances are attempts to strengthen formal groups by linking them into a network of similar groups outside of the school. Teacher organizations of the association or union variety are examples. Although the manifest purposes of informal and formal group structures may vary depending upon the nature of the group and its location, latent purposes are the same: Groups exist to help teachers make a better adjustment to their school lives by satisfying human needs and by protecting teachers from a potentially, if not actually, insensitive and hostile organization.

In this section the nature of teacher militancy—teacher power—is examined by exploring what individuals seek from teacher-organization membership. Simple economics reminds us that teachers must pay for that which they hope to gain, and whether the price of teacher organization or any other group membership is worth it or not is an important consideration. We do not assume that teachers are united by organizational membership in a common cause, but, rather, we assume that such membership represents a convenient coalition between two groups of educators who ultimately seek opposite gains from such membership.

Teacher Militancy—Teacher Power

Teacher militancy needs to be understood from within the broader framework of social problems facing us today. Among these are the civil rights movement, the youth movement, women's liberation, the problem of urban America, and the prevailing drive for increased control over one's life.

It should be remembered that militancy is a means to power, and power permits teachers to express greater influence on matters which relate to the schooling. Teachers have always had some individual power—particularly over students. Indeed, the power to modify or change student behavior may be the core of the teacher-student relationship. However, since power is a neutral phenomenon which enables a person to influence another for good or for bad, students may benefit or be harmed as a result of the individual power which teachers have.[10] Teacher power expressed in the form of teacher militancy is derived from group membership. This group power not only increases individual teacher power over students but expands the influence system to any and every other aspect of the educational enterprise. As in the case of individual teacher power, this expanded group influence has the potential for improving or harming American education, depending upon the direction and means of expression.

What Do Teachers Seek from Teacher-Organization Membership?

Perhaps the most deceiving aspect of the teacher-organization movement is the appearance of unity among teachers. What superficially appears as a homogeneous group united in a common cause is really a heterogeneous group bound together in a makeshift coalition. What holds this coalition together is a common interest in factors which have been described earlier in this chapter and in other chapters as hygienic. All teachers are interested in the economic advancement of the education occupations, in improving the conditions of work, in achieving reasonable guarantees that they will be protected from abuses by administrators and community members, and in being treated fairly. Therefore, hygiene seekers and motivation seekers are united in reacting against educational occupations which have not kept pace in providing economic and other work benefits to teachers.

This common interest in hygiene factors, once a strong basis for a teacher coalition, will continue to weaken as (1) many teachers feel that they have achieved reasonable equity in hygienic conditions, and (2) the public reaches the point where it feels that additional major investments in hygienic conditions are not worth the returns it gets from the services of teachers. These positions are likely to be arrived at simultaneously because of standardized procedures for dispersing hygienic rewards—the standard salary schedule is a prime example. It is doubtful whether the public will continue to buy this standardization as salaries continue to rise. Motivation seekers and hygiene seekers may be united in reacting against poor hygiene, but motivation seekers will be alone in reacting against a school bureaucracy which is ineffective in meeting their personal and professional needs for competency development, esteem, autonomy, and self-actualization. The focus of militancy in the future may very well be in that direction. If this is the case, teachers will be more concerned with accumulating additional shares in the school enterprise. They will likely focus more intensely on policy decisions; assuming additional and perhaps all of the responsibility for school matters relating to educational programs and instruction; participating more actively in personnel functions such as recruitment, selection, orientation, and in-service; and assuming the lion's share of responsibility for evaluation and supervision. All of these developments promise greater satisfaction for motivation seekers but at the same time require additional investments from hygiene seekers. Those hygiene seekers who lack the psychological readiness or professional competency for becoming junior partners in the school enterprise will be threatened by such developments. For these reasons, one can expect hygiene seekers to be reluctant to move in this direction, and thus to continue their power coalition with motivation seekers. This difference will constitute the basis for a new struggle in education—the outcome may well be determined by the direction which collective negotiations in education takes in the next several years. At present, hygiene seeking seems to be the focus of this process. Two points are emphasized before moving on to discuss bureaucratic and professional characteristics of teacher organizations:

1. The divisions among teachers are not conveniently clear-cut by organizational affiliations, such as union versus associations, but by

basic motivational orientation and commitment levels of teachers as they relate to their jobs. Thus union teachers have more in common with their motivational and commitment counterparts in professional associations than with other union members and vice versa.

2. School executives and school boards do not automatically lose power and influence as teachers gain power and influence. There is no fixed power pie to be distributed—power distribution is not necessarily a win-lose proposition. Current thinking[11] suggests an open power system in the school which permits power expansion. That is, if group A increases its influence, the total amount of influence for the school increases—not only to permit A's influence expansion but the expansion of other groups as well. This relationship suggests that gains in teacher influence potentially increase influence of school executives.

Bureaucratic and Professional Tendencies of Teacher Organizations

The professionalization of the educational occupations is a militant process. The sociologist Ronald Corwin, an effective champion of this position, argues as follows:

> Professional associations were, of course, originally formed in order to free vocations from lay control; and the efforts of teachers to professionalize are no exception. The process of professionalizing publicly-supported vocations, then, is likely to be militant. It represents a challenge to the traditional ideologies of control by laymen and their administrative representatives. The professionalization of any vocation (including school administration) will involve boundary disputes among laymen, the professionals, and public administrators. These boundary disputes, it should be noted, also infect the vocation itself, breaking it into segments or coalitions which compete among themselves: one, a small but active militant leadership group, spearheads the movement, while other coalitions constitute small groups of supporters and the opposition. Each segment then attempts to control the conditions of work in terms of its own definitions.[12]

As any group approaches professionalism, it must develop, define, and defend certain areas of ability and expertness. This process continues until the professional group has legitimately established an exclusive influence or ability monopoly over its area of reference. When groups which aspire to professionalism conduct their activities in cooperative ways and within organizational structures (as opposed to private practice or to entrepreneurial activity), militancy, expressed in the form of conflict, is inevitable. This conflict results from the interface of professional values which

(*Legal Model*) Administrator-Dominated Bureaucratic Schools	(*Professional Model*) Administrator-Teacher Partnership: The Professional Bureaucracy
(Potential for student self-actualization increases)	⟶

Figure 8-1   The promise of teacher militancy.

individuals hold or would like to hold, and bureaucratic values and tendencies which are often found in school structures. Teacher organizations are the means to structuring this conflict in a systematic way. More importantly, gains made by teacher organizations as a result of this conflict are official ones and, therefore, serve to legitimize influence and ability monopolies for teachers. If teachers, through organizational efforts, win the right to vote on the addition or deletion of courses from the high school curriculum, they have legitimized one influence pattern which relates to the administration of the school's educational program.

Illegal strikes and brinksmanship tactics often used by teacher organizations as a means to win concessions are not necessarily contrary to this position. These are nothing more than symptoms of organizational immaturity. As organizations increase in power, they also assume more responsibility for restraint and self-discipline as well as concern for the welfare of other parties. For example, the labor movement as a whole has moved in just a few decades from violent anarchism to responsible legitimacy as its power and influence in society have increased. T. George Harris supports this position as follows: ". . . there is fraud in the notion that responsibility breeds power, it's the other way around."[13]

What has been described, then, is exactly the promise to educators which teacher organizations offer—systematic professionalization of the education occupations.[14] This process may take several forms, but it is directed at moving schools from fairly pronounced bureaucratic tendencies which are incapable of nurturing professional employees, to new bureaucratic forms which are able to support and nourish a human organization, professional in outlook and motivation seeking in orientation. This relationship is illustrated in Figure 8-1.

The professional bureaucracy[15] offers great promise to American education, for its utilizes the natural bureaucratic tendencies of most organizations in support of professional efforts. There are certain organizational and individual needs which all organizational inhabitants have and which are efficiently met by the school's bureaucratic mechanism. Among these are the regular and prompt distribution of paychecks, the making of room assignments, the allocation of supplies, the arrangement of students into convenient collectivities, the facilitation of communication networks, the providing of reasonable protection from parents, the programming of certain decisions which teachers find annoying or time consuming, and the accumulation and storage of information such as student records which facilitates professional decision-making. As routine tasks of the type described previously are categorized, programmed, systematized, and structured by the school's bureaucracy, teachers and other professional workers are left free to express themselves as full partners in the school enterprise through the complexities of the school's instructional system, educational program matters, counseling and guidance work, cocurricular activities, and stimulating student self-actualization.

There is a danger, in this kind of development, that the school might be transformed from a strong administrator-dominated bureaucracy to a strong teacher-dominated bureaucracy. Both of these organizational forms are inconsistent with the humanistic ends of American education. The effects on young people would be the same regardless of who dominates the school bureaucracy. Nothing is gained from this power transfer and indeed schools may lose something, for the tyranny of many may be worse than the tyranny of a select group. This danger is illustrated in Figure 8-2.

The movement from an administrator-dominated bureaucracy to a strong teacher-dominated bureaucracy is best described by a curvilinear rather than a linear relationship. Both ends of the continuum describe extreme forms of bureaucracy for schools, with the professional bureaucracy assuming a middle position. Probably the motivation-seeking–hygiene-seeking coalition of teachers can move only so far from the administrator-dominated bureaucracy. When this critical point is reached, two alternatives must be faced: (1) to move to the professional bureaucracy, or (2) to short-circuit this form and instead move to the teacher-dominated bureaucracy. The first alternative depends upon motivation seekers dominating in influence, whereas the second depends upon hygiene seekers dominating.

Present indications from collective negotiations and other teacher-organization activities suggest that hygiene seeking is dominating and that the danger of short-circuiting the establishment of a professional bureaucracy is near. Teacher organizations are still largely concerned with conditions of work; and the results of their bargaining activities often result in dramatic increases in rules, in procedures, in programming decision-making, in defining in detail the nature of work, and so on. The elimination of

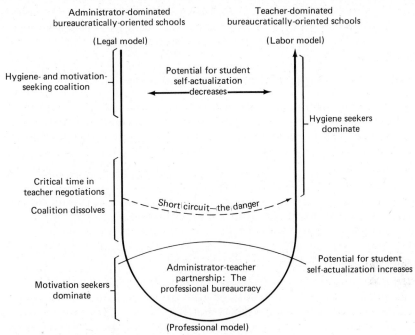

Figure 8-2   The danger of teacher militancy.

discretion on the part of teachers and administrators retards development of a professional bureaucracy.[16]

COLLECTIVE NEGOTIATIONS FOR PROFESSIONALS

Negotiating or bargaining represents a form of participatory decision-making in education. School executives negotiate and bargain almost continuously in school and out of school with board members, teachers, students, community groups, and legislators. The bargaining process, of course, has become more formalized and substantially accelerated since the early sixties, with the rise in importance and power of teacher groups. This formalization has increased the visibility of power too. This in turn has aggravated the frequency and intensity of conflict between school executives and teachers. The aggressiveness of parent groups and increased pressures for community participation by vocal minority groups promise even more conflict in the decade ahead. Bargaining as a form of decision-making, in other words, will continue to increase in importance, and sophisticated understanding of this process is an important dimension of administrative effectiveness for school executives.

In this section several forms of collective bargaining, each appropriate for given circumstances, are examined. Consideration is also given to the questions of power and ethics.

DIFFERENTIATING FORMS OF BARGAINING

The processes through which decisions are reached in a bargaining relationship depend upon (1) attitudes which each of the groups holds for the other; (2) the perceived availability of resources which constitute the bargaining issue (money, time, power, responsibility, control, protection, influence); and (3) the extent to which the parties perceive the outcome of bargaining to be fixed or variable. One form of bargaining emerges when teachers and school executives are mutually distrustful, when the focus on bargaining is on the distribution of limited resources, and when each party is committed to reference groups to settle for a position better than that possible for both. Another form of bargaining is appropriate when teachers and school executives trust each other, when teachers and school executives identify with similar goals and aspirations for the school, when the distribution of resources is not fixed, and when the outcome of bargaining strengthens the position of both parties.

The concept of bargaining in education has historically been associated with the first form, in which a conflict of interest between parties is assumed. As a result, the process of bargaining has emerged as a game with a winner and a loser. Walton and McKersie[17] provide a differentiated bargaining framework of social interaction which characterizes modern organizations. In this effort they identify four types of bargaining: distributive, integrative, attitudinal, and intraorganizational. Each of the types will now be described briefly.

Distributive Bargaining

This type of bargaining is characterized by winning and losing, the allocation of scarce resources, and a fixed-sum payoff for negotiation, with each party attempting to maximize his share. Whenever a gain is made by one party, a loss is incurred by the other; thus distributive bargaining is a self-oriented process. Negotiable items are considered as issues rather than problems, and conflict of interest is assumed. The rules of the game permit bluffing, threatening, misrepresenting one's position (normally called "lying"), manipulating, and so on. The focus of distributive bargaining is on conflict resolution rather than on problem solving, and the process often results in a stalemate which is resolved through compromise. Unfortunately, compromise frequently sacrifices the best solution to educational problems and issues in order to provide satisfaction of the self-interest which negotiating parties represent.

Distributive bargaining will always have a place in education as long as the economic and physical dimensions of the education occupations are characterized by scarce resources. Indeed, this form of bargaining is and will probably remain as the means to settle factors and conditions which we have described as hygienic—providing for our lower-order needs and contributing to the first-level decision. (These factors are listed in Table 7-1 and include salaries, benefits, leave, course loads, grievance procedures, protection from parents, and other conditions-of-work factors.)

Integrative Bargaining

The nature of the bargaining process in education is remaining relatively stable (primarily distributive), but the content of bargaining is shifting. Many teachers are no longer content with negotiating the conditions of work and have become increasingly interested in negotiating the work itself, as expressed in school goals, developing instructional strategies, allocating responsibilities, formulating policy, protecting professional rights, and extending professional immunity, privileges, and influence. As the focus of bargaining changes, so must the process of bargaining.

Integrative bargaining is an alternative bargaining process which seems more suitable to this shifting emphasis. This type of bargaining is characterized by a problem-solving orientation which assumes the possibility of increasing shares of influence to all parties. The variable-sum payoff rather than a fixed-sum one means that the win-lose element is substantially reduced. The focus then is not on increasing one's own advantage over another but on increasing the total amount of advantage available to all. Expanding advantage to various parties is assumed as the school increases its effectiveness in achieving its goals.

Attitudinal Bargaining

Fundamental to the integrative approach is mutual respect among parties and mutual commitment to school effectiveness. Thus attitudinal bargaining, a type of bargaining which concerns the maintenance or restructuring of attitudes the parties have toward each other, must be employed before and during integrative bargaining. Unless school executives respect the ability authority which teachers bring to educational problems and are willing to consider them as partners in the educational process, the bargaining format will be exclusively distributive rather than distributive and integrative. No less important is the recognition by teachers of the abilities, perspectives, and responsibilities which school executives have in relation to educational problems. At another level, any mental blocks that school executives have about labor unions, militancy, the strike, the professional right of teachers to be involved in educational decision-making, and the job right of teachers to be involved in work decision-making can only be disruptive of bargaining processes. Teachers who have illusions about legal aspects of school functioning, who are infatuated with anarchy, who are plagued with images of school executives as robot bureaucrats enslaved by their organization or power-hungry despots out to enslave school inhabitants also institutionalize distributive bargaining as a negotiating process monopoly.

Intraorganizational Bargaining

Intraorganizational bargaining is the process of achieving flexible consensus within the administrative group, parent group, or student group before the actual bargaining takes place. As interest groups work to achieve internal consensus, they are typically engaged in problem solving, which better prepares them for inter-bargaining efforts. Indeed, administrators should avoid negotiating with any group which does not exhibit some evidence of intraorganizational bargaining.

A major crisis may face education at the intraorganizational level, as motivation-oriented teachers and hygiene-oriented teachers struggle with what the focus of bargaining will be in the future. As illustrated in Figure 8-1, hygiene seekers will push for maintaining distributive bargaining, with its emphasis on work conditions, whereas motivation seekers will be more likely to favor integrative bargaining, with its emphasis on the work of education itself. Administrators and schools have much to gain by legitimizing and encouraging the integrative process. Figures 8-3 and 8-4 show the present focus of bargaining in education and a new focus which suggests a mature profession of education.

POWER AND ETHICS

When one discusses alternatives to the distributive model of collective bargaining, power is de-emphasized. This is misleading,

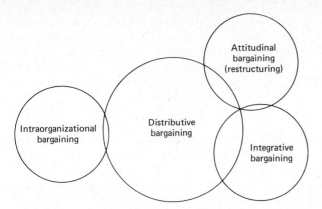

Figure 8-3   The present focus of professional negotiations in education. (Symptoms of immaturity of the education professions.)

for power is fundamental to each of the bargaining types discussed, although in each case it may be expressed differently or may emerge from a different source. For example, in distributive bargaining the capacity to bargain is often expressed through coercive (reward and punishment), political, legal, and gamesmanship means. Integrative bargaining, on the other hand, relies heavily on power expressed in thinking creatively, exhibiting expert knowledge, and advancing viable solutions to educational problems.

The importance of power in bargaining should not be underestimated, nor should it be idolized. Regardless of how agreements are reached between two parties, the daily interpretation and application of this agreement involves not power but ethics. Furthermore, in preparing for bargaining and during the bargaining process itself, the concept of bargaining in good faith is dependent upon ethics. Ethical matters should not be taken lightly in public organizations such as schools, for alienation of the local and general public upon whom we depend for support is always a consequence.

IMPLICATIONS FOR ADMINISTRATIVE EFFECTIVENESS

The future direction of teacher organizations depends less on teachers than on school executives. We can do much to help ensure that the professional bureaucracy is not short-circuited in favor of a teacher-dominated bureaucracy. Hanging on to the last remnants of the administrator-dominated bureaucracy will encourage short-circuiting. Legitimizing the professional bureaucracy depends upon the following conditions:

1. Administrators need to open and expand reward systems for motivation seekers. Indeed, the reward system should favor

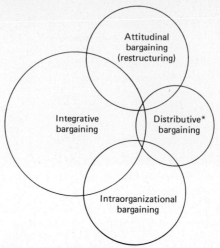

Attitudinal
bargaining
(restructuring)

Integrative
bargaining

Distributive*
bargaining

Intraorganizational
bargaining

*Distributive bargaining as compared with other forms is deemphasized here; however, at an absolute level, economic and conditions-of-work factors maintain their importance.

Figure 8-4   A proposed focus of professional negotiations in education. (Symptoms of maturity of the education professions.)

the motivation orientation, and shares in the educational enterprise should keep pace with investment commitments which individual teachers make.

2. Hygiene seekers need to be managed more effectively. They should not be expected to perform or to invest at the same levels as motivation seekers, and rewards need to be adjusted accordingly. Not everyone should be required to participate actively, and this group should not suffer sanctions for its reluctance. By the same token, fair and competent supervision for these groups needs to be increased. Indeed, working with other hygiene seekers as part of a team, under the supervision of motivation seekers, may be the solution. Thus—while they actively teach—long-range planning, creative problem solving, curriculum development, and so on, are the responsibility of others. As hygiene seekers increase commitment and investment levels, they should share in the expanded reward system enjoyed by motivation seekers.

3. Selection procedures need to be improved so that a proper balance in commitment levels among teachers is achieved. Administrative effectiveness suffers if low-commitment teachers dominate by sheer numbers.

4. Perhaps most important of all—administrative and supervisory positions are not the places for hygiene seekers

Administrators often favor teachers who reinforce their own self-images. The school cannot afford a bias which favors hygiene seeking.

This chapter concludes Part II, "The Human System." In Part III the emphasis shifts from questions of values and human motivation to those of organization, structure, and leadership.

Notes

1. This chapter deals primarily with patterns of adjustment of teachers, but such behavior is readily transferable to student adjustment and school executive adjustment.
2. Walter S. Neff, *Work and Human Behavior* (New York: Atherton, 1968), pp. 207–16. The five categories are empirically established in W. S. Neff and M. Koltuv, "Toleration for Psychiatric Rehabilitation as a Function of Coping Style," *Journal of Counseling Psychology*, 31 (1967):364–370.
3. Several other combinations of task and person exist which yield an array of leadership styles. See for example Chapter 14.
4. See, for example, Robert K. Merton, "Patterns of Influence, Local and Cosmopolitan Influentials," *Social Theory and Social Structure*, rev. ed. (Glencoe, Ill.: Free Press, 1957), chap. 10; and Alvin W. Gouldner, "Cosmopolitans and Locals: Toward an Analysis of Latent Social Roles, I and II," *Administrative Science Quarterly* 2 (December 1957):281–306, and 3 (March 1958):444–480. The cosmopolitan and local orientations are summarized in Robert E. Jewett, "An Educational Theory Model: Theory of Local and Cosmopolitan Influentials," Center for the Construction of Theory in Education, Ohio State University. Occasional Paper No. 63-140, June 1963. Our discussion is based primarily on the two Gouldner articles and, to some extent, the Jewitt summary.
5. Gouldner, "Cosmopolitans and Locals," p. 448.
6. Ibid., p. 449.
7. Ibid., p. 450.
8. Robert Presthus, *The Organizational Society* (New York: Alfred Knopf, 1962). This discussion is based on and follows closely Chapters 6, 7, and 8.
9. Ibid., p. 258.
10. For a startling collection of critical incidents which describe power abuses of teachers as they relate to students, see Sam Leles, "Evolving a Theory of Effectiveness in Education," unpublished doctoral dissertation, Ohio State University, 1967. Some of these are reported in Leles, "Teacher Power—What's It All About?" *Theory into Practice*, College of Education, Ohio State University, vol. 7, no. 2 (April 1968).
11. C. G. Smith and A. Tannenbaum, "Organizational Control Structure: A Comparative Analysis," *Human Relations* 41, no. 4 (November 1963): 299–316. Robert Ohm discusses power expansion in reference to

schools in his "Collective Negotiations: Implications for Research," in *Collective Negotiations and Educational Administration*, Roy Allen and John Schmid, eds. (Fayetteville: College of Education, University of Arkansas and University Council for Educational Administration, 1967), pp. 1–21.

12. Ronald Corwin, "Professional Persons in Public Organizations," *Educational Administration Quarterly* 1 (1965):4.

13. Quoted in "The Young Are Captives of Each Other: A Conversation with David Riesman and T. George Harris," *Psychology Today* 3, no. 5 (October 1969):31.

14. It is commonly assumed that professional groups in addition to being well trained, having control over selection and the policing of colleagues, and possessing skills not commonly held by others are also first and foremost client serving. Professionalization of the education occupations, therefore, should be directed first and foremost at improving the services available to students. Although professionalization does not imply that teachers will forsake or let up on demands in terms of work hygiene, it encompasses much more than this.

15. See, for example, Eugene Litwak, "Models of Bureaucracy Which Permit Conflict," *American Journal of Sociology* 57 (1961):177–184.

16. Discretion is a critical component of the professional bureaucracy. This is clearly illustrated by Bell's discretionary model of organization. See Gerald D. Bell, "Formality Versus Flexibility in Complex Organizations," in *Organization and Human Behavior: A Book of Readings*, Gerald D. Bell, ed. (Englewood Cliffs, N.J.: Prentice-Hall, 1967), pp. 97–106.

17. Richard E. Walton and Robert B. McKersie, *A Behavioral Theory of Labor Negotiation* (New York: McGraw-Hill, 1965).

Part III
THE
ORGANIZATIONAL
SYSTEM

Chapter 9
The School Executive's
Work Context

The school executive functions within the context of both a formal and an informal organization. Interaction between the two affects the overall working relationships in the school. Although not denying the importance of the informal organization, in this chapter we focus primarily on selected characteristics of the formal organization of the school.

Although the school is similar to other organizations in many ways, its special mission in society gives it a certain uniqueness. A number of characteristics differentiate the school from organizations in general. First, the school is a professionally oriented organization. That is, school members are manifestly concerned with the education of children and youth and are, by and large, professionals as opposed to skilled, semiskilled, or unskilled workers. Conflict between professional and employee orientations, preferences, values, and assumptions will be examined more specifically in a later section of this chapter.[1] Second, the school's clients, the pupils, typically do not have a choice in determining the services they receive from the school nor which school they will attend. Legal codes require at least minimal participation.[2] Similarly for public schools, school personnel have only a limited choice of pupils served and individual teachers typically are assigned a group of pupils. Third, the amount of financial support a school receives is generally related to local wealth and the number of students. This is not to say that school executives are not concerned with organizational goal achievement, such as pupil learning. Rather, the point is that differences among schools and school districts in per pupil expenditures are not directly attributable to goal achievement.

A fourth unique characteristic presents an interesting paradox. Schools suffer from goal ambiguity. Although the stated goal of the school is "to provide learning experiences for children and youth"—and no citizen or administrator would challenge this general goal—yet the means by which it is to be accomplished are not universally agreed upon. Indeed, considerable confusion ensues when a group attempts to define what is meant by this goal.

Finally, the unique, dual status of pupils places the school in an unusual situation. Pupils are consumers of the services provided by schools, but, as already noted, they have little voice in the nature of the educational services provided. The fact that their parents and other citizens collectively hold the ultimate responsibility to act in their behalf exacerbates the school organization–pupil relationship. Pupils are also organization members, and the accomplishment of school goals is directly related to their performing membership functions. Their lot is quite different from that of lowest organizational members in business, industrial, military, and religious organizations. Clerks, assembly-line workers, recruits, and the laity are not minors, and although there are constraints on the organization's capacity to terminate the relationship, continued membership rests largely on a minimum level of performance.

It is within such a formally defined, unique structure that we find school executives. It is likely that many, if not most, of their personally and professionally frustrating problems could be attributed to these identifying characteristics of the school. On one level, the overwhelming demand for regularized, predictable functioning inhibits attention to individual needs of clients. On a second level, the same demand restricts the extent to which teachers are able to be involved to their satisfaction and to have the freedom of autonomous behavior. We now move to an analysis of this demand and its dysfunctional effects.

THE SCHOOL'S ORGANIZATIONAL STRUCTURE

All organizations exist to accomplish purposes. The ways in which organizations arrange role relationships to accomplish these purposes determine the organizational structure. The eminent sociologist Max Weber studied and wrote about the questions of organizational authority and structural arrangements.[3] Of the three pure types of authority he identified—legal, traditional, and charismatic—he perceived legal authority as a fundamental building block of the classical bureaucracy, "capable of attaining the highest degree of efficiency and in this sense formally the most rational means of carrying out imperative control over human beings."[4] As Abbott asserts, and we agree, "The American schools have been particularly receptive to the bureaucratic ideology, albeit perhaps unwittingly."[5]

According to Weber's formulations, the distinctive characteristics of a bureaucracy are:

1. A well-defined hierarchy of offices. Organizational authority is allocated to and through these offices, which also have specified functions. The organizational chart outlines the hierarchical authority. Position titles, although not specific job descriptions, usually furnish an important clue as to what "competence" is associated with that office.

2. Selection of officeholders on the basis of technical qualifications. Certificates, licenses, and diplomas provide evidence that one has achieved a minimum level of qualification. Incumbents are appointed rather than elected to office.

3. Remuneration received in the form of fixed salaries, with officeholders treating the office as the primary, if not sole, occupation and considering it a career. Most educational administrators in public schools do not moonlight; thus the salary they receive is their only income. Most are also considered to be waiting and working for a promotion.

4. Officeholders are subject to organizationally developed rules and regulations in the conduct of their offices. Thus predictability is increased by assuring a reasonable degree of stability.

5. Rules and regulations that are impersonal in nature. That is, officeholders are expected to perform their functions quite independently of their personal selves.[6]

These characteristics can be readily applied to schools. One should not necessarily attribute negative connotations to either the

The Organizational System

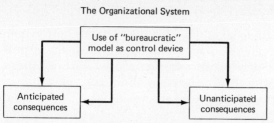

Figure 9-1 The general bureaucracy model. (Source: From James G. March and Herbert A. Simon, *Organizations* [New York: John Wiley, 1958], p. 37.)

characteristics or the schools to which they apply. Indeed, the school would be unable to exist without some such basic features. The problem arises when an organization adheres too rigidly to the bureaucratic formulation.

Dysfunctional Effects of Bureaucratic Organization

There are a number of negative as well as positive effects of formal organizational structures which approach the bureaucratic model.[7] As can be seen in Figure 9-1, both the anticipated and unanticipated consequences of the use of the bureaucratic model reinforce its continued use. We would say that the use of impersonal rules and regulations, a clearly defined hierarchy of offices, each of which is the primary occupation of the incumbent, and the other distinctive characteristics of a bureaucracy, generally produce predictable results which reinforce their continued use. Unfortunately, organizations which overemphasize structure, hierarchy, and rules also assume the risk of evoking unanticipated consequences which also reinforce their continued use. Thus the process becomes a closed spiral, with the organization increasingly relying on practices and procedures derived from bureaucratic principles.

Of the three models of unanticipated consequences presented and analyzed by March and Simon,[8] the most readily understood is their "simplified Gouldner model." (Gouldner was a sociologist who recognized that bureaucratic rule usage has both an intended and unintended effect on organizational dynamics. He developed a schematic to illustrate the dual effects.) An adaption of this model appears as Figure 9-2.

The Gouldner model suggests that an intentioned result of the use of rules is to reduce the visibility of power relations. School executives use policies, rules, and procedures to increase control over events and the reliability of behavior. One of the results of the

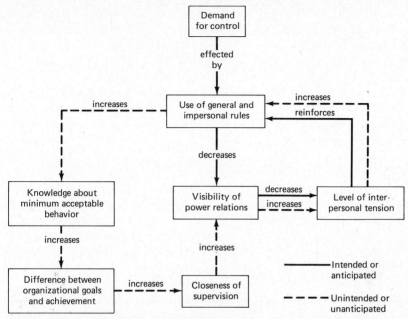

Figure 9-2   An adaptation of the simplified Gouldner model of unanticipated consequences. (Source: From James G. March and Herbert A. Simon,
Organizations [New York: John Wiley, 1958], p. 45.)

use of such general and impersonal rules is that the school executive is not constantly responding to questions relative to organizational functioning. Thus visibility of the person in charge is
decreased.

In the absence of continuous rulings on questions raised, we
would expect the level of interpersonal tension to be reduced in the
organization. That is, teachers are more likely to feel relaxed when
authority is less conspicuous. We would further expect that the
school executive would assess this positive, intentioned effect and
continue to utilize the rules approach.

There are other possible, if not probable, results of the use of
general and impersonal rules. One might hypothesize, however,
that these would occur only if there were continual and accelerat-
ing use of rules. The Gouldner model identifies only one such
unintended consequence—subordinates gain knowledge about
minimum organizationally acceptable behavior. Because of the
filtering of messages that occurs in the process of communication, it
is likely that some subordinates will not "hear" the rule but will
think it is intended for everyone else. In any event, the gap
between organizational goals (as perceived and accepted by school

executives) and their achievement is widened. This, in turn, leads to closer supervision. The school executive is then more visible as a power figure than before, and the subordinates react with increased tension. Again, the school executive obtains feedback, analyzes the problem, and increases the use of general and impersonal rules. The reader may be able to think of not only other variables affecting the Gouldner model, but other actions which have unintended and dysfunctional, as well as intended and functional, effects.

A STRUCTURAL-FUNCTIONAL APPROACH TO SCHOOLS

Let us now turn to a theoretical framework which links organizational arrangement variables (structural variables) with end result variables (functional variables). After reviewing and summarizing much of the organizational theory literature, Jerald Hage proposed an axiomatic theory of organizations; four means (structural characteristics) and four ends which seem to pervade the literature of organizational operation were identified.[9]

Implicit (if not explicit) in bureaucracy are the structural dimensions of complexity (specialization by function of officeholders), centralization-decentralization of decision-making (hierarchy of authority), formalization (rules and regulations), and stratification (assignment of varying degrees of status to the offices). These are the four structural or means variables in the Hage formulation. The four ends variables in the formulation are adaptiveness, production, efficiency, and job satisfaction.

These eight variables are clearly concerns of the school executive. One is continually confronted with decisions relating to one or more of them. Indeed, one may conceptualize the executive function as that of systematically establishing or reinforcing priorities among the ends and/or altering one of the means. The eight Hage variables are presented and defined in Table 9-1.

Structural Characteristics

School executives vary in the extent to which they can alter the structure of their organization (affect the means). Legally, complexity is related to state certification requirements for teachers and administrators. However, new specialists are created as individuals enter a school, assume certain responsibilities, and concentrate their efforts on those responsibilities. Indeed, person specialization (as opposed to task specialization)[10] develops independently of formalized training. This can be illustrated in the area of federal

TABLE 9-1 THE EIGHT VARIABLES IN HAGE'S AXIOMATIC THEORY
OF ORGANIZATIONS

VARIABLE	INDICATORS[a]
ORGANIZATIONAL MEANS	
Complexity (specialization)	Number of occupational specialties
	Level of training required
Centralization (hierarchy of authority)	Proportion of jobs that participate in decision-making
	Number of areas in which decisions are made by decision-makers
Formalization (standardization)	Proportion of jobs that are codified
	Range of variation allowed within jobs
Stratification (status system)	Differences in income and prestige among jobs
	Rate of mobility between low- and high-ranking jobs or status levels
ORGANIZATIONAL ENDS	
Adaptiveness (flexibility)	Number of new programs in a year[b]
	Number of new techniques in a year
Production (effectiveness)	Number of units produced per year
	Rate of increase in units produced per year
Efficiency (cost)	Cost per unit of output per year
	Amount of idle resources per year
Job satisfaction (morale)	Satisfaction with working conditions
	Rate of turnover in job occupants per year

SOURCE: From Jerald Hage, "An Axiomatic Theory of Organizations," *Administrative Science Quarterly* 10 (December 1965): 293.
[a] Two indicators are used for each variable because of the possibility of errors in measurement. In general, the first indicator should be the stronger one, with the second accounting for exceptions.
[b] The time unit of a year is used to level out random variation resulting from specific and idiosyncratic organizational events. This time period also has the advantage of corresponding to one which is used by many organizations in the compilation of their records.

programs. Consider the following example: A teacher, fresh from a state university master's program, is employed to encourage and assist with the development of proposals to obtain federal funds. The teacher becomes familiar with the guidelines governing the awarding of funds, visits the state department office through which the funds are distributed, attends conferences surrounding the legislation, establishes contacts with federal officials, and examines the local educational system to determine goodness of fit of needs and resources. Two years later, programs have been initiated, the role functions (delineated previously) continue to be performed, new legislation is enacted, and at that point only this individual is in a position to assess intelligently the new legislation for the school district and make decisions with respect to it; a specialist has been developed by virtue of experience rather than training. If the emerging specialist performed role functions well, his or her district has been able not only to obtain its share of the federal funds, but these funds have made an educational difference.

State laws and rules also place limits on the school's freedom to decentralize. Boards of education have legal authority for making certain decisions. Participation in decision-making may be granted to teachers and even students, but ultimately the decision resides with board members. It has long been recognized, if not widely practiced, that school executives should involve as many people in decisions as possible.[11] The Hage theory predicts decreases in production and efficiency, but increases in adaptiveness and job satisfaction resulting from decentralized decision-making. An obvious effect of the teacher militancy movement is to increase the number of decision areas in which teachers are involved.

The functions and dysfunctions of relying on rules and procedures—an index of formalization—were illustrated earlier via the Gouldner model. Two additional points regarding emphasis on rules and procedures merit mention here. First, only because there have been certain key preservice experiences common to most teachers and school executives is it possible to operate school organizations with the relatively small number of rules and procedures that now exist. High entry-exit rates among staff, the increasing size and complexity of schools, and the diversity of backgrounds of faculty members—all work against administration without rules. Second, that students have fewer common experiences—both among themselves and with faculty—probably accounts, in part, for the felt need to regulate their behavior more closely. It should be noted that, as a result of negotiations, the school appears to be increasing rather than decreasing in formalization. Only in relation to student dress, grooming, and behavior codes does there seem to be a movement away from school rules and procedures.

The extent to which a school is stratified is easy for an administrator to assess. Teachers are stratified only to the extent that training and experience determine salary. (Differentiated staffing plans[12] increase stratification among teachers and those could be expected to result in dysfunctions as well as functional gains for the organization.) Movement from one salary level to another among teachers is not only easy, it is assured. It is between the major divisions or levels in the educational organization that stratification is more problematic. Barnard[13] identifies the beneficial and disruptive effects of differentiating rewards and status between and among individuals as follows.[14]

Beneficial Effects	Disruptive Effects
1. Recognizes differential abilities	1. Leads to distorted evaluation of individuals
2. Recognizes differential difficulty of various kinds of work	2. Restricts the circulation of the elite
3. Recognizes differential importance of various kinds of work	3. Distorts the system of distributive justice
4. Recognizes the value of formal status as a social or organizational tool	4. Exaggerates administration to the detriment of leadership and morale
5. Protects the integrity of the individual	5. Exalts the symbolic functions beyond the level of sustainment (Attitudes and behaviors come to be expected which status incumbents cannot fulfill.)
	6. Limits the adaptability of an organization

Two factors have tended to blur or mediate the stratification system in schools, at least until recently: (1) a professional feeling of togetherness among educators; (2) the fact that each aspiring teacher is potentially an administrator—as the administrative and supervisory components have increased, almost without exception the new positions have been filled with ex-teachers (or guidance personnel), and, of course, all administrators were once teachers. In summary, school systems vary in the degree of stratification, but there are unique circumstances which prevent the negative effects from disabling the organization.

Despite the maze of legal regulations, certification standards, local expectations, and financial restrictions, executives are able to vary the structural dimensions to create an organizational environment best suited to accomplish school system functions. It is not, then, a question of new professional specialist positions or not, centralized decision-making structure or not, formal rules or not, status systems or not. Rather, it is the school executive's responsibility to arrange for structural dimensions in light of internal assumptions, the motivations (needs) of those in his school, and the effects of varying structure on the functions of the school.

Figure 9-3   Explicit-implicit ends continuum.

Organizational Ends

A distinction between implicit and explicit organizational ends of the school is helpful. The most explicit (expressed) organizational end is to provide learning experiences for children and young people—to produce educated clients. Less explicit but obvious is the end of providing the learning experiences as cheaply as possible—the end of efficiency. Less explicit and obvious still is the end of adapting the organizational arrangements, curricular content, procedures, and materials to new demands and new developments. The least explicit organizational end, job satisfaction, is similar, if not identical, to the group maintenance function of leadership. No school can afford to have job satisfaction as its major explicit goal; however, a minimum level of satisfaction is essential for sustained effectiveness. On an explicit-implicit continuum, the four organizational ends from the Hage formulation are depicted in Figure 9-3.

The obvious problem for the school executive, in terms of overall school effectiveness, is the effective balancing of achievement emphasis among the four organizational ends (goals). Such balancing may well be accomplished by reducing major goals to minor goals. Newell, Shaw, and Simon point out that progress is affected by following this approach, which they term *"The principle of subgoal reduction:* Make progress by substituting for the achievement of a set of easier goals."[15] An illustration of how this principle encourages, if not forces, balance is as follows:

Major goal The "education" of all children in the school.
Subgoal 1 The employment and retention of competent staff.
Subgoal 2 The creation and maintenance of a satisfying school climate.
Subgoal 3 The involvement of personnel in decisions which affect them.
Subgoal 4 The establishment of a procedure or a structure to identify key decision areas and personnel to be involved.

In the preceding list, four subgoals are substituted for the one major goal. If one assumes a positive relationship between input (staff) and output (education of children), subgoal 1 identifies employment and retention of competent staff as activities for the school executive to achieve the major goal. The existence of a satisfying school climate is conducive to attracting and retaining competent staff. One of the components of a satisfying school climate is the involvement of personnel in decisions affecting their work and work relationships. Establishing a mechanism that enables the accomplishment of subgoal 3 represents adaptive behavior on the part of the executive and the organization. Three of the four ends, production, satisfaction, and adaptiveness are, thus, explicitly involved in the illustration. The fourth, efficiency, is implicitly involved; available dollars that can be utilized to employ and retain competent staff members (as well as support their efforts) sets one portion of the efficiency equation. The crucial efficiency question concerns the quality level of education the school's public will tolerate and support.

School executives have a unique problem with respect to the balance question independent of the explicit-implicit difference. Since schools are public and service organizations, they are subjected to pressures and constraints by external groups which affect all of the ends (goals) of the school, although these groups hold legitimate, vested interests only in the explicit goal of educated children. This pressure is also due, in part, to the lack of certainty about the professionalization of educational personnel. For example, many of the complaints school patrons make about staff members' dress, political opinions, personal life habits and preferences, and work hours are absurd, but clearly have implications for the school executive's efforts toward achieving school ends. Indeed, these complaints have the effect of forcing the school executive to emphasize structure or means rather than ends.

In summary, school executives functioning in formal organizations have four ends toward which they strive with varying degrees of commitment: to produce (to increase performance efforts toward school goals); to produce efficiently; to adapt programs, procedures, and technologies continually; and to maintain satisfaction of personnel. These ends are accomplished by structuring the organization in certain specific ways. Interaction between means and ends (structure and function) is not always compatible, though, and frequently results in conflict. Let us now turn our attention to conflict in organizations.

STRUCTURAL-FUNCTIONAL CONFLICT

The two categories of conflict which will be identified, defined, and discussed at this point have already been treated from a different perspective in earlier chapters. They are used here specifically to illustrate difficulties which school executives face in the implementation of administrative organization. Simply stated, the categories of conflict are the individual-organization conflict of which Argyris[16] has written so cogently and the bureaucratic-professional orientation conflict proposed by Corwin.[17]

Individual-Organization Conflict

Argyris's thesis is that the demands organizations make of the individual are in basic conflict with the individual's desire and need to achieve self-actualization. In structural-functional terms, this means that organizational decision-making structures and rules inhibit the optimum satisfaction of individuals.[18] A direct relationship between structure and function is thus evident. This relationship is an inherent one, especially in schools as they are now conceived and operated. Conflict of this type operates more forcefully on teachers and pupils than on school executives, since their behavior is more specified. For instance, freedom of physical movement is greater for principals than for teachers, since the latter are required to remain with children. The demands of preparing students to succeed in the next grade, in high school, in college, or even in the next examination restricts the behavior of teachers in another way. Similarly, the school's requirement—legitimate, no doubt—that certain materials be used at specified times and in prescribed ways impinges on the freedom of teachers to develop more fully their professional potential.

Since the school is concerned with quality (of the education pupils receive) as well as quantity (number of pupils served), both objectives require attention from administrators. In large measure, the problem is reduced to a question of formality versus flexibility in the school structure.[19] The indirect relationship between demand for control through decision-making structures and formalization and for quality production through the satisfaction of its members has been blurred by conflicting research evidence. MacKay reports that Canadian teachers have been less satisfied in school organizations with bureaucratic authority relationships. He concludes that such relationships lead to staff members not performing up to capacity, reduction in productivity, and poor organizational decisions.[20] Hage hypothesizes a negative relationship between production and satisfaction and cites supporting evidence.[21] Common sense suggests that satisfied employees produce more. In any event, the organization-individual conflict may be analyzed in structural-functional terms. School executives are encouraged to examine and test informally the nature of the relationship between organization and individual in their schools.

Historically, teachers have expressed the conflict between themselves and the school in individual-organization terms: "You can't beat the system." "The administration just won't listen." "It doesn't matter what I say." Recognizing that it would be impossible to eliminate all such complaints, still the frequency and regularity with which they are voiced strongly suggest a measure of validity in them. Another way of conceptualizing this conflict has been proposed and empirically observed by Corwin.[22] Let us now turn to that formulation.

Bureaucratic-Professional Conflict

Noting that the individual-organization formulation has been less than totally satisfactory in explaining organizational tensions, Corwin suggests an alternative: the examination of conflict stemming from competing bureaucratic and professional orientations. Assuming that teachers are professional employees and would exhibit an orientation typical of other professionals,[23] Corwin suggests that there are two distinctly different views toward organizational characteristics or bureaucratic principles.[24] These views were measured in terms of three organizational characteristics: standardization of work, specialization of jobs, and authority.[25] In other words, according to Corwin, conflict arises—not because individuals oppose specialization, standardization, and centralization but—because these characteristics imply something different for professionally oriented persons than for bureaucratically oriented persons. The differences are delineated in Table 9-2.

It should be noted that Corwin sees the distinctions not as one set of orientations held by school executives and another held by teachers, but as independent sets of competing orientations available to both school executives and teachers. That is not to say that one group does not tend toward one or the other orientation. Because of the functional responsibility of school executives, we would expect them to rate higher on the bureaucratic orientation.

Corwin developed an instrument of assessing the strength of the two orientations and administered it to 284 teachers in seven secondary schools. The independence of the two orientations was validated in that the "professional scale scores of the sample were not significantly correlated with total employee scale scores. . . ."[26] Interviews were also conducted with 143 teachers to ascertain

TABLE 9-2 ORGANIZATIONAL CHARACTERISTICS AND
BUREAUCRATIC-PROFESSIONAL ORIENTATIONS OR EXPECTATIONS

ORGANIZATIONAL CHARACTERISTICS	BUREAUCRATIC EXPECTATIONS	PROFESSIONAL EXPECTATIONS
Standardization	Stress on uniformity of clients' problems	Stress on uniqueness of clients' problems
	Stress on records and files	Stress on research and change
	Rules stated as universals—and specific	Rules stated as alternatives and diffuse
Specialization	Stress on efficiency of techniques—task orientation	Stress on achievement of goals—client orientation
	Skill based primarily on practice	Skill based primarily on monopoly of knowledge
Authority	Decisions concerning application of rules of routine problems	Decisions concerning policy in professional matter and unique problems
	Rules sanctioned by the public	Rules sanctioned by legally sanctioned professions
	Loyalty to organization and to superiors	Loyalty to professional associations and clients
	Authority from office (position)	Authority from personal competence

SOURCE: Adapted from Ronald G. Corwin, "Professional Persons in Public Organizations," *Educational Administration Quarterly* 1 (Autumn 1965): 7.

friction incidents within the school involving other teachers or staff members. The testing and the interviews showed the following:

> There was a significant rank order correlation (rho = .91) between the mean professional orientation of the seven schools and their rates of conflict per interview. . . .
> Finally, persons who held simultaneously high-professional and low-employee orientations had higher rates of conflict than persons who held low-professional and high-employee orientations, or any of the other possible role combinations.[27]

Corwin relates this conflict to organizations on a structural-functional basis when he writes:

> It seems likely that if the sources of organizational tension are

structural, then potential solutions to organizational problems also will be found at that level. . . . Hence, those who regard the problem [administrators in organizations with professional employees] simply as one of creating "good administration," ignore the very condition that professionalization is designed to remedy—that, under benevolent authoritarian administration, the status of the teacher's authority still depends on the discretion of the administration.[28]

THE SCHOOL AS ORGANIZATION: A PROPOSAL FOR SCHOOL EXECUTIVES

Implicit in the discussion of organizational variables and constraints is the desirability, necessity, and—perhaps—inevitability of change in organizational arrangements. School executives, students, and professors of educational administration, however, are often prone to chart the organization. Ask a school superintendent about the district's administrative organization, and a chart complete with clear line and staff distinctions, is produced. We shall not totally disappoint those who find charting to be useful. Our proposed organizational structure will include a diagram. Our proposal will consist largely, however, of stating principles for school executives to consider in developing or modifying their structural work context.

It may be well to pause at this point and distinguish between a set of principles derived from specific value-laden ideas and a set derived from relatively value-free ideas. Stated differently, a distinction can be made between a proposal for "how to do it" that is based on fundamental values and beliefs about human potential and relationships and one that is based totally on current realities. That is the essential distinction between a normative theory, which this book represents, and a strict situational theory with task or organizational effectiveness as *the* controlling, dependent variable.[29] Of course no proposal is ever quite a pure type. Proposals based on "normative theory" have some latitude for interpreting situations and structuring behavior accordingly. Similarly, principles based purely on situational theory have value bases that exclude certain structures and behaviors. Our proposal is predominantly value based while permitting, even encouraging, attention to the nature of work to be accomplished and expertise of organizational members involved.

The proposal has three key features, two explicit and one implicit. The first explicit feature is that school executives are human links in the complex organizational chain.[30] Our unwillingness to chart an organizational structure should alert the reader to the second explicit feature, the flexibility or the temporary character of the structure. The implicit feature is that the proposal generally recognizes the inevitability of specialist-generalist, bureaucratic-professional orientation conflicts. An obvious result of defining a structure is to reduce authority or responsibility conflicts. The existence of the American court structure, for example, reduces conflict over who determines the constitutionality of laws, but not whether laws are constitutional or not. Actually, the court structure—like our proposed flexible organizational structure— legitimizes the presence of different points of view and provides for their resolution.

Human Links

Moser's conclusion that the principal is "a man in the middle" (following a study of expectations for school principals held by superintendents and teachers)[31] applies structurally to all school executives. We are not unaware of the necessity for the superordinate position in a school organization. To dramatize the difference between the usual and what we propose, however, we shall depict links and groups horizontally or in the round rather than vertically. Two examples of school executives as human links appear in Figure 9-4 in the form of basic decision-making structures.

Except for the hint given by traditional titles—for example, superintendent, principal—there is no way of identifying the flow of decision-making power. The examples in Figure 9-4 clearly indicate participants for decisions at various places within the structure. Intergroup coordination is effected through the human link, and links are effective if recognized as legitimate by members of both groups. Implications for decision-making about staff selection are obvious. The selection of principal A (in example 1) would be participated in by chairpersons 1–4, student groups 1–2, the two assistant principals, principals B–E, and central office administration. It is appropriate here to acknowledge the ambiguity surrounding the theoretical and operational definition of participation, as well as the difference between its definition(s) and what is, indeed, practiced. The point to be made with this proposal is that it suggests guidelines for structure which improve the opportunity for a school to emphasize job satisfaction and adaptability.[32]

Two additional points should be made with respect to the human link model. First, if such a model is followed, the traditional groupings of teachers and students—for example, departments and student councils—would need to be complemented by task forces

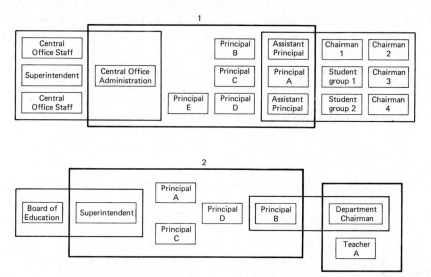

Figure 9-4   The school executive as human link: two examples.

or temporary committees. Second, the placement of principal, assistant principal, and department chairperson in the same permanent work group would eliminate the need for distinguishing whether they are line or staff.

Principles for Structural Arrangements

Recognizing that school executives have functional responsibilities which come from legal requirements and from decisions of the work group of which they are members, it is necessary to establish some guidelines for the organization.

1. Initial decisions about employment of staff, allocation of resources, development and modification of programs, and evaluation of staff and program should be made by the work group most directly affected.
2. Operational and evaluative procedures should focus on goal achievement (behaviors, tasks, functions to be performed) rather than control.
3. Functional responsibilities should be assigned on the basis of competence rather than position. This requires that more attention be given to what constitutes competence, given a certain function.

4. Rewards should be based on job performance rather than on location in a school's structure.

Following the means-ends analysis presented earlier, it is assumed that school executives do not specifically organize in terms of each of the four organizational ends: job satisfaction, adaptiveness, production, and efficiency. Rather, an organization is arranged according to structural characteristics (means) to effect maximum accomplishment of ends as determined at some point in time. However, since the organization is dynamic—both in terms of personnel, resources, and climate and in terms of placement on any of the implied continua (e.g., centralization-decentralization)—the school executive cannot play out the "watchmaker theory." That is, the executive cannot create a structure, set it in motion, allow it to run, and merely be about the performance of other administrative responsibilities. The structure requires observation and intervention. Indeed, decisions about the organizational structure—even the initial arrangement—may be the most important decisions the school executive has to make.

Notes

1. See, for example, Ronald G. Corwin "Professional Persons in Public Organizations," *Educational Administration Quarterly* 1 (Autumn 1965):1–22; Ronald G. Corwin, "The Professional Employee: A Study of Nursing Roles," *American Journal of Sociology* 66 (May 1961): 604–615; Norman J. Boyan, "The Emergent Role of the Teacher in the Authority Structure of the School," in *Collective Negotiations and Educational Administration*, R. Allen and J. Schmid, eds. (Fayetteville: University of Arkansas Press, 1967), pp. 1–21; and Eugene Litwak, "Models of Bureaucracy Which Permit Conflict," *American Journal of Sociology* 67, no. 2 (September 1961): 77–184.
2. A number of scholars have used choice of membership (and other dimensions) to develop useful typologies of organizations and have discussed their effects on organizational functioning. See, for example, Amatai Etzioni, *A Comparative Analysis of Complex Organizations* (New York: Free Press, 1961); Peter M. Blau and W. Richard Scott, *Formal Organizations: A Comparative Approach* (San Francisco: Chandler, 1962); Richard O. Carlson, "Environment Constraints and Organizational Consequences: The Public School and Its Clients," in *NSSE Yearbook*, Daniel E. Griffiths, ed., vol. 63, Part II (Chicago: The Society, 1964), pp. 261–302.
3. Max Weber, *The Theory of Social and Economic Organization*, A. M. Henderson and Talcott Parsons, trans., Talcot Parsons, ed. (New York: Free Press, 1947), pp. 324–363.
4. Ibid., p. 337. Imperative control might be considered synonymous with authority; see ibid., p. 152, n. 83.

5. Max. G. Abbott, "Hierarchical Impediments to Innovation in Educational Organizations," *Change Perspectives in Educational Administration* (Auburn, Ala.: School of Education, Auburn University, 1965), pp. 40–53.

6. Adapted from Weber, *Theory of Social and Economic Organization*, pp. 333–35.

7. See, for example, James G. March and Herbert A. Simon, *Organizations* (New York: John Wiley, 1958), p. 37.

8. Ibid., p. 45.

9. Jerald Hage, "An Axiomatic Theory of Organizations," *Administrative Science Quarterly* 10 (December 1965):289–320; Jerald Hage and Michael Aiken, *Social Change in Complex Organizations* (New York: Random House, 1970); and Jerald Hage, *Communication and Organizational Control* (New York: John Wiley and Sons, 1974). In the books, Hage (and Aiken in the first) uses the variables in the axiomatic theory to examine program change—an indicator of *adaptability*—and communications.

10. Victor Thompson, *Modern Organization* (New York: Knopf, 1961), chap. 3.

11. Jack R. Gibb, "Dynamics of Leadership," in *In Search of Leaders* (Washington, D.C.: American Association for Higher Education, NEA, 1967), pp. 55–56; Rensis Likert, *The Human Organization: Its Management and Value* (New York: McGraw-Hill, 1967).

12. See, for example, M. John Rend and Fenwick English, "Towards a Differentiated Teaching Staff," *Phi Delta Kappan* 49 (January 1968): 264–268; and Anthony F. Gregorc, "Satisfaction from Teaching," *Educational Forum* 35 (March 1971):307–313.

13. Chester I. Barnard, "Functions and Pathologies of Status Systems in Formal Organizations," in *Industry and Society*, William F. Whyte, ed. (New York: McGraw-Hill, 1946), pp. 46–83.

14. Ibid., pp. 52–83.

15. A. Newell, J. C. Shaw, and H. A. Simon, "A General Problem-Solving Program for a Computer," *Computers and Automation* 8 (July 1959):10.

16. Chris Argyris, "Individual Actualization in Complex Organizations," *Mental Hygiene* 44 (April 1960): 226–37, and Argyris, "Personality and Organization Theory Revisited," *Administrative Science Quarterly* 18 (June 1973):141–67.

17. Corwin, "Professional Persons in Public Organizations." For more extensive treatment of the research reported and additional discussing of the more general topic of "professional militants," see Ronald Corwin, *Militant Professionalism* (New York: Appleton-Century-Crofts, 1970), and *Education in Crisis* (New York: John Wiley and Sons, Inc., 1974), especially chaps. 5 and 6.

18. Two works that forcefully describe schools and the special characteristics of teachers in them are: Seymour B. Sarason, *The Culture of the School and the Problem of Change* (Boston: Allyn and Bacon, Inc., 1971), and Dan C. Lortic, *Schoolteacher: A Sociological Study* (Chicago: University of Chicago Press, 1975).

19. Gerald D. Bell, "Formality Versus Flexibility in Complex Organizations," in *Organizations and Human Behavior: A Book of Readings,* Gerald D. Bell, ed. (Englewood Cliffs, N.J.: Prentice-Hall, 1967), pp. 97–106.
20. D. A. MacKay, "Should Schools Be Bureaucratic?" *The Canadian Administrator* 14, no. 2 (November 1964):7–8.
21. Hage, "An Axiomatic Theory."
22. Corwin, "Professional Persons in Public Organizations."
23. For a discussion of professionals, see Ernest Greenwood, "Attributes of a Profession," *Social Work* 2 (July 1957): 30–40; Howard S. Becker, "The Nature of a Profession," *Education for the Professions.* Sixty-first *NSSE Yearbook,* Part II (Chicago: University of Chicago Press, 1962).
24. Corwin, "Professional Persons in Public Organizations."
25. In terms of the Hage theory, these would be complexity, formalization, and centralization, respectively.
26. Corwin, "Professional Persons in Public Organizations," p. 10.
27. Ibid., p. 15.
28. Ibid., p. 16.
29. There is increasing attention given to the development of situational (contingency) theories of organization. The Hage theory is implicitly a contingency theory at the point of using it to make major decisions about structural features of organizations. See, for example, John P. Langdale, "Toward a Contingency Theory for Designing Work Organizations," *Journal of Applied Behavioral Science* 12 (April/May/June 1976):199–214; Paul R. Lawrence and Jay W. Lorsch, *Organization and Environment: Managing Differentiation and Integration* (Boston: Division of Research, Graduate School of Business Administration, Harvard University, 1967); and Jay W. Lorsch and John J. Morse, *Organizations and Their Members: A Contingency Approach* (New York: Harper & Row, Publishers, 1974).
30. See Likert's linking-pin and overlapping-groups concepts in Rensis Likert, *New Patterns of Management* (New York: McGraw-Hill, 1961), or Rensis Likert. *The Human Organization* (New York: McGraw-Hill Book Company, 1967). For a report on an organization designed specifically on overlapping work groups and linking pins see *Harvard Business Review* 55 (January–February 1977): 117–127—an interview with John F. Donnelly, Donnelly Mirrors, Holland, Michigan.
31. Robert P. Moser, "The Leadership Patterns of School Superintendents and School Principals," *Administrator's Notebook* 6, no. 1 (September 1957).
32. The point we wish to make is made by Keith Goldhammer when he says, "We are professionals who have meshing roles, and the role of the superintendent in meshing with his principals is to see that the conditions are most favorable for them to do a creative, sound, professional job." See Paul L. Houts, "A Conversation with Keith Goldhammer," *National Elementary Principal Journal* 52 (March–April 1974): 27–34.

Chapter 10
Authority and the School Executive

Although administrative subordinates, supervisors, teachers, students, and parents accept—in varying degrees—the suggestions, orders, and decisions of the school executive, it is well—in the absence of the "perfect" school executive—that not all administrative decisions are unquestioningly accepted. This is organizationally healthy. With respect to the acceptance of administrative action, however, the question of why school members do accept administrative suggestions, orders, and decisions remains. It is this question to which this chapter is addressed. The discussion proceeds as follows. First, we define the central concept of authority and place it in perspective in regard to the school executive's authority. The contradictory concepts of fixed and variable sums of organizational authority are introduced and related to the school executive's concern with subordinates. The chapter concludes with an approach to operating the authority system.

AUTHORITY DEFINED AND PLACED IN CONTEXT

We are concerned with the authority system within the school organization and how it is related to the accomplishment of school goals. We define authority of a school executive as "the potential capacity to effect movement toward goal achievement."[1] The fact that administrative authority resides in the school executive position rather than the teacher position is due in large part to the circumstances under which schools developed in American society.

Early American public schools were creatures of the colonial town legislatures. Teacher and pupil positions were established; authority with respect to pupil control was placed in the teacher position; and the decisions about who would do what, to whom, for how long, under what conditions, and for what remuneration were reserved for town selectmen. Thus, although "the teacher was the school," authority in American public schools was reserved to an administrative level from their inception.

As schools increased in size, the states began to take seriously the education function. It became necessary for the authority of the town selectmen—organizational ancestors of the modern school board or board of education—to be transferred to a professional educator, a headmaster or master teacher. Originally a part-time function, the headmaster position evolved into the principal position as we know it today, at first fracturing and finally severing the teaching/administration functional marriage. Simultaneous growth in the numbers of schools, resulting in school district systems, gave rise to the central office administrative cadre. The key point here is that the development of the school executive strata was initiated by a statutorily created lay body. School administration until the advent of teacher militancy and collective bargaining was able to discharge its distinct functions with relatively little intraschool challenge to its authority because its membership emerged from the larger teacher membership and its functions were facilitating in nature.

Complexities associated with operating schools—securing adequate financial resources, attracting, retaining, and continually upgrading organizational members, determining and establishing priorities among goals, developing instructional programs, and carrying out a host of other functions—sparked growth in the number of administrative positions. Continued and further legal legitimation for school executives is evidenced by specialized certification requirements and programs aimed at preparing individuals for every conceivable position. Thus school executives have both a historical and legally derived charge to effect goal achievement in their schools.

In this time of questioning authority—first, by teachers and, more recently, by pupils, parents and other citizens, individually and collectively—it is of no small consequence that the analysis of authority sources presented in this chapter might well have been the same had teachers originally been granted the responsibility for developing the administrative functions. It is a simple organizational fact that administrative functions have to be performed. However, perhaps teachers would be more willing to accept authority (perceive it as more legitimate or consider the incumbent more competent) if they had been permitted to provide for the conduct of administration. As collective bargaining has developed, there have been calls from teacher leaders for educational leadership to be performed by a teacher while leaving building management functions to an administrator (principal). That idea did not originate with teacher organization leaders, however. Moehlman suggested, over two decades ago in the "democratic administration" period, that a school faculty would ideally choose its principal from its own ranks.[2] Let us now move to the main focus of this chapter and map out the sources of authority of school executives.

SOURCES OF AUTHORITY

Three formulations which illustrate the origins of authority as defined earlier are presented and developed in this section. A two-dimensional framework suggested by Guba[3] is followed by a four-base typology developed and empirically tested by Peabody.[4] The third formulation is French and Raven's analysis of five kinds of social power derived from relationships between two actors.[5] The logic of this order is to move from the simple to the more complex.

Role-and Person-Based Authority

In discussing internal administrative relationships, Guba suggests that the administrator has actuating force (authority) derived from two sources—the role and person dimensions of the administrative social system—both of which can be utilized to effect goal achievement.[6] The role dimension is realized through the placing of the administrator in a school role which carries ascribed or delegated authority for role-related activities. As noted in Chapter 7, the school organization is essentially bureaucratic, with a chief characteristic being a hierarchy of authority which flows from the top of the school to the bottom. The amount of organizational authority members have is dependent upon their place in the hierarchy. This authority, furthermore, is conferred independent of the individual. Thus superintendents, assistant superintendents, directors, principals, assistant principals, and other school executives are able to direct subordinates in their activities, in part, due to their position and attendant status; subordinates comply because "the principal says" or "he or she is the boss."

Despite stereotyping attempts by teachers, parents, and others, each school executive is a unique individual.[7] Experience, training, personality, and personal appearance are variables which differentiate between and among school executives. The extent to which subordinates react positively to attempts at movement toward goal achievement initiated by a particular administrator may have a positive or a negative force. Whether or not the executive deliberately utilizes the person dimension does not negate its existence. It is somewhat ironic that the true bureaucrat who works so hard at depersonalizing role performance (and authority) presents a personal image of a faceless, colorless, cold fish. This practice, in turn, has negative implications for effectiveness; authority is diminished rather than increased. Schematically, the administrator's sources of authority are depicted in Figure 10-1.

Authority of a school executive may be expressed algebraically as follows:

$$A = f(R + P)$$
where
A = Authority
f = function of
R = Role delegated
P = Person achieved

Intuitively and experientially, this formulation seems to capture reality. Probably everyone could identify instances when they observed (or sensed) one or more of the possible authority combinations being utilized or reacted to. Perhaps the formulation can be further clarified by offering some incidents.

1. A parent initially refuses to accept the authority of a school principal with respect to the disciplining of a child. Principal and parent meet and no new evidence is presented, but the parent leaves the conference perfectly willing to accept the principal's authority because "the principal is sincere and a real fine person."
2. A teacher questions the assignment of a pupil to class. The principal meets with the teacher and says, "You will admit this pupil to your classroom"—and the teacher does. (It has already been noted that role authority in this and related decision areas is being challenged by teachers through the negotiations process. The manner in which role authority is

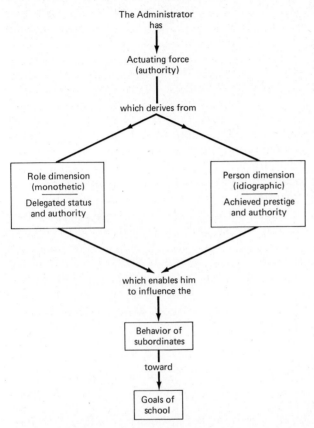

Figure 10-1   Role and person dimensions of authority. (Source: A modification of Figure 1 [Model of Internal Administrative Relationships] from Egon G. Guba, "Knowledge of Internal Administration—What Do We Know," in *Administrative Theory as a Guide to Action,* Roald F. Campbell and James M. Lipham, eds. [Chicago: Midwest Administration Center, University of Chicago, 1960], p. 124.)

exercised has much to do with whether a staff member is satisfied and elects to remain in the school. Neither of these is at issue here.)

3. An administrative council meeting is in progress and an issue arises about which subordinate administrators are less than enthusiastic. The superintendent implies that, even though group opinion will be sampled, the superintendent's office supports the issue—and no opposition is voiced.

4. An administrative council meeting is in progress, and a question of administrative procedure is raised. Open and free discussion ensues. The superintendent suggests a solu-

tion and explains why it would be the best, citing previous experience. All subordinate administrators enthusiastically and sincerely agree that "this is the way it should be done."

Incidents 1 and 4 exemplify effectively exercised authority deriving from the person dimension. We can only believe that the parent was willing to accept the principal's authority because of personal qualities which became evident in the conference and that the subordinate administrators accepted the proposed procedure due to perceived knowledge of the superintendent.

The teacher and subordinate administrators in incidents 2 and 3 are responding to role authority. There are, of course, occasions when the exercise of role-derived authority has positive connotations even though attention is directed to its use—for example, two groups of teachers present proposals for an educational program to a principal with the reminder that it is "the principal's decision."

Just as there is a difference between the kind of authority exercised in incidents 1 and 4 as compared with 2 and 3, so are there also differences within the two groupings. The parent's reaction (incident 1) was prompted by an aspect of the person-based authority different from the one to which subordinate administrators (incident 4) responded. Similarly, there is a suggestion of a more subtle distinction between role-based authority exercised with respect to the teacher (incident 2) and subordinate administrators (incident 3). A framework which would magnify these distinctions and offer some empirical evidence should be instructive at this point. We now present and discuss such a formulation.

Formal and Functional Authority Bases

Peabody's approach to authority[8] merits attention for at least three reasons. First, while it is constructed on a dichotomy between formal and functional authority (somewhat analogous to the role-person distinction made by Guba), each of these concepts is further divided, resulting in four distinct bases of authority available to school executives. Thus finer distinctions are possible relative to why organization members perform job-related tasks. Second, Peabody's approach synthesizes a large amount of significant literature related to authority and authority systems in organizations. Third, data about authority relations in three public service agencies, including an elementary school, are reported.

The bases of formal and functional authority, according to Peabody, can be distinguished in the following way. Formal authority bases are comprised of "legitimacy, position, and the sanctions inherent in the office," whereas functional authority bases are comprised of "professional competence, experience, and human relations skills, which support or compete with formal authority."[9] Victor Thompson has suggested that the reduction in functional ability resulting from the growth of bureaucratization and specialization, has created the major problem for modern organizations, a condition he labels the "ability-authority gap."[10] In the ideal bureaucratic organization, conflict would be nonexistent since in any superordinate-subordinate relationship the superordinate would have competencies greater than those of the subordinate. This ideal is far from realized in organizations, including schools; and that this is so is nowhere more clearly illustrated than in the secondary school, where principals with specialized training in administration are hierarchically superior to personnel with specialized training in English, foreign language, guidance, and the like.

Formal authority bases are subclassified as legitimacy and position bases, and functional authority bases as competence and person bases. From the definitions or descriptions of these sources of authority identified and discussed by Peabody (and presented in Table 10-1, in which Peabody categorizes, according to his own system, the positions of five other authorities), we may differentiate among the four bases of authority as follows:

1. Authority of legitimacy—potential capacity to effect movement toward goal achievement accruing from acceptance by subordinates of legally constituted order. (The principal relies on the school code, similar documents, and generalized norms and traditions.)
2. Authority of position—potential capacity to effect movement toward goal achievement accruing from position and its inherent sanctions and rewards. (The principal relies on delegated authority.)
3. Authority of competence—potential capacity to effect movement toward goal achievement accruing from knowledge and skill gained through training or experience. (The principal knows more about schedule making than the teachers.)
4. Authority of person—potential capacity to effect movement toward goal achievement accruing from personal characteristics or mystique. (The principal has a way with teachers.)

As previously noted, the possession and utilization of one authority base may reinforce another and, thus, the total of a school executive's authority appears greater than the sum of its parts. The

TABLE 10-1   THE BASES OF AUTHORITY

	FORMAL AUTHORITY		FUNCTIONAL AUTHORITY	
	LEGITIMACY	POSITION	COMPE- TENCE	PERSON
Weber[a]	Legal	—	Rational author- ity	Traditional authority
	Legal order	Hierarchi- cal office	Technical knowl- edge, experi- ence	Charismatic authority
Urwick[b]		Formal, conferred by the organiza- tion	Technical, implicit in spe- cial knowl- edge or skill	Personal, conferred by senior- ity or popularity
Simon[c]	Authority of legiti- macy, social approval	Authority of sanc- tions	Authority of con- fidence (techni- cal com- pe- tence)	Techniques of persua- sion (as distinct from au- thority)
Bennis[d]		Role in- cum- bency	Knowl- edge of perfor- mance criteria	Knowledge of the hu- man aspect of adminis- tration
Presthus[e]	Generalized deference toward authority	Formal role or posi- tion	Technical exper- tise	Rapport with subordi- nates, ability to mediate individual needs

SOURCE: From Robert L. Peabody, "Perceptions of Organizational Authority: A Comparative Analysis," *Administrative Science Quarterly* 6 (March 1962): 467.
[a] Max Weber, *The Theory of Social and Economic Organization*, A. M. Henderson and Talcott Parsons, trans., Talcott Parsons, ed. (Oxford: Oxford University Press, 1947), pp. 328, 339.
[b] L. Urwick, *The Elements of Administration* (New York: Harper & Row, Publishers, 1947), p. 42.
[c] Herbert A. Simon, "Authority," in Conrad M. Arensberg et al., eds., *Research in Industrial Human Relations* (New York: Harper & Row, Publishers, 1957), pp. 104–6; H. A. Simon, D. W. Smithburg, V. A. Thompson, *Public Administration* (New York, Alfred A. Knopf, 1950), pp. 189–201.
[d] Warren G. Bennis, Leadership Theory and Administrative Behavior: The Problem of Authority, *Administrative Science Quarterly* 4 (1959): 288–89.
[e] Robert V. Presthus, "Authority in Organizations," *Public Administration Review* 20 (1960): 88–91.

highly competent superintendent with a supportive board of education and attractive personal characteristics has virtually unlimited
capacity to bring about the goal-oriented behavior of an administrative staff. It should be obvious that competence and person authority are not restricted (in schools) to administrators, even with
respect to areas of activity typically reserved for administrative
responsibility. This was implied earlier in terms of the negative
consequences for administrators of the ability-authority gap. We
will return to this problem later in this chapter to consider it in a
positive context. Our focus presently is on school executives who
occupy formal administrative positions.

An exploratory interview study of authority relations in a
country welfare department, a police department, and an elementary school was conducted by Peabody.[11] The questions asked in
the interviews were aimed at discovering what authority bases
were operating to move the work of the organization. The findings
strongly supported the four authority bases developed from the
literature. No teacher perceived an authority base other than one of
the four; only 4 percent of the responses of welfare workers and 6
percent of policemen's responses indicated a perceived base different from the bases of legitimacy, position, competence, and
person.

Of particular interest in this study are the perceptions of
elementary school teachers. These are reported in Table 10-2. Of
some interest is the fact that only 22 percent of the welfare workers
and 15 percent of the policemen reported authority of competence
as important, as compared with 45 percent of the teachers.

By way of footnote to the Peabody findings, it is surprising that
only 15 percent of the teachers mentioned authority of person as
important. It is surprising in view of the widespread concern of
school executives for personal characteristics. We can only speculate that certain of the personal qualities deemed so important to
success in educational administration (i.e., interpersonal relations)
are perceived as competencies rather than personal qualities.[12]

While the Guba and Peabody analyses identify dimensions of
an authority reservoir and imply or suggest why these dimensions
comprise the administrator's potential capacity, the French and
Raven framework, the last to be used in our discussion of authority,
focuses on the reasons for accepting authority.

Since, in the French and Raven[13] analysis, the concept of five
bases of social power—reward, coercive, legitimate, referent, and
expert—are referred to as "power" rather than "authority," it is well
to return to the opening paragraphs of this chapter. Here, concerned with why organizational members accept administrative

TABLE 10-2 PERCEPTIONS OF BASES OF AUTHORITY IN AN ELEMENTARY SCHOOL

BASES OF AUTHORITY	PERCENT OF TEACHERS REPORTING $(N = 20)^a$
Authority of legitimacy	35
Authority of position	60[b]
Authority of competence	45
Authority of person	15
Other sources	0
No source specified	15

SOURCE: Adapted from Table 2, "Perceptions of the Bases of Authority in Three Public Service Organizations," in Robert L. Peabody, "Perceptions of Organizational Authority: A Comparative Analysis," *Administrative Science Quarterly*, 6 (March 1962): 477.
[a] Percentages total more than 100 percent because some respondents reported more than one base.
[b] The nature of one-fourth of these responses indicates that teachers were responding in terms of authority in their position.

direction, we defined "authority" as the "potential capacity to effect movement toward goal achievement." Although we could as well have used "power" to mean precisely what "authority" has been defined to mean, the selection was made in favor of "authority" because it has more positive connotations than "power." However, so as not to adulterate unnecessarily the present discussion, we shall employ the word "power" rather than "authority" in delineating the French and Raven framework and reporting the research findings.

According to the French and Raven formulation, students, teachers, and administrators respond affirmatively to their superior because of the perception of rewards or coercion which can be used, because the superior is making a legitimate request, or because he or she is seen as an important referent or expert. Specifically, the five types of power available to the school executive are:

1. Reward—subordinates perceive that the school executive can withhold, permit, or increase rewards.
2. Coercive—subordinates perceive that the school executive can distribute punishment (e.g., dismissal, undesirable assignments). Coercion at one extreme would involve physical force.
3. Legitimate—subordinates perceive that the school executive, by virtue of position and status within a duly constituted hierarchy, has the right to expect what is expected.
4. Referent—subordinates perceive the school executive as a desirable and appropriate human model and want to be perceived reciprocally—thus demands are accepted.

5. Expert—subordinates perceive the school executive to possess relevant expertise.[14]

Using these concepts, we are able to analyze in a different manner the incidents reported earlier. For instance, the parent yielded to the principal's authority (incident 1) because of referent power. It is equally obvious that the teacher accepted the child in class (incident 2) because of the veiled threat of punishment—coercive power. The superintendent's success with the administrative council (incident 3) appears to have been due to the perceived legitimacy of position. Without additional information about the behavior pattern of this superintendent, to attribute the "silent victory" to the threat of reward or coercion would be unwarranted. Unquestionably, the principal motivation behind the acceptance by the subordinate administrators of the superintendent's procedural suggestion (incident 4) was their perception of the superintendent as an expert.

We would expect that of the four school executives described in these incidents, the expert superintendent is in the best position to utilize potential capacity in the future. Peabody's findings suggest that the perception of expertise (authority of competence) by teachers is important in terms of why they accept school decisions. If the 15 percent of teachers reporting authority of position referring to their own positional authority is removed from the percentages reported in Table 10-2 (see table footnote b), then authority of competence is as important to teachers as any of the other authority bases. Two studies using the French and Raven dimensions bear directly on the question.

Bachman, Bowers, and Marcus[15] report results of investigations in 36 branch offices of a national sales firm, 12 liberal arts colleges, 40 life insurance agencies, 40 electrical appliance manufacturing firms, and 21 work groups in a utility company. They sought to determine why the subordinates (salespeople, faculty, agents, production workers, and semiskilled installation and repair personnel, respectively) complied with the requests of superiors. Respondents were asked to rank[16] the importance of the five reasons for complaince. The "he," "his," and "him" in the statements refer to the superior (office manager, academic dean, regional manager, production foreman, and first-line foreman, respectively). The five choices were:

1. Legitimate power: "He has a legitimate right, considering his position, to expect that his suggestions will be carried out."
2. Expert power: "I respect his competence and good judgment about things with which he is more experienced than I."

TABLE 10-3 MEAN RANKINGS OF POWER BASES[a]

| | ORGANIZATIONS | | |
| | 1 | 2 | 3 |
BASES OF POWER	SALES FIRM BRANCH OFFICE	LIBERAL ARTS COLLEGES	INSURANCE AGENCIES
Legitimate	4.1	3.6	3.3
Expert	3.5	4.1	3.8
Referent	2.9	3.5	2.5
Reward	2.7	2.3	2.8
Coercive	1.9	1.6	1.8

SOURCE: Adapted from Jerald G. Bachman, David G. Bowers, and Philip M. Marcus, "Bases of Supervisory Power: A Comparative Study in Five Organizational Settings," in Arnold S. Tannenbaum, *Control in Organizations* (New York: McGraw-Hill, 1968), p. 234.
[a] 5.0 = highest and 1.0 = lowest possible score. Respondents in organizations 1 and 2 used a ranking procedure; those in 3 used a rating (1–5 scale) procedure.

3. Referent power: "I admire him for his personal qualities, and want to act in a way that merits his respect and admiration."
4. Reward power: "He can give special help and benefits to those who cooperate with him."
5. Coercive power: "He can apply pressure to penalize those who do not cooperate."[17]

Without exception, either legitimate or expert power bases were the two most important reasons given for complying with superiors' requests. Subordinate in four of the five organizations ranked coercive power as least important; respondents in the utility company were the exception. Of most interest to us are the rankings by the white collar, semiprofessional, and professional subordinates in sales firms, insurance agencies, and colleges. Mean rankings of the five power bases in these three organizations are reported in Table 10-3.

Unless one is willing totally to disregard self-report data, clearly respondents in liberal arts colleges prefer to comply with the requests of their superior when expert power is the based utilized. The preferred power bases in the sales firm branch offices and the insurance agencies are legitimate and expert, respectively.

Findings from a study by Hornstein and others[18] are supportive of the Bachman results. Furthermore, they relate directly to school executives, since the research was conducted among public school teachers. The investigators correlated rankings of the bases of power of principals (derived from questions used by Bachman) with three other measures obtained from 325 elementary school teachers in 14 schools representing two school systems. The three other measures were: (1) satisfaction with the principal, (2) evaluation of the school system, and (3) perception of student satisfaction with the teacher. Of interest and relevance to our analysis is Hornstein's finding that reliance on expert power was associated with (1) more favorable evaluations of the school system, (2) greater satisfaction with the principal, and (3) a tendency to perceive students to be more satisfied with their teachers.[19]

Ivancevich[20] investigated interrelationships among the amount of control exercised by managers, power bases utilized, and satisfaction in 34 insurance agencies. Two findings are relevant to the present discussion. The first is that legitimate, expert, and referent (in that order) were the power bases of managers that agents perceived to be used most—mean ratings were computed for the five French and Raven power bases.[21] Second, and most important, the correlations between power bases used and three measures of satisfaction were significantly positive for referent and expert than for the other bases; all six were about 0.70. The power base with the next highest correlation was reward, about 0.30.[22]

Isherwood[23] studied authority bases of the secondary principal and related the use of different bases to teachers' loyalty to the principal, teachers' job satisfaction, and teachers' sense of powerlessness. His authority bases were Weber's[24] traditional, legal, and charismatic and expertise, normative, and human relations skills which more or less combine Peabody's competence and person and French and Raven's expert and referent bases. Factor analysis revealed two factors: *formal authority*—traditional and legal; and *informal authority*—charismatic, expertise, normative, and human relations skills. He found significant positive relationships between teachers' loyalty to the principal and teachers' job satisfaction and the use of informal authority, r = 0.78 and 0.42, respectively. The respective correlations with the use of formal authority were −0.54 and −0.77. Teachers' sense of powerlessness was significantly, positively related to the use of formal authority, r = 0.61, and significantly, negatively related to the use of informal authority, −0.46. Both Ivancevich and Isherwood conclude, and we concur, that the use of expert and reference or informal power/authority bases has positive implications for organizations and school executives.

Some Research Caveats

Numerous questions about authority (power) in schools are suggested by the results just reported. The first and most obvious has to do with authority relations among administrators. Respondents in the Bachman, Hornstein, Ivancevich, and Isherwood studies were technical-level subordinates responding to their immediate superior. The question is whether there are differences between administrator reaction and teacher reaction to the utilization of various power sources by their respective superiors.

A second question for research concerns the amount of interaction between the subordinates and their superior and among the subordinates. We would hypothesize that the amount of interaction and preference for expert authority would correlate strongly and positively. This suggests that if expert authority is mutually preferred (by superior and subordinates), administrative functions of executive positions have to be defined so that it is possible for school executives to bring to the position, or develop on the job, distinctive expertise. Similarly, it suggests that certain authority functions, which have long been within the domain of school executives, have to be performed by someone else. For instance, consider the principal as master teacher. This is a much easier role, from an expert authority point of view, for the elementary principal to perform than for the secondary school principal, although obviously a secondary principal can be selected from the ranks of master teachers regardless of teaching area.

Finally, practicing school executives might examine the mode (or modes) or gaining compliance in their organizations, immediate and extended. For example, principals might study compliance patterns in their schools or districts. The examination need not be highly formalized or systematized. By using focused random observations it is possible to obtain crude measures of authority modes and their relationships to equally crude measures of performance and other variables. In short, the school executive might engage in reflection and simple experimentation utilizing the authority concepts as tools.

Before offering more specific suggestions for organizing and operating the authority system, a consideration of the concepts of fixed and variable sums of power is in order. Since the proposal for changes in the authority system involves reduction in authority of school executives in the traditional sense, the definition and discussion of these concepts are important. (It is well to reemphasize that our definition of authority as "the potential capacity to effect movement toward total achievement" allows us to use the words "authority" and "power" virtually synonymously in the following discussion.)[25]

FIXED AND VARIABLE POWER SUMS

Logically, we can conceive of there being X amount of authority available to school executives in school system Z at any point in time. As a corollary, since not all organizational authority resides in school executive positions, we can also conceive of there being Y amount of authority available to subordinates (teachers primarily, although building-level and second-line central office administrators are subordinates as well) in school system Z at the same point in time. Mechanic[26] suggests that a number of factors—expertise, effort and interest, attractiveness, location and position, coalitions, and rules—are sources of power of organizational members in subordinate positions. Becker[27] and Washburne[28] report that public school teachers have various sources of authority relation to administrators and others. The question is whether the sum of X and Y is fixed or variable. If it is fixed, then a gain for subordinates is a loss for school executives; if it is variable, there need not be a loss.

Fixed or variable power is a relevant issue, since, as a practical matter, the particular "theory" presented throughout this book involves increased participation of members of the school organization. Collective bargaining in education has clearly modified the formal decision-making relationships between teachers on the one hand and administrators and school boards on the other. Although contract specifics vary, that modification has been more or less restricted to salary and working conditions. That is, of course, a somewhat ambiguous term. As enrollments have declined, teachers have been anxious to bargain decision rules and procedures for reductions in professional staff. Evaluation processes and procedures have increasingly found their way into contracts between teachers and school boards. Depending on how one defines working conditions, those two issues are or are not included. The point about collective bargaining and the participation of teachers and other professional staff members is that collective bargaining does not involve, for the most part, issues in schools that relate to what is taught, to whom, how is it taught, and in what configuration.[29]

A number of social scientists take the view that authority/social power within organizations is not a fixed amount.[30] Research in business, industrial, union, and voluntary organizations summarized by Smith and Tannenbaum[31] led them to conclude that the level of total organizational control, related to organizational goal achievement, is variable. They further concluded that perceived increases in control by subordinates were not necessarily accompanied by perceived decreases for superiors. Likert[32] reported that the sum total of influence in departments in business and industrial organizations was increased by changes in the leadership approach used. Lammers, noting the finding cited and suggesting that management increases the likelihood of its decisions being effected by ceding power to subordinates, sums up the argument: ". . . managers and managed in organizations can at the same time come to influence each other more effectively and thereby generate joint power as the outcome of a better command by the organization over its technical, economic, and human resources in the service of certain objectives."[33] McMahon[34] studied participation and power equalization as perceived by top-, middle-, and first-level managers in 12 plants in a large manufacturing corporation. He found a significant interaction between participative and power-equalized management systems, namely, that plants high on *both* participation and power equalization were superior to those characterized by only one of the variables. His conclusion echoes that of Lammers: ". . . a high degree of mutual interaction and influence is a necessary prerequisite for an effective power equalized system. While participation is more desirable than a lack thereof the incremental impact of a more egalitarian distribution is clearly an important consideration as the interaction effect demonstrates."[35]

Advocacy and evidence in educational administration is less strong. Ohm and Ohm and Monahan[36] support the variable-sum concept. Willower[37] investigated the effect of differential strengths of collective bargaining agencies (teachers' organization) on the distribution of influence in school districts as perceived by teachers. Ten Pennsylvania school districts were identified, five with strong and five with weak local teachers' associations. Teachers were selected and administered an instrument to assess their perception of the distribution of influence (within the district) of the school board, the superintendent, principals, and teachers. He found that there were differences in perceived influence at the various levels: board, superintendent, principals, teachers. Only at the board level was there any difference related to strong and weak teachers' association districts, however; boards in strong districts were perceived to have significantly more influence than boards in weak districts. These findings are mixed with respect to the issue of the fixed-variable power sum. On the one hand, teachers' associations characterized as strong could be assumed to have more impact on certain decisions but apparently that had no effect on the general distribution of influence to principals and the superintendent, and increased the influence of boards of education. On the one hand, teachers did not perceive themselves to have increased their influence either.

Belasco, Milstein, and Zaccarine[38] studied relationships between teacher participation in decision-making and perceived influence of superiors on those decisions in two western New York school districts in 1968. Measures of the extent of teacher participation in 11 decision areas were obtained from teachers as were their perceptions of the amount of influence their principal and superintendent had over their daily activities. The major hypothesis—no relationship between teachers' participation and perceived degree of control of their superintendent and principal over their teaching activities—was rejected. Correlational analysis revealed that the more teachers participated, the less influence they attributed to their principal and superintendent over daily activities of teachers. When analyses were performed by elementary and secondary teachers, however, there was no relationship between secondary teacher perceptions of participation in decision-making and perceived influence of principals and superintendents. Thus results from the secondary teachers supported the variable power sum hypothesis and results from elementary teachers did not.

There are two other reasons why we support the variable power sum concept, recognizing that evidence in schools is mixed. One relates to the school as an open system,[39] and the other is the dynamic, interacting nature of authority bases.

The school organization—its goals, priorities, structures, and internal relationships—is in constant interaction with other forces and groups (e.g., the school board, the PTA, the community). It is subject to influence from, and capable of having an impact on, the interacting groups, with the result that the amount of authority for effecting goals may increase or decrease.

Consider two examples: control of student behavior, dress, and grooming; and financial resources available for education. For whatever basic reasons, challenges to the school's methods and level of control of students' behavior and grooming have resulted in reduced authority for the school.[40] It is important to note that in this particular case all of the control-directed behavior of the school was allegedly aimed at effecting goal achievement. Indeed, until recently the courts upheld school dress and grooming codes on the argument that deviant dress and grooming was disruptive of the educational process. In our second example, forceful, vocal demands of teachers—concurrent, if not in harmony with, requests and pleas from boards of education and school executives—have, we believe, increased the level of financial resources for the support of public education. More importantly, the school's total potential capacity, relative to the community, to effect movement toward goal achievement (authority) has been increased—both for any specified time and generally over time.

The amount of authority held by an administrator at any point in time may be stated, after Peabody's formulation, as a function of the magnitude of position, legitimate, competence, and person bases ($A = f [Po \times L \times C \times Pe]$). Although the precise interaction effects are unknown, it is apparent that subordinates are less likely to question the position or legitimate authority of a school executive when the executive performs activities in a competent, expert manner. Conversely, the position or legitimate authority is more subject to question when competence is lacking.

This "face validity" question seems analogous to the traditional professor/practitioner quarrel. The aura of suspicion surrounding professors of educational administration generally—and, particularly, those who have not practiced educational administration—seems attributable to the feeling that one cannot be legitimated in a position as professor unless a minimum level of competence has been demonstrated in practicing the subject. The analogy is not perfect, of course. The relationship between professor and practitioner is not a superior-subordinate one. Their roles are quite distinct and different. Nevertheless, the professor with successful practice experience is perceived by administrators to be more legitimate than one without that experience. Position authority is therefore increased.

A PROPOSAL FOR CHANGE IN AUTHORITY RELATIONS

As noted at the beginning of this chapter, the prevailing distribution pattern of authority in schools derives from formal decisions by state legislatures and their agents, boards of education. Organizational authority of school executives below the superintendent level has been assigned also within the guidelines established by state legislatures and boards of education, in large part by the superintendent. Thus the formal authority bases—position and legitimate—result from deliberate, structural decisions. Competence-derived authority has been organizationally sanctioned (less explicitly but directly, nonetheless) in that training and experience requirements have been established to ensure minimum levels of expertise in the performance of administrative activities. Furthermore, in selecting school executives, attention is given to those characteristics which make it easier to accomplish the school's work. Thus the school assumes some responsibility for increasing even the person authority of school executives.

This analysis is not to suggest sinister, conspiratorial behavior on the part of state legislatures, school boards, and school superintendents. On the contrary, such behavior represents rational, logical action aimed at effecting the goals of the school. Our purpose in making such an analysis is to highlight the formal, organizational environment within which the school executive's authority functions, as well as to point out that change in authority distribution demands recognition and sanction, if not initiation, from the formal organization. Some change (e.g., style of leadership) is possible without changes in organizational arrangements, but the basic problem is structural.[41] It is, of course, a functional problem as well—in terms of organizationally prescribed role relationships.[42] At the risk of overgeneralization and oversimplification, however, we suggest that the bases of authority utilized in a school are largely determined by school executives within formalized arrangements.

Professional/Collegial Authority Relations

Our proposal for change in the authority system rests heavily on both a positive attitude toward, and a continuous restructuring in the direction of "collegial" or professional authority relations. Entirely consistent with research findings reported concerning preferred authority, the primary characteristic of collegial authority relations is its distribution based on demonstrated knowledge or competence.[43] For persons initially entering positions in education, this distribution is probably best determined by examining preparation and practice experiences. If implemented perfectly by school executives, this proposal would entail redistributing authority within the organization any time the specific decision task or position changed. The reader experienced in administration will recognize that this is consistent with current effective practice. For example, the central administration grants more autonomy (positional authority) to principal A, who has demonstrated competence as a building-level administrator, than to principal B, who is a beginner. Obviously, similar examples could be cited within central administration and within a building unit.

For numerous reasons it is not realistic to expect perfect, ideal, or extreme implementation of this proposal. The school cannot perform its function, educating large numbers of children and young people, if its authority system is in a state of perpetual change. Systematic study to determine decision areas for which authority is most appropriately assigned to a particular role, or set of roles, is a necessity, however.

In our view, school executives can approximate a more ideal authority system without negating the legally established administration–school-board–community relationships. Nor would acceptance and movement toward implementation reduce the school executive to an educational ideas eunuch or clerical assistant. The assignment of administrative authority would be predicated on expertise to the extent possible. The nature and the scope of the activities for which expertise is required are crucial questions. Since currently authority of school executives includes the prerogative to alter the basic authority system, the initiative for exploring alternative arrangements to effect a competence-based authority system rests in their hands. Interestingly, rather than contradicting the professional negotiating movement, our proposal capitalizes on it as a vehicle for making the alterations. That is, if one views the professional negotiations movement generally as an orderly (granted its operation is disorderly at times) procedure by which those previously without authority are seeking to increase their areas of authority, such negotiations become an advantage rather than a disadvantage.[44]

Implications for Change in Authority Bases

Implementation of change in an authority system which approximates collegial authority relations would have positive consequences for the four authority bases. Thus administrative authority would be strengthened rather than weakened. Furthermore, the potential for expanding the sum total of authority available to school organizations would be increased.

Position authority would be more changed than diminished. School authority demands would focus on facilitating, coordinating, arranging, structuring, and process seeking rather than on directing and deciding.

Legitimate authority would be more accepted, since assigned (position) authority activities would be perceived as more appropriate. Moreover, if the professional negotiations movement assists in the redeployment of the authority system, as we suggest it might, subordinates (teachers particularly) might well have been instrumental in creating the authority configuration and the nature of its component activities and, thus, would perceive administrative action as doubly legitimate.

Competence authority logically would be increased when activities outside the purview of a school executive's competence are excluded from his role. Pre- and in-service training could focus on those needed competencies with more intensity than before.

Person authority, the base least affected directly by the expertise/organizational authority conflict currently experienced by school executives, could be utilized more openly in a positive manner.

Greater objective and subjective unity among professional educators, in our view, can only lead to an increase in the total number and kind of authority areas over which the school is responsible. The total amount of authority is, thus, expanded.

Notes

1. Although authority may be defined otherwise, these definitions do not depend on differentiating authority from power. That the definition of authority does not rely on its differentiation from power is most clearly demonstrated by reference to: Herbert Danzger, "Community Power Structure: Problems and Continuities," *American Sociological Review* 29 (October 1964):707–717—power is defined as "potential capacity for action" (p. 715); Robert L. Peabody "Perceptions of Organizational Authority: A Comparative Analysis," *Administrative Science Quarterly* 6 (March 1962):463–482—implicitly, authority is defined as we have defined it; John R. P. French, Jr., and Bertram Raven, "The Bases of Social Power," in *Group Dynamics: Research and Theory*, 3rd ed., Dorwin Cartwright and Alvin Zander (ed.) (New York: Harper & Row, 1968), pp. 259–69—power refers to the potential of "O to influence P in A" (p. 261); and Fred D. Carver, "Eroding Power Bases of the School Principal," *Illinois Elementary Principal* (May 1969): 11–14—principal position is analyzed in power terms with power defined as "the common sense notion of the 'ability to get things done' " (p. 11).
2. Arthur B. Moehlman, *School Administration: Its Development, Principals, and Function in the United States* (Boston: Houghton Mifflin, 1951), pp. 274–75.
3. Egon G. Guba, "Research in Internal Administration—What Do We Know?" in *Administrative Theory as a Guide to Action*, Roald F. Campbell and James M. Lipham (eds.) (Chicago: Midwest Administration, University of Chicago, 1960), pp. 113–30.
4. Peabody, "Perceptions of Organizational Authority."
5. French and Raven, "The Bases of Social Power."
6. Guba, "Research in Internal Administration," p. 123. The complete social systems model from which the Guba formulation is derived can be found in Jacob W. Getzels and Egon G. Guba, "Social Behavior and the Administrative Process," *School Review* 65 (Winter 1957):423–41.
7. There are, of course, many personal and professional characteristics on which school executives are quite similar. Our present purpose is not to describe personal variables of school executives as a group.
8. Peabody, "Perceptions of Organizational Authority."
9. Ibid., pp. 466–67.
10. Victor A. Thompson, *Modern Organizations* (New York: Knopf, 1965), p. 6; "Hierarchy, Specialization, and Organizational Conflict," *Administrative Science Quarterly* 5 (March 1961):485–521; and Melville Dalton, "Conflicts Between Staff and Line Managerial Officers," *American Sociological Review* 15 (June 1950):342–351.
11. Peabody, "Perceptions of Organizational Authority," pp. 465–72.
12. One of the authors recently asked a highly successful suburban school superintendent with a doctor's degree in educational administration to name the single most important variable for success as a school executive. With no hesitation or qualification he replied, "The charisma of interpersonal relationships."

13. French and Raven, "The Bases of Social Power," pp. 465–72.

14. Ibid., pp. 262–68.

15. Jerald G. Bachman, David G. Bowers, and Philip M. Marcus, "Bases of Supervisory Power: A Comparative Study in Five Organizational Settings," in Arnold S. Tannenbaum, *Control in Organizations* (New York: McGraw-Hill, 1968), pp. 229–38.

16. Actually, insurance agents and production workers rated the five reasons on a five-point scale rather than ranking them from five to one, with five high and one low (ibid., p. 232).

17. Ibid.

18. Harvey A. Hornstein, D. M. Callahan, E. Fisch, and B. A. Benedict, "Influence and Satisfaction in Organizations: A Replication," *Sociology of Education* 41 (Fall 1968): 380–389.

19. Ibid., p. 385. Unfortunately, the mean rankings were not reported.

20. John M. Ivancevich, "An Analysis of Control, Bases of Control, and Satisfaction in an Organizational Setting," *Academy of Management Journal* 13 (December 1970): 427–436.

21. Ibid., p. 434.

22. Ibid., p. 435.

23. Geoffrey B. Isherwood, "The Principal and His Authority: An Empirical Study," *The High School Journal* 56 (March 1973):291–303.

24. Max Weber, *The Theory of Social and Economic Organization*, A. M. Henderson and Talcott Parsons, trans., Talcott Parsons, ed. (New York: Free Press, 1947), chap. 4.

25. Parsons suggests that although authority may be thought of as the "institutional counterpart of power," "authority is not a circulating medium." See Talcott Parsons, "On the Concept of Political Power," *Proceedings of the American Philosophical Society* 107, no. 3 (June 19, 1963): 244. One implication of this distinction is that formal redistribution of authority within school organizations is essential in conflicts among school executives, and between school executives and teachers, over the use of potential capacity. This will be implicit throughout the remainder of this chapter.

26. David Mechanic, "Sources of Power of Lower Participants in Complex Organizations," *Administrative Science Quarterly* 7 (December 1962): 349–364.

27. Howard S. Becker, "The Teacher in the Authority System of the Public School," *Journal of Educational Sociology* 27 (November 1953):128–141.

28. Chandler Washburne, "The Teacher in the Authority System," *Journal of Educational Sociology* 30 (May 1957):390–394.

29. Issues that would come under the rubric of expressive activities as defined by Etzioni; see Amitai Etzioni, *Modern Organization* (Englewood Cliffs, N.J.: Prentice-Hall, Inc., 1964).

30. See, for example, Parsons, "On the Concept of Political Power;" Rensis Likert, *New Patterns of Management* (New York: McGraw-Hill, 1961); C. J. Lammers, "Power and Participation in Decision Making in Formal Organizations," *American Journal of Sociology* 73 (September

1967):201–216; Arnold S. Tannenbaum, *Control in Organizations* (New York: McGraw-Hill, 1968).

31. C. G. Smith and A. S. Tannenbaum, "Organization Control Structure: A Comparative Analysis," *Human Relations* 16 (November 1963); 299–316. See also Tannenbaum, *Control in Organizations.*

32. Likert, *New Patterns of Management.*

33. Lammers, "Power and Participation in Decision Making," p. 204.

34. J. Timothy McMahon, "Participative and Power Equalized Organization Systems," *Human Relations* 29 (March 1976):203–214.

35. Ibid., p. 212.

36. R. E. Ohm, "Collective Negotiations: Implications for Research," in *Collective Negotiations and Educational Administration*, Roy B. Allen and John Schmid, eds. (Columbus, Ohio: University Council for Educational Administration, 1966), pp. 97–113; and R. E. Ohm and W. G. Monahan, "Power and Stress in Organizational Response to Collective Action," in *Negotiations in the Schools*, R. E. Ohm and O. D. Johns, eds. (Norman: College of Education, University of Oklahoma, 1965), pp. 71–76.

37. Donald J. Willower, "Relationships Between Teacher Union Strength and the Distribution of Influence Attributed to Hierarchical Levels in School Districts," *Peabody Journal of Education* 52 (January 1975): 150–154.

38. James A. Belasco, Mike Milstein, and Paul Zaccarine, "Participation and Control: The Tannenbaum Hypothesis Revisited," *Planning and Changing*, 6 (Fall-Winter 1976):135–148.

39. For a cogent discussion of the concept of systems, and especially open systems, see Daniel E. Griffiths, "Administrative Theory and Change in Organizations," in *Innovations in Education*, Matthew Miles, ed. (New York: Teachers College Press, 1964), pp. 425–36.

40. One might counter with the argument that the externally induced change in authority relations between school executives and students represents a demand for different methods of utilizing authority, rather than a reduction in the level of authority. Since we prefer not to argue that question, suffice it to say that the open system concept would nonetheless be illustrated.

41. Mary Parker Follet's statement that "The division of power is not the thing to be considered, but that method of organization which will generate power," expresses our point well; see H. C. Metcalf and L. Urwich, eds., *Dynamic Administration: the Collected Papers of Mary Parker Follett* (London: Pitman Publishers, 1941), p. 111. Nowhere is the necessity for organizational recognition and sanction illustrated better than in the professional negotiations movement when failure to recognize formally the teachers' organization temporarily cuts off the negotiations process and effectively blocks the drive for power equalization on the part of teachers.

42. We shall examine complex role relationships in Chapter 9, just as structural characteristics were discussed in Chapter 7. The proposal which follows obviously spans both sets of concepts.

43. Norman J. Boyan, "The Emergent Role of the Teacher and the Authority Structure of the School," in *Collective Negotiations and Educational Administration*, Roy B. Allen and John Schmid, eds. (Columbus, Ohio: University Council for Educational Administration, 1966), p. 4.

44. The advantages accure from the impact of integrative bargaining which grows out of and, to some extent, operates concurrently with adversarial bargaining. See Richard Walton and Robert McKersie, *A Behavioral Theory of Labor Negotiations* (New York: McGraw-Hill, 1965); or George Madden, "A Theoretical Basis for Differentiation Forms of Collective Bargaining in Education," *Educational Administration Quarterly* 5 (Spring 1969): 76–90.

Chapter 11
School Executives and
Role Relationships

The school executive function is the articulation of organizationally determined demands with needs and aspirations of groups and individuals so that the manifest goals of the school are achieved. This is possible for the school executive today only because the school is a relatively known quantity to those who work in it. Administrators, teachers, and most students enter the school with generally similar images of what it is all about. Simply stated, the school is the formal educating institution in the community: Children and young poeple come to school to grow and mature intellectually, socially, emotionally, and physically; teachers assist in the process by developing, structuring, and presenting materials; administrators plan for, coordinate, appraise the effectiveness of the teacher-pupil relationship, and act as arbiters when disputes arise.[1] Over time the school has developed mechanisms aimed at making the induction of members orderly, painless, and relatively simple. Half-day kindergarten, short days for primary school children, in-service days prior to the beginning of a school year, student teaching, administrative internships, administrative assistant positions, PTA meetings—are all examples of such mechanisms. More fundamentally, programs to prepare administrators, teachers, counselors, and other professionals for schools may be as important for their socialization as for skill development. It is, thus, not necessary for the school executive to reconstruct the history of educational organizations and operations for new administrators, teachers and pupils before beginning the task of articulating demands, needs, and aspirations.

The executive process, routine, and function is, of course, less simply practiced than described. None of the organizational members with whom the school executive interacts is void of notions about how the articulation should occur. Only at the most fundamental level is it valid to say that members (or their constituent group) hold precisely the same notions of how the executive function should be performed. For example, teachers think the principal exists to support them against pupils, parents, other administrators, and the board of education. Central office administrators "know" that the principal was installed to ensure that teachers perform effective teaching-learning activities, satisfy parents, and control pupils. Parents are certain that the principal protects pupils, controls teachers, and fights central office bureaucracy. Finally, pupils increasingly suspect that the principal imposes illegitimate demands on them, at the same time offering some recourse against unsatisfactory teachers.

Two problems are readily apparent from these examples. First, the principal cannot possibly be what all think, know, or suspect, since one image often conflicts with another. Second, much is expected of the principal, perhaps too much. We might say that the images are of a superperson. It is easy to understand at a superficial level, at any rate, why the performance of the principal and other administrators, measured against absolute standards, is inevitably less than optimum.

CONCEPTUAL TOOLS

We have been discussing one of the problems of school executives in nontechnical language. Implicitly our discussion has involved the concepts of *social system, role, role set, role expectations,* and *role conflict.* It is our purpose in this chapter to delineate and define these concepts in relation to the school executive's function and to suggest basic strategy for job performance which would seem to use consistent with maximizing the goals of the school. The literature contains many excellent references on the concepts which we shall use as analytical tools.[2] We do not propose to review the theoretical and empirical research literature per se, however. Our concern is with providing a conceptual framework which will hopefully enable the school executive to better understand the role within the school environment and, thus, function more effectively. We conclude the chapter by suggesting an ideal behavioral model for role performance.

To proceed, it is necessary to specify and define the conceptual tools which we shall utilize. We define and discuss, in turn, the key concepts we have just mentioned.

Social System

Since the late fifties, many students of educational administration have been introduced to the concept of social system through the Getzels-Guba social process theory.[3] Social system, as the setting for administrative behavior, is the first-order concept in that theoretical model. It is an appropriate beginning concept for our purpose as well. We may define it very simply as "two or more persons interacting toward a goal (or goals) about which there is some agreement." Applying this definition of social system to a school district, we arrive at the following definition: The school district social system is "all members of a school organization working to achieve the goals of the school district." If we wished to relate the concept of social system specifically to a school building or some other unit of the school district, we need only think of a different membership and goals that are less global. We could, of course, conceive of larger units (e.g., the state or national education system), by making similar changes.

Our attention is directed to three characteristics of social systems in their simplest forms: (1) they consist of individuals; (2) there is interaction between and among individuals; and (3) interaction is not randomly directed—it is aimed at the achievement of goals. Given these characteristics, it seems reasonable that a particular social system could emerge in a variety of ways—for instance, a larger social system may create a subsystem which assumes the characteristics of its creator, or like-minded individuals may voluntarily join together to achieve certain goals. Modern formal educational entities (e.g., school districts, building units, and classrooms) are of the first variety. They were created by the larger social system, the community. Rotary International, the Woodlawn Organization, Operation Push, local drama groups, and bridge clubs are examples of the latter type.

Logically, although not explicit in the original definition, social systems may be more or less permanent. The school district and building organizations are among the more permanent of school social systems. Specific districts, or attendance units, are sometimes consolidated out of existence, but only so that larger or different districts or building units may be created. School executives, thus, function in social systems which are formally created for generally agreed-upon purposes and which are more or less permanent. Thus although by definition the social system world of the school executive is inhabited by individuals, the nature of the origin, permanence, and purpose of this world is such that the interaction of these individuals is neither random nor totally idiosyncratic. It is, in large measure, structured. This fact leads, in turn, to the second major concept to be defined, namely, the concept of role.

ROLES, EXPECTATIONS, SETS, AND CONFLICT

When an individual is appointed to a school organization, that individual assumes a positional identity: superintendent, principal, teacher, student. These are all identities which, in the relatively permanent and formally created social system of the school, carry with them certain generally agreed-upon images. To return to the opening paragraphs of this chapter, these agreed-upon identity images are of the type used there to describe the principal of a school. It should be noted, furthermore, that there is a relational character to these identities or images; that is, they do not exist independent of other identities. Thus the definition of role proposed by Getzels, Lipham, and Campbell is most useful: ". . . the structural or normative elements defining the behavior or role incumbents or actors, that is, their mutual rights and obligations."[4] Or, stated in terms we have been using, a role can be defined as "the images held for an individual's relational behavior when that individual is operating in a particular position."

Two independent but related characteristics are implicitly intended in our definition. The first is that a role occupant (e.g., Clare Jones, principal) is bounded by a particular context but is not confined in terms of relational behavior to any other one role occupant. Second, and conversely, images of a particular relational behavior may be held by any other role occupant in the social system.

This means that board members, the superintendent, teachers, other principals, and pupils are image holders and role definers for our imaginary principal, Clare Jones. Whenever a role occupant engages in job-related behavior, in other words, that individual is engaging in role performance.

Role Expectations

In the Getzels, Lipham, and Campbell formulation, roles are defined in terms of expectations, that is, "certain normative rights and duties."[5] Gross, Mason, and McEachern, furthermore, define role expectations as "an evaluative standard applied to an incumbent of a position."[6] Thus our imaginary principal, Clare Jones, is subject to expectations for behavior (as principal) held by all the other role occupants in the school. Central office administrators "expect" the principal to supervise teachers, teachers "expect" the principal to supervise teachers, teachers "expect" the principal to support them against pupils, and so on.

Role Set

Earlier we pointed out that a role occupant may have interaction with a number of other role occupants. Our definition of role explicitly involves more than one individual. We could isolate for any particular role all other roles with which there are relationships. This would comprise, for the role in question, the family of roles or, in the langage of Merton[7] and Katz and Kahn,[8] the "role set." Ther concept of role set is illustrated in Figure 11-1.

Role Conflict

Role conflict may be defined as "mutually contradictory expectations for a role occupant's behavior." Gross, Mason, and McEachern's example of the superintendent who perceives that teachers expect him to obtain more salary for them from the board, while board members expect him to convince teachers to accept less, although anachronistic in an age of professional negotiations, illustrates the definition clearly and succinctly.[9] The opportunity for role conflict of this type is great, since there are numerous role definers for any given role. Furthermore, there may be a division within a role-definer group, resulting in mutually contradictory expectations. Instructor-student interaction at the university level can be used to illustrate this point. The instructor is confronted with a group of graduate students concerned with determining the content focus of a semester course. One-half of the group expects the instructor to determine the important content to be examined. The other half expects the instructor to permit the students to determine the content. It may not be possible to meet the expectations of both. Both examples of role conflict just cited are termed "intra-role conflict."

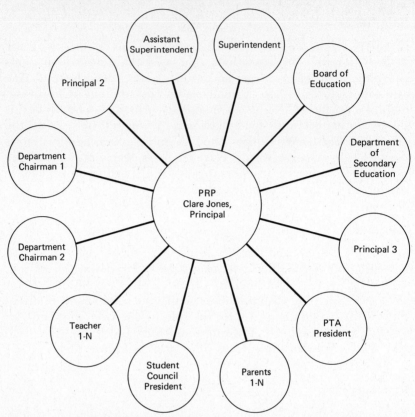

PRP = Pivotal Role Player (role under analysis).
Other circles = Role occupants in or directly related to the social system of Clare Jones, Principal.

Figure 11-1 Illustration of role set. (Source: Adapted from Warren B. Bennis, *Changing Organizations* [New York: McGraw-Hill 1966], p. 193.)

A second type of role conflict is called "inter-role conflict." This exists when mutually contradictory expectations are held for two roles, both of which are occupied by the same individual. Our principal, Clare Jones, may experience this type of conflict as the additional roles of parent and spouse are assumed. There are two major differences between this type of conflict and the previous type. The first difference is that the focus of inter-role conflict is on larger, more basic elements in terms of expectations. One of the earliest empirical tests of the social process theory was conducted by Getzels and Guba at Air University, Maxwell Air Force Base.[10] They hypothesized, and their data supported the hypothesis, that the officer and instructor role was basically in conflict. Without moving to specific behavioral expectations, certain roles just seem not to go together. In public schools, the building-level chief-executive role of principal and the student-service-oriented role of counselor are generally perceived to be in conflict and are among the first to be separated when size of school permits. Obviously, the principal role is not entirely inconsistent with the counselor role. There is, however, a generalized role conception—pattern of images—held for the principal role which is substantially different from that for the counselor.

The second major difference between intra- and inter-role conflict is that inter-role conflict may involve two or more social systems. Intra-role conflict, in contrast, exsits within a single social system. In the discussion of the social system concept, we noted that virtually all social systems are at one and the same time sub- and suprasystems. Thus the school district social system is a subsystem of the larger community and a suprasystem to each building-level subsystem. A superintendent of schools also occupies different roles in different systems: for instance, a parent and a spouse in the family social system; a church member in a religious social system; and, of course, a superintendent in the school district social system.

Except for principal-counselor, department chairperson-teacher, and superintendent-principal dual roles, job-related roles in school organizations are largely single purpose in nature. That the principal is a member of the district social system and the building-level subsystem does not change the basic job-related role. Since each single-purpose role has many role definers, there are abundant sources of conflict. This conflict, however, is of the intra-role rather that the inter-role variety.

This leads logically to an identification of two different sets of potential conflict situations: one for role occupants and the other for role occupants as individuals. Our purpose is not to discuss all possible potential conflicts for role occupants. Again, we refer the reader to the most complete explication of the Getzels-Guba theoretical formulation, in which the authors systematically present empirical evidence bearing on dozens of specific conflict types and their consequences.[11] The set of potential conflicts involving role occupants as individuals consists of two primary types: (1) conflict between role expectations and individual needs and aspirations—usually termed role-personality conflict; and (2) conflict between individuals attributable to conditions other than role expectations—interpersonal conflict.

The distinction between certain role conflicts and role-personality conflicts is less than clear in some instances. Consider the following example:

> Our hypothetical principal, Clare Jones, is expected by the district superintendent and board of education to be responsible for preparing and administering the school budget. In no uncertain terms, they communicate personal accountability for its accuracy, educational efficacy, and ultimate effectiveness. The department chairpersons and faculty members in Principals Jones's school are knowledgable about the expectations and are in general agreement except that they want to participate too. Principal Jones accurately perceives the expectations and proceeds to meet them. The behavioral approach taken is largely determined by the principal's philosophy, beliefs, assumptions about education and teachers, and of course, personality. As the actual budget-making process ensues, disagreement is encountered over both procedures and substantive decisions. The principal recognizes the disaffection but is unable to say whether it is due to differences between superintendent-board expectation and what faculty members and department chairs expect relative to budget preparation or to differences between what teachers expect and personal style in carrying out the expected tasks.

The purpose of the illustration is to demonstrate how interrelated the social and psychological variables are. Had the superintendent and board explicitly stated how Principal Jones was to proceed with budget development, we would be in a better position to decide the nature of the conflict, if any, which might exist. If the superintendent and board expected that teachers not be involved, and teachers expected to be involved, then the conflict is of the role variety. If both role-definer groups expected teachers to be involved, but Principal Jones felt a need to be in complete control and did not believe teachers were capable of contributing to budget development, then the conflict is of the role-personality type. Pure interpersonal conflict is theoretically and practically easier to understand than role/role-personality conflict, although the underlying reasons may be quite complex. Indeed, two individuals, occupying the same or different roles, may be interpersonally incompatible to the point of causing dysfunction to either or both.

SUBROLE OCCUPANCY

By definition the school executive's role involves interaction with other role occupants. As noted earlier, if one identified all role relationships for a particular role occupant, a family of interacting

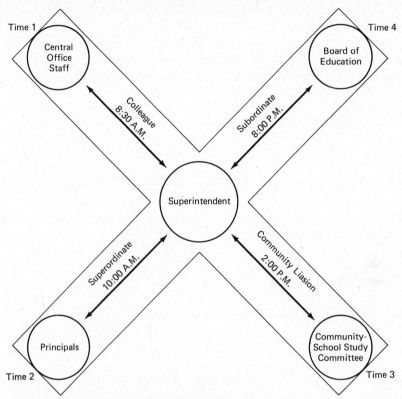

Time 1.   Executive council discussion and planning session.
Time 2.   Building-level administrators budget development meeting.
Time 3.   Community-school study committee meeting—information exchange and mutual idea testing.
Time 4.   Biweekly board of education meeting.

Figure 11-2   Illustration of subrole occupancy of a school superintendent.

roles, the role set, would be created. By classifying the interacting roles as organizationally equal to, above, or below the school executive role in question, we create three distinct subroles for the school executive: colleague, superordinate, and subordinate. A fourth subrole is that of community liaison. Any school executive is, thus, simultaneously occupying, if not performing, four subroles, each of which impinges on or has implications for the others. These subroles are illustrated in Figure 11-2, with a superintendent as the focal role and with times of subrole occupancy added.

Colleague Subrole

The reader may question the designation of the 8:30 A.M. session with central office staff as a colleague subrole for superintendent X.

It is probable that in most interaction with central office staff, the superintendent is in the superordinate subrole. The nature of formal organization (and expectations of board members, citizens in the community, the superintendent, and the central office staff) determines the relationship. Conversely, management philosophy, values, beliefs, and personal needs of superintendents and central office staff members operate to induce the colleague relationship for certain purposes. Thus it may be more accurate to conceive of the superintendent–central office office staff role relationships as virtually simultaneous colleague-superordinate role performance. For example, the superintendent defines a problem situation (superordinate behavior), solicits open discussion and deliberation among equals (colleague behavior), and ultimately makes the final decision or suggests the procedure by which the final decision is to be made (superordinate behavior).

Superordinate Subrole

The superordinate subrole is the characteristic school executive subrole. Chief among the generalized set of expectations for superordinate role performance is, for example, that superintendent X has the rights, privileges, and organizational authority to structure the activity at the 10:00 A.M. building-level administrators' meeting. As a result of the emergent power-equalization movement by teachers, however, much more open, free communication, supportive behavior, and meaningful participation in decisions are certain to be expected of the superordinate in the future.

Subordinate Subrole

Superintendent X may not think of the relationship to the board of education as we have diagrammed it in Figure 11-2. The extent to which the superintendent-board role interaction emphasizes the former as subordinate is a function of three major sets of variables. The first of these is the amount of agreement between the community and the school district about goals for the school. Internal board agreement about school goals, means, and satisfactions comprises a second set of variables. Resource levels make up the third set of variables. Whether or not the subordinate character of the superintendent-board role relationship is emphasized, all of the potential conflicts earlier identified exist. Their scope and intensity levels are merely increased or decreased.

Community-Liaison Subrole

The liaison subrole of superintendent X represented in Figure 11-2 is not generally so neatly characterized nor performed as in our example of a community-school study committee meeting. In fact, it permeates the total role performance of the school executive, manifesting itself formally in planned contacts but also surfacing in unplanned interactions with individuals and groups of citizens. The myriad of citizen groups with which the school executive must communicate about school concerns is astounding. Increasingly, community liaison is becoming institutionalized as a primary subrole for the school executive. The creation of an ombudsman, an administrative assistant for school-community relations, a community information officer, or whatever, does not negate the necessity for attention to this subrole by all school executives. Nor does it remove the potential for role, personality, philosophy, and interpersonal conflicts. Thus the community liaison subrole would seem to provide a formal, ready structure through which expectations for schools generally, and school executives specifically, could be made explicit. The popularity of the community school concept, which deliberately links not only school executives but total schools to the citizens in the comunity, is clear evidence that effective performance of this subrole is important.[12]

Subrole Occupancy and Conflict

Pervading our discussion of subroles of the school executive was an implicit suggestion of the ubiquitous nature of all of the conflict types: intra-role conflict—contradictory expectations by two or more role-definer groups or two or more individuals within a role-definer group; role-personality conflict—contradiction between expectations for behavior and personality characteristics, values, assumptions, beliefs; and interpersonal conflict—disagreement between occupants of the same or different roles deriving from differences in personal characteristics of qualities. The propositions which follow summarize our suggested relationships between subrole performance and conflict types.

1. In general, the more the emphasis on either the superordinate or subordinate subrole, the greater the probability of any type of conflict.
2. In general, the more the emphasis on the coordinate subrole, the greater the probability of role-personality or interpersonal conflict.

3. In general, the more the emphasis on the community liaison subrole, the greater the probability of inter-role, intra-role and role-personality conflict.

Subrole Occupancy and Position in the School Hierarchy

Some propositions which relate the concept of role to position in the hierarchy of the school are listed next. They are divided into propositions regarding three levels—institutional, managerial, and technical. (The institutional level refers to the board of education; the managerial level refers to the administrative component of the school system; and the technical level refers to the instructional function.)[13]

Institutional Level

1. The closer an administrative position is to the board of education:
    a. the less the emphasis on the subordinate subrole vis-à-vis the board of education.
    b. the more the emphasis on the superordinate subrole vis-à-vis school administrators lower in the hierarchy.
    c. the more the emphasis on the community liaison subrole.
2. Emphasis on the colleague subrole is independent of the distance from the board of education.

Managerial Level

1. The higher a position is in the administrative hierarchy, the more the emphasis on the superordinate subrole.
2. The higher a position is in the administrative hierarchy, the less the emphasis on the subordinate subrole.
3. Emphasis on the colleague and community liaison subroles is independent of position in the administrative hierarchy.

Technical Level

1. The closer an administrative position is to the teacher role:
    a. the more the emphasis on the colleague subrole vis-à-vis teachers.
    b. the less the emphasis on the subordinate subrole vis-à-vis school executives.
    c. the less the emphasis on the superordinate subrole vis-à-vis teachers.
    d. the more the emphasis on the community liaison subrole.

ROLE PERFORMANCE AND THE EXECUTIVE FUNCTION: ALTERNATIVE STYLES

Scholars who have studied role performance of managers, leaders, and administrators[14] have consistently reported two general behavioral orientations: (1) task and (2) person. In role analysis terminology, this means that an administrator might emphasize, for self and subordinates, the performance of task expectations more than the satisfaction of needs and aspirations, resulting in a task-oriented style of administrative performance. An opposite ordering of emphases in role performance results in an opposite style. The two orientations are not mutually exclusive, however, and the maximization of both results in the highest level of goal achievement for the social system.

We shall briefly discuss three stereotyped styles of administrative performance followed by a model for role performance leading to the effective articulation of demands and needs, interests and aspirations and, thereby, goal achievement. The stereotypes and the suggested role model focus attention on the school executive in the performance of the characteristic superordinate subrole.

The Taskmaster

This is the school executive who is "all business"—and if necessary at the expense of need satisfaction. Acceptance of and strict adherence to expectations characterize job behavior. This school executive type is not averse to work being accomplished in a cordial manner. Indeed, work is more acceptable if people are pleasant. Minimum hours, due dates for reports, attendance at meetings, participation in specified deliberations, following curriculum guides and reading lists are only the minimum that should be performed by teachers—observes the taskmaster principal. District personnel policy relating to leaves; the selection, adoption, and use of textbooks and other materials; graduation requirements; student behavior; administrator, teacher, and student leaving school; the use of school facilities; and teacher-student ratios clearly outline behavior for the principal, teacher, student, and parent according to the taskmaster superintendent, director of instruction, or assistant superintendent.

Although all of the types of conflict are potentially present for the taskmaster, those pitting organizational demands against personal needs are easy to resolve. Conflicts in expectations between role-definer groups or within a role-definer group, though more difficult, are resolved by looking to the job demand (what the school organization spells out, for example, in job descriptions and responsibilities) for cues. Interpersonal conflicts are similarly decided. Expectations conflicts related to basic goals are, of course, the most difficult to deal with (as they are for any administrator). Again, the tendency of the taskmaster is to search for an answer in the direction of the established patterns.

As noted earlier, as long as expectations are met (tasks are accomplished), interpersonal relationships between the taskmaster and others may be quite pleasant. There is nothing inherent in the taskmaster's role performance to inhibit genuinely warm human interactions. The point is that all interacting roles in the role set understand perfectly what decisions will be on any but the most complex problem. The fact that the "pure" taskmaster exists only on paper is a reminder that school executives are indeed human beings and that the executive function is an articulation of two concerns, organizationally determined demands and needs and aspirations of groups, rather that an advocacy of one. Now for a look at the taskmaster's counterpart.

The Sympathizer

In role relationships, the sympathizer refuses to permit organizational demands to obstruct attention to personal needs, interests, and aspirations. That expectations, organizational demands, are met seems more a function of prior recognition and acceptance of the tasks by subordinates, than of the sympathizer's administration. Rules, procedures, patterns of performing are for suspending if they conflict with an individual's desires. Meetings called for the purpose of identifying, delineating, or resolving problems are as likely to be devoted to extraneous matters or to expressions of personal or group ego gratification. The sympathizer's zealous concern for people gives the appearance of indecisiveness.

The sympathizer can be expected to relate well to virtually anyone, especially initially. Thus the colleague, subordinate, and community liaison subroles are generally easier to perform whereas the superordinate subrole is most difficult. It is not that this school executive refuses to acknowledge the organizational demands for uniform and focused task performance. Efforts are made to accomplish them, but not at the expense of individual concern. In contrast to the taskmaster, intra-role and interpersonal conflicts are resolved by weighing the effects on individuals. Goal conflicts affecting expectations are resolved by finding the alternative with least disruption to individual or group needs. The sympathizer may or may not be the back-pounding, handshaking, "don't you worry" type. Quiet, dignified individuals may also be sympathizers. The sympathizer is, as is the taskmaster, quite predictable in terms of role behavior.

The Calculator

The calculator recognizes the essence of the legitimate executive function and, at optimum performance, calculates the points of potential conflict between organizational demands and individual needs, interests, and aspirations and systematically moves between the two poles. In unexpected or unyielding situations, conflicted issues or decisions are willingly negotiated. Although intra-role and interpersonal conflict situations are not easy to resolve, this pattern of administrative behavior provides a good model from which to test alternatives. If there were no negative connotations attached to the label used to identify characterization, the calculator might well be taken as the model of successful administration. The characterization in fact conforms to the commonly heard role description of the successful politician.

A major difficulty with the calculator's role performance is the tendency to emphasize organizational demands when performing the subordinate subrole, and individual needs, interests, and aspirations when performing the superordinate subrole.[15] In other words, the calculator may come to view the behavioral performance of the two subroles in quite different perspectives. These perspectives revolve around individual needs, interests, and aspirations, however, and assume a general tendency to reject the taskmaster style. Thus the calculator style changes when one moves to the satisfaction of individual needs.

It should be recalled here that in instances involving the individual need dimension, we have the choice as posed by Miles[16] of human relations or human resources (see Chapter 3). Accepting the two concerns of the executive function as legitimate and the problem of selecting a role-performance style as important, we shall now sketch out an approach to role performance that is oriented toward human resources with respect to individual needs, interests, and aspirations, while at the same time recognizing organizational demands.

THE HUMAN RESOURCES DEVELOPER:
A MODEL FOR ROLE PERFORMANCE

The human resources developer role model for school executives is consistent with the earlier sections of the book. It is implicit, in our judgment, in the expectations for ideal administrative role performance described in the work of Getzels, Lipham, and Campbell;[17] in the Theory Y manager one would create from McGregor's writings[18] (see also Chapter 3); and in the management system 4 manager in Likert's *The Human Organization*.[19] Acceptance of this model for role performance and movement toward its implementation do not remove the potential for conflict discussed earlier. It does, however, provide a school executive with a different benchmark against which to measure behavior—a set of criteria which can be applied in order to resolve for each executive the conflicts encountered. Briefly, the legitimate executive function performed by the human resources developer is "creating an environment in which the total resources of his department (organization) can be utilized."[20]

The human resources developer model of role performance for school executives rests on three sets of assumptions or propositions: (1) about personal needs and interests or role occupants in the school executive's role set; (2) about school executive's behavior relative to participation; and (3) about expectations for processes and ends related to all role occupants in the executive's role set, particularly subordinates. Adapting Miles's human resources model[21] to school executives, particulars of these sets of propositions are as follows:

About Personal Needs and Interests

1. Most school personnel with whom the school executive interacts share common needs for belonging and respect, and desire to contribute effectively and creatively to the accomplishment of worthwhile objectives.
2. A majority of students, teachers, and administrators are capable of exercising far more initiative, responsibility, and creativity than presently possible the way roles are defined.
3. These untapped capabilities represent wasted resources available to the school.

About School Executive Behavior

1. The school executive's basic task is to create an environment in which all school personnel can contribute their full range of talent to the accomplishment of school goals. More specifically, the task is to uncover and tap creative resources of occupants of all interacting roles, especially if the executive is concerned with subordinates.
2. The school executive should allow and encourage subordinates and colleagues to participate, not only in routine decisions, but in important matters as well. The more

important the decision to the school, the greater should be the effort to tap resources of subordinates and colleagues.

3. The school executive should attempt continually to expand the areas over which subordinates exercise self-direction and self-control as they demonstrate greater insight and ability.

About Expectations for Processes and Ends

1. The overall quality of decision-making and performance will improve as the school executive utilizes the full range of experiences, insight and ability in the school system.

2. Subordinates and colleagues will exercise repsonsible self-direction and self-control in the accomplishment of those worthwhile objectives that they understand and have helped establish. Obviously, since the school is a formally established social system, limits are placed on the extent to which teachers and school executives are free to define objectives. It seems reasonable to believe, however, that most educators have accepted the general goals for which the educational institution strives.

3. Subordinate and colleague satisfaction will increase as a by-product of improved performance and the opportunity to contribute creatively to this improvement.

Participation is the key to improved decision-making, control, satisfaction, and morale.[22] Another way of emphasizing the same point is to say that expectations (for school executive role performance) which recognize the integrated nature of organizational demands, and personal needs and interests, convey the idea of utilization of subordinates and colleagues because that is the way both are best accomplished.

Perhaps the most powerful argument for the human resources developer as a model for school executive role performance is that pointed out in Miles's research. He found overwhelming support among middle- and upper-level managers in business and industry for human resources management to be applied by their superiors to them. If the model "applies" from above, why is it not applicable horizontally and below? The human resources developer model for role performance thus suggests an approach for the school executive to follow for self-behavior, as well as for defining expectations for other interacting roles in the school social system.

Notes

1. The "idealized" conception of the school is more or less accurate for individuals, schools, and groups in society. We assert, however, that

the survival of *the school,* and public schools as the dominant type, rests on a generalized acceptance of that characterization.

2. See, for example, Neal Gross, Ward Mason, and Alexander McEachern, *Explorations in Role Analysis* (New York: John Wiley, 1958); Jacob Getzels, James M. Lipham, and Roald F. Campbell, *Educational Administration as a Social Process* (New York: Harper & Row, 1968); Daniel Katz and Robert L. Kahn, *The Social Psychology of Organizations* (New York: John Wiley, 1966); Warren Bennis, *Changing Organizations* (New York: McGraw-Hill, 1966); and Robert Owens, *Organizational Behavior in Schools* (Englewood Cliffs, N.J.: Prentice-Hall, 1970), chaps. 3 and 4. Our set of concepts, their definitions, and the ensuing discussion rely heavily on formulations developed by the first four authors.

3. See, for example, Jacob W. Getzels, "A Psycho-sociological Framework for the Study of Administration," *Harvard Educational Review* 22 (Fall 1952):235–246; Jacob W. Getzels and Egon G. Guba, "Social Behavior and the Administrative Process," *The School Review* 65 (Winter 1957):423–441; Egon G. Guba, "Research in Internal Administration—What Do We Know?" in *Administrative Theory as a Guide to Action*, R. F. Campbell and J. M. Lipham, eds. (Chicago: Midwest Administration Center, University of Chicago, 1960), chap. 7; Jacob W. Getzels and Egon G. Guba, "Role, Role Conflict and Effectiveness: An Empirical Study," *American Sociological Review* 19 (April 1954):164–175.

4. Getzels, Lipham, and Campbell, *Educational Administration as a Social Process*, p. 60.

5. Ibid., p. 61.

6. Gross, Mason, and McEachern, *Explorations in Role Analysis*, p. 58.

7. R. K. Merton, *Social Theory and Social Structure*, rev. ed. (New York: The Free Press, 1957).

8. Katz and Kahn, *Social Psychology of Organizations*, pp. 174–75.

9. Gross, Mason, and McEachern, *Explorations in Role Analysis*, p. 249.

10. Getzels and Guba, "Role, Role Conflict, and Effectiveness," pp. 164–75.

11. Getzels, Lipham, and Campbell, *Educational Administration as a Social Process*. We have deliberately not examined the individual, his personality, needs, motives, beliefs, values and assumptions—the "other" dimension of the Getzels-Guba model—in much detail in this chapter, since the entire first section of the book is largely devoted to those concerns.

12. See, for example, Clyde M. Campbell, ed., *Toward Perfection in Learning* (Midland, Mich.: Pendell Publishing Company, 1969); or *The Community School: Fifty-second Yearbook of the National Society for the Study of Education* (Chicago: The Society [University of Chicago Press], 1953).

13. See Talcott Parsons, "Some Ingredients of a General Theory of Formal Organization," in *Administrative Theory in Education*, Andrew W. Halpin, ed. (Chicago: Midwest Administration Center, University of Chicago, 1958), pp. 40–72.

14. Robert Blake and Jane Mouton, *The Managerial Grid* (Houston, Tex.: Gulf Publishing Co., 1964); David G. Bowers and Stanely E. Seashore, "Predicting Organizational Effectiveness with a Four-Factor Theory of Leadership," *Administrative Science Quarterly* 11 (September 1966): 238–264; Andrew W. Halpin, *Theory and Research in Administration* (New York: Macmillan, 1966), chap. 3; and Egon G. Guba and Charles E. Bidwell, *Administrative Relationships* (Chicago: Midwest Administration Center, University of Chicago, 1957); Fred Fiedler, *A Theory of Leadership Effectiveness* (New York: McGraw-Hill, 1967); W. J. Reddin, *Managerial Effectiveness* (New York: McGraw-Hill, 1970); and Philip E. Gates, Kenneth H. Blanchard, and Paul Hersey, "Diagnosing Educational Leadership Problems: A Situational Approach," *Educational Leadership* 33 (February 1977):348–354.

15. See Robert Moser, "The Leadership Patterns of School Superintendents and School Principals," *Administrator's Notebook* 6 (September 1957).

16. Raymond E. Miles, "Human Relations or Human Resources," *Harvard Business Review* 43 (July–August 1965): 148–52, 154, 156, 158, 160, 163.

17. Getzels, Lipham, and Campbell, *Educational Administration as a Social Process.*

18. Douglas McGregor, *The Human Side of Enterprise* (New York: McGraw-Hill, 1960); or Douglas McGregor, "The Human Side of Enterprise," *The Management Review* 46 (November 1957):22–28, 88–92.

19. Rensis Likert, *The Human Organization* (New York: McGraw-Hill, 1967).

20. Miles, "Human Relations or Human Resources," p. 150.

21. Ibid., p. 151.

22. Ibid., p. 152. Participation and participative management are much overused and advocated as the general cure-all for administrative behavior. We do not intend to suggest its use in that sense. Throughout the book are guidelines for effective use of participation. The best single reference that contains specific guidelines for participation of subordinates, with the *school* as the social system, is Edwin M. Bridges, "A Model for Shared Decision Making in the School Principalship," *Educational Administration Quarterly* 3 (Winter 1967): 49–61; also see Arthur Blumberg, William Wayson, and Wilford Weber, "The Elementary School Cabinet," *Educational Administration Quarterly* 5 (Autumn 1969):39–52.

Part IV
THE POLITICAL SYSTEM

Chapter 12
The School as a Political System

Perhaps the most significant advance in the development of administrative thought in the past decade has been the more widespread recognition of the political aspects of life in educational organizations. Political scientists have added yet another set of lenses through which one might more adequately view organizational and administrative phenomena. The result has been expansive in not only providing scholars in educational administration with additional theoretical concepts but in providing practicing administrators with insights which strike a comfortable cord with their own visions of reality. Of course, viewing the school as a political system is not a substitute for but an enhancement of other views.

In Chapter 4 the phrases "organizational and management platforms" were used to suggest the set of biases administrators bring to decision-making. These biases are visions of reality, theories, beliefs, models, and paradigms which to a large extent *govern* what school executives see, what they decide and what they do. The thought that platforms are often implicit and/or latent should not distract from the notion that school executives work from such theoretical underpinnings.

One aspect of a school executive's management platform is the overall view he or she has as to how organizations work. In this section we begin our analysis of the school's political system by examining three such views or "conceptual models" of organizational functioning which can color an administrator's vision of reality. The models are proposed by Graham T. Allison as part of his now classic study of the Cuban Missile Crisis of 1962.[1] In that study Allison showed that the particular model internalized by the analyst governs his explanation of the crisis and its associated events. Two of the models, *rational policy* and *organizational process*, are treated informally elsewhere in this book and here will be only summarized. The third model, the *politics* model, will be discussed in greater detail. In each case models will be applied to the analysis of the school as an organization.

THE RATIONAL MODEL

In explaining organizational events using Allison's discussion of the rational model one assumes that events occur as largely purposive acts of a unified school or school district. Basically, schools have objectives and missions. These objectives and missions have identifiable rationales which can be understood. In attempting to achieve objectives the school as a unitary organization can identify best choices and make decisions accordingly. In explaining actions of a particular school, one need only determine how the school could have rationally chosen that action.

Rational choice is defined in economic terms as value maximizing. The rational school and school executive select the alternative whose consequences rank highest given school goals, objectives, and missions. Classical management images of school executives as influential and independent entrepreneurs with high moral standards and extraordinary vision are compatible with the rational model of organizational analysis. Interestingly, management images of teachers and administrators working in concert as autonomous groups of professionals with high moral standards and extraordinary vision are also compatible with this image.

THE ORGANIZATIONAL PROCESS MODEL

In explaining organizational events using Allison's discussion of the organizational process model, one assumes that events occur as largely purposive acts from a coordinated, indeed orchestrated, entity known as an organization. Whereas the rational model viewed the school as a unitary concept capable of rational decision-making, central coordination, being completely informed and value maximizing, the organizational process model views the school as consisting of a complex array of often divergent subparts. Organizational activity requires that the behavior of large numbers of individuals be coordinated. Coordination is accomplished by developing organizational routines such as standard operating procedures, flow charts, and other manifestations of rules which specify behavior. Organizational routines are stored in the organization's memory and are subject to recall by executives in response to particular problems they face. Organizational events, then, are explained as logically selected organizational routines. Viewing the school as a bureaucracy and its executives as organization men and women is compatible with the organizational process model of organizational analysis.

THE POLITICAL MODEL

In explaining organizational events using Allison's discussion of the political model, one assumes that events occur as a result of diverse groups, each bargaining to improve its own position. Leaders of organizations are not seen as a monolithic group, Allison suggests, but rather each in his or her own right is a player in a highly competitive game known as politics. This game of politics is played by bargaining in regularized ways among players in the hierarchy.
In Allison's words:

> In contrast with Model I, the ... politics model sees no unitary actor but rather many actors as players, who focus not on a single strategic issue but on many diverse ... problems as well, in terms of no consistent set of strategic objectives but rather according to various conceptions of ... organizational, and personal goals making ... decisions not by rational choice but by the pulling and hauling that is politics.[2]

In contrast to the rational and organizational models whose outcomes are viewed as solutions to problems, the political model views outcomes as resulting from intraorganizational phenomena such as compromise, coalition, competition, and confusion. The process is political in that the activity from which outcomes emerge is bargaining. Many players are involved in this bargaining, and power is widely distributed. The tactic of coalition, for example, is practiced in order to concentrate sufficient power to act.
In summarizing the play of the game of politics Allison notes:

> Actions emerge neither as the calculated choice of a unified group nor as a formal summary of leaders' preferences. Rather the context of

shared power but separate judgments concerning important choices determines that politics is the mechanism of choice. Note the *environment* in which the game is played: inordinate uncertainty about what must be done, the necessity that something be done and crucial consequences of whatever is done. These features force responsible men to become active players. The *pace of the game*—hundreds of issues, numerous games, and multiple channels—compels players to fight to "get others' attention," to make them "see the facts," to assure that they "take the time to think seriously about the broader issue." The *structure of the game*—power shared by individuals with separate responsibilities—validates each player's feeling that "others don't see my problem," and "others must be persuaded to look at the issue from a less parochial perspective." The *rules of the game*—he who hesitates loses his chance to play at that point, and he who is uncertain about his recommendation is overpowered by others who are sure—pressures players to come down on one side of a 51–49 issue and play. The *rewards of the game*—effectiveness, i.e., impact on outcomes, as the immediate measure of performance—encourages hard play.[3]

It would be a mistake to assume that the political model represents an exclusive image of how organizations work, but views which do not give sufficient attention to this model will not only miss the mark in providing accurate descriptions of reality but will result in distortions as well.

ORGANIZATIONS AS POLITICAL COALITIONS

Following James March,[4] organizations can be viewed as political coalitions and administrators as political brokers. As a political coalition, the form, shape, goals, mission, and structure of an organization are not givens but negotiated. Though March was speaking specifically of the business firm, his comments seem even more appropriate to public organizations.[5]

March suggests that though individuals have goals, collectivities do not. Given this observation, the theorist's problem is to "identify some concept of organizational goals that is consistent with the apparent denial of their existence."[6] Viewing organizations as coalitions helps in this effort. Further, within the organization, individuals frequently join together into subcoalitions. Coalition members in schools would include teachers, chairpersons, supervisors, administrators, janitors, students, the school board, the PTA, the teachers' union, the central office, volunteers, interest groups, regulatory agencies, and municipal departments.

Schools, according to this view, are concerned with a set of potential and actual participants which makes demands on the system. These demands are the price the system must pay if it wishes to maintain the coalition as relatively domesticated—that is, being able to carry on an acceptable pattern of interaction with the system. Demands take the form of money, attention, involvement, personal treatment, and other resources deemed important by coalition members. Demands are sometimes complementary and sometimes contradictory. When contradictory, meeting demand A forecloses or makes difficult meeting demand B. Consider a group of parents who want the school to stress its educative function of teaching responsibility and self-discipline on the one hand and maintain its custodial function of student control on the other.

If the school cannot maintain some semblance of coalition with important members, it is likely that competing coalitions will be established outside of accepted patterns of interaction. As competing coalitions gain in strength, they replace established coalitions. A principal who loses the support of only a few teachers and parents can survive. But as the number of disenchanted teachers or parents increases or if the two smaller groups gain enough strength by joining forces, the principal is replaced and the school's social order disturbed.

Administrators try to use the organization to maximize their own interests and needs. They face the problem of selecting a coalition of participants so that demands required as the price for participation do not compromise the return they seek. A principal who seeks support from teachers for a program of staff development at the cost of losing access to teachers' classrooms might find the trade-off as jeopardizing not only his immediate intent but future options as well. A cost-benefit analysis is conducted whereby the administrator assesses whether the benefits accrued by participating in a coalition with person A justify the demands which must be provided.

March suggests that the coalition nature of organizations is political in four critical ways. "First, the focus of attention shifts from the owners (and their objectives) to the actual, operating organizers of the coalition—whoever they may be."[7] Schools in particular are public organizations with few rules governing who can play the game of bargaining, and indeed since many of the players are outside of direct authority of administrators (tenured teachers, parents, alumni, the mayor, juvenile sections of the police department, NAACP, citizens for basic education, etc.), bargaining cannot be avoided. "Second, the theory emphasizes the non-uniqueness of short run solutions to the coalition problem. At any point in time, there are a number of possible coalitions that are viable (that is, their total value exceeds their total cost of maintenance)."[8] This phenomenon encourages the establishment of ad hoc coalitions and permits administrators some latitude in maintaining favorable coalitions by making them tenuous. The administrator as artful broker is sensitive to which coalitions have long-term implications and which are more expendable. Further, the cost of dissolving today's coalition against possible loss of future participation by individuals cannot go unnoticed. "Third, the theory does not solve the problem of conflict by simple payments to participants and agreement as a superordinate goal. Rather it emphasizes the importance of policy demands and payments and of sequential rather than simultaneous mediation of demands."[9] Demands differ and no standard payoff can assure a happy array of coalitions. Dealing with conflicting demands is a political process. Conflict, however, is often managed by separating conflicting goals and payments. The high school principal who works with the counseling department at nine, the college-prep academic departments at ten, and the distributive-education department at eleven is dealing with conflicting interests sequentially.

"Fourth, the theory emphasizes the importance of institutional constraints on the solution of coalition problems."[10] Active and potential participants in coalitions are not free to make any demand they wish, and administrators are limited in payments available. Coalitions are struck *within* institutional boundaries on the one hand and environmental constraints on the other. Budgetary constraints, codes of ethics, case law policies and other administrative precedents, and the school code are examples of constraints on coalition demands and payment. The administrator as artful broker uses these constraints to best advantage in managing coalitions.

Victor Baldridge proposes five assumptions about conflict, interest group, and decision processes which he believes are central in viewing schools as political systems:

1. Conflict is natural, and is to be expected in a dynamic organization. Conflict is not abnormal, nor is it necessarily a symptom of a breakdown in the organization's community.
2. The organization is fragmented into many power blocs and interest groups, and it is natural that they will try to influence policy so that their values and goals are given primary consideration.
3. In all organizations small groups of political elites govern most of the major decisions. However, this does not mean that one elite group governs everything; the decisions may be divided up, with different elite groups controlling different decisions.
4. Formal authority, as prescribed by the bureaucratic system, is severely limited by the political pressure and bargaining tactics that groups can exert against authorities. Decisions are not simply bureaucratic orders, but are instead negotiated compromises among competing groups. Officials are not free simply to order decisions;

instead they have to jockey between interest groups, hoping to build viable compromises among powerful blocs.

5. External interest groups have a great deal of influence over the organization, and internal groups do not have the power to make policies in a vacuum.[11]

According to Baldridge, the assumptions suggest that organizational analysis shifts from the execution of policy to the more central political process of policy formulation. The debate over goals, values, and strategies that accompany policy formulation and how these issues are resolved are keys to understanding organizations.

Certainly Allison's explication of the political model of organizational analysis, March's conceptualization of organizations as political coalitions, and Baldridge's assumption in viewing schools as political systems provide stark contrasts to traditional professional-bureaucratic images of schools as organizations.

THE SCHOOL AS A POLITICAL SYSTEM

Power is readily accessible in schools to those willing and able to tap appropriate sources.[12] It is true that persons with authority derived from their position have a distinct advantage in acquiring and using some sources of power, but nevertheless power monopolies tend not to exist.[13] Increased reliance on functional authority, participatory decision-making and other power-equalization strategies have enabled teachers, for example, to become more powerful. Further, as schools move away from bureaucratically oriented images of structure and functioning, power equalization increases.

As power equalization increases in the school, the *potential* for expressing political behavior increases. Political scientists tend to define politics as self-serving behavior, protecting one's own domain, building support through a constituency, influencing and maneuvering and/or coalition building. The acquisition and the maintenance of power seem central to this view. In the discussion which follows, our attention will be on organizational politics and political behavior within the school as an organization. *Organizational politics* is defined, after Robbins, as *internal* to the organization and as any behavior by an organizational member that is *self-serving*. In his words, "when individuals act to enhance their own position, regardless of costs to the organization or to others, they are acting politically."[14] A more neutral definition describes politics as the structure and process of using authority and power to effect goals and other major aspects of the organization. Following this definition, decisions are viewed less as rational or formal products and more as outputs of compromises, bargaining, and accommodation.

Political behavior associated with organizational politics differs from political behavior associated with government and political science in their broadest sense. The former is more concerned with activities of individuals inside the organization. The latter is more concerned with external constitutencies. In this context political behavior is often dysfunctional to the organization though at times one's self-interest may coincide with organizational purposes.

One can debate the benefits and evils of political behavior in schools. To simplify matters, schools benefit when the match between self- and organizational interests are high and suffer when this match is low. Though political behavior may be functional at a given point in time, it is too risky to be encouraged as a widespread strategy. Political behavior is based on self-interest rather than organizational norms, goals, and beliefs; and though benefits accrue when the two are matched, organizational goals are likely to be sacrificed when self-interest so mandates.

Political behavior, of course, involves the exercise of power, but power in itself is a form of neutral organizational energy capable of fueling both positive and negative actions. Though many people are able to influence the decision-making process in schools—that is, they are able to exercise power—it is the motivation they bring to this effort which determines whether they are exhibiting political behavior.

The relationships between power and motivation are illustrated in Figure 12-1. School executives, for example, who in exercising power to influence decision-making are motivated primarily out of self-interest are displaying political behavior in an organizational context. They intend to be the prime beneficiary of the decisions that are made. Coincidentally, the decisions may also substantially benefit the school, but since their intent is self-serving, this is political behavior nevertheless. Should circumstances change so that school interests are not served by self-interest, then self-interest, being the prime motivation, is likely to dominate providing that this choice does not jeopardize future self-interest options. By the same token, when school interests are the prime motivation, the school, or typically both the school and the individual tend to benefit and this is the normal exercise of power known as leadership.[15]

One fact remains clear. Political behavior exists in schools and indeed its *potential* for expression *increases* as power equalization

ORGANIZA-TIONAL ENERGY		PRIME MOTIVA-TION	PRIME BENEFICIARY	ACTION
Power	+	Self-serving ends (either self-advancement or defense) →	The individual only or coincidentally the individual and school →	Political behavior in an organizational context
Power	+	School ends (either organizational advancement or defense) →	School only or typically school and individual →	Leadership behavior in an organizational context

Figure 12-1   Combining power and motivation.

increases and school roles become more ambiguous. Faced with the prospect of increases in political behavior in the school, school executives can slow down or suppress such behavior by reversing the trend toward power equalization and by clear clarification of roles. But this strategy suggests a return to more classical and bureaucratically oriented schools, which provide again a different set of problems as discussed in Part III. A second alternative is to "manage" political behavior so that normatively it becomes less popular and where self-interest does exist, it matches more closely school interests. These strategies are summarized and school consequences suggested in Figure 12-2. Note that both strategies, the reduction of ambiguity and the increasing of commitment, can reduce political behavior, but their consequences for school differ. Decreasing ambiguity by making more explicit organizational arrangements and requirements reduces the school's problem-solving and adaptive qualities and increases member alientation. Opposite consequences are suggested for the more normative strategy.

TOWARD A THEORY OF ORGANIZATIONAL PATRIOTISM

The collective psychology of individuals and the information-processing capabilities of organizations are consistently underestimated by organizational analysts. Schools cannot be studied merely as inanimate structures, coalitions, and technologies or as input, thru-put, and output systems governed by natural laws. A more adequate view of the school is that of a cultural-bound information-processing system which takes on human qualities. In this sense, organizations are not natural but artificial. This

ADMINISTRATIVE STRATEGIES	POLITICAL BEHAVIOR	SCHOOL CONSEQUENCES
1. Decrease ambiguity by increasing organizational structure constraints, specificity in roles and objectives, standardization and reliability in work flow and other manifestations of bureaucracy.	→ Reduced. →	The school's adaptive capacities decrease, and alienation of actual and potential members increases.
2. Increase the match between self and organizational interests by increasing commitment to the school's organizational, educational, and management platforms.	→ Reduced. →	The school's adaptive capacities increase, and alienation of actual and potential members decreases.

Figure 12-2   Managing political behavior in schools.

metaphor is elaborated in our discussion of artificial intelligence in organizations, which appears in Chapter 4. Louis R. Pondy, for example, states:

> Conceptually, the status of an organization shifts from that of an objective reality to one which in the extreme is phenomenologically represented in the subjective experience of individual participants or more moderately is a socially constructed reality. Given such a conception, to endow such concepts as technology with measurable and perceivable attributes is questionable. Instead, we need to study how participants themselves come to invoke categories such as "organization" and "technology" as a means of making sense of their experience. The resulting meanings will frequently be "stored" in organizational myths and metaphors to provide rationales for both membership and activity in organizations. The role that institutional leaders play in the creation of myths and metaphors is a worthwhile focus for study.[16]

Significant is Pondy's suggestion that organizations should be viewed from the perspective of extreme phenomenology as represented in the subjective experience of individual participants. He and others[17] argue that organizations create meanings which are stored in myths and metaphors. These myths and metaphors become normative compliance tools which govern individual behavior.[18] Indeed, organizational members who honor these myths and metaphors are being patriotic to the organization. Schools which are thought of as progressive, flexible, and open view teachers who espouse these virtues in word and deed as being more patriotic than teachers who do not. And indeed when myths and metaphors encourage slavish attention to basic education, tight control and strong discipline and these characteristics therefore dominate the school culture, then the characteristics become the requirements of patriotism. The converse would be true in schools characterized by a humanistic culture. Myths and metaphors are implicit in the organizational, educational, and managerial platforms of schools.

Organizational patriotism can be defined as commitment and loyalty to the characteristics which give a school its unique meaning. This meaning is part of the school's culture and is implicit in its governing platforms. Goals, sense of mission, philosophy, accepted ways of operating, and image are examples of such characteristics. The more explicit these are and the more patriotic are members to them, the more likely that school interests and self-interest will be matched. Political behavior, of course, will still exist but is managed by norms of patriotism.[19]

Some have argued that most organizational myths are unrealistic and unattainable. Should this matter? Probably not. Our national patriotism prevails though its myths (liberty, equality, and fraternity, for example) are unattainable. And so it is with schools. Missions, hopes and ideals are destined to be unreached but they represent the common rallying cry, nevertheless, for organizational members and become the backbone of normative compliance strategies. The issue, as March would put it, is optimism, not hope.

> In a similar way, we may ask the educator to separate his optimism from his hopes. Neither the teacher nor the educational administrator has profound basis for hope. The world is probably cruel. But hope is not required for attacking educational windmills, only a commitment to the classical traditions of knight-errantry in schools—enthusiasm, intelligence, imagination, and devotion to the future. The roles we accept define the battles we fight; and we find optimism in the joys of that dependence.
>
> Indeed, we can make a stronger claim. To be optimistic is the nature of education. The terminology is archaic. We have grown to accept the modern idea that human actions, institutions, and traditions are justified by expectations of their consequences; and we have come to view optimism without hope as an unfortunate surrender to Pollyanna. But education unconditionally celebrates life. It is an arbitrary assertion of optimism. It echoes an ancient conception by which I do what I do because that is what is appropriate to my nature; and my nature is not simply a tautological summary of what I do but an understanding of the essence of my destiny, an interpretation of my history, and an assertion of my humanity.[20]

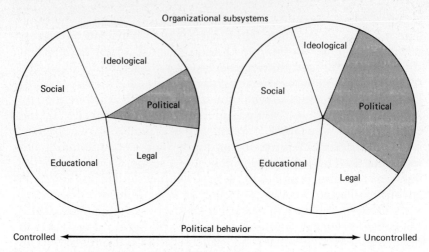

Figure 12-3   Controlling political behavior.

Roger describes five subsystems found with various degrees of emphasis in all organizations: ideological, social, technical (educational), judicial (legal), and political.[21] The subsystems are not operationally discrete but nevertheless can be readily differentiated. We suggest as a basic proposition that the more manifest the ideological, legal, educational, and social subsystems are, and the greater the degree of commitment to them, the less chance of dysfunctional behavior in the political system. Since many aspects of the legal system are fixed or given, the relationship suggested previously is likely to be stronger for the ideological, social, and educational systems.

To the extent that the propositions we propose are true, then dysfunctional political behavior can be controlled by making more explicit and increasing commitment to the ideological, social, and educational systems. These relationships are illustrated in Figure 12-3. In the school, the ideological system is comprised of the assumptions, values, and beliefs which represent platforms from which organizational decisions are made. Theory Y assumptions, for example, as part of a school's management platform would belong in the ideological system. The social system includes the attachments, relationships, loyalties, and norms which characterize the school's human organization. The higher the group loyalty, the greater the support and the more trust which exist within the group and between the group and school executives, the less likely will dysfunctional political behavior be expressed. The educational system includes the intents, assumptions, values, and beliefs which comprise the school's educational platform. The more explicit this platform and the more agreement which exists over educational intents, the less likely will dysfunctional political behavior be expressed.

Though idealistically one might speak of eliminating political behavior in schools, realistically the emphasis should be more on building a better match between such behavior and the norms which comprise the school's ideological, social, and educational systems. The more explicit the norms and the more patriotic are actual and potential organizational members, the more likely that self-interest will conform to school purposes than purposes to self-interest. Questions of organizational and self-interests aside, power equalization among actual and potential participants in schools suggests that the decision-making process is likely to be fairly open and susceptible to influence from a variety of sources. Conflict, whether it results from loyal opposition expressed by a "patriot" or outright hostility from organizational "rebels" will be present and in abundance as a natural aspect of life in modern school organizations.

CONFLICT IN ORGANIZATIONS

The political system's view has contributed a great deal to more fully understanding the role and nature of conflict in organizations. Traditionally, conflict has been viewed as an organizaton evil to be suppressed and preferably eliminated. Bureaucratic images of schools, for example, prescribe that by making explicit organizational requirements (elaborate job descriptions, clear-cut lines of authority, detailed rules and regulations, etc.) and by careful recruitment of those willing to accept authority, conflict in organizations can be eliminated. Those who advocate professional images of schools seem more accepting of conflict but overemphasize the importance of its resolution. Political views of schools as organizations seek to find the good in conflict and suggest even that without conflict the very survival of the organization is threatened. Coser, for example, argues that since conflict fights against routine and stimulates innovation, it has long-range benefits to society.[22] And Robbins, in proposing his conflict-survival model, sees organizational *survival* as being dependent upon the organization's *adaptive* abilities. Adaptation is possible through *change* and change in turn is stimulated by *conflict*.[23]

From a political point of view, the management of conflict does *not* necessarily mean the resolving of conflict. Resolution is only one option, desirable in some instances but not in others. A second option, also desirable in some instances but not in others, is to create or stimulate conflict. Though the literature is rich in conflict resolution,[24] not enough attention has been given to conflict stimulation as a conflict management strategy. Two such strategies suggested by Robbins are manipulating communications channels (repressing information, overloading channels, using nontraditional channels, ambiguous communication) and altering structural arrangements (job redefinition, consolidation of units, decentralizing of units or otherwise redistributing power).[25] These strategies raise ethical questions which are partially resolved by examining the motivation of the conflict stimulator. Conflict stimulated to enhance self-interest is quite different from that stimulated to enhance school objectives. Further, common decency requires sensitivity in one's management style and a concern for the personal and professional welfare of those likely to be involved in the stimulated conflict. The goal is to improve school effectiveness, not to create "winners" and "losers."

In viewing conflict internal to the organization, Pondy[26] identifies three types:

First is *bargaining* conflict among individuals and groups with specific interests who are competing for scarce resources. Two high schools in the same district competing with each other to obtain more resources (perhaps expansion of programs and staff, new band uniforms, the agricultural education classroom and garage, or a change in school boundaries which increases the number of desirable students) from the central office and school board might be an example.

Second is *bureaucratic* conflict between individuals and groups at different levels of the hierarchy who are competing for scarce resources. An example is found within the high school, where the department chairpersons as a group bargain with the principal, his administrative staff, and his administration-dominated committee structures to obtain more rights and prerogatives against pressures for more centralization. The subordinate or the subordinate group seeks to protect itself from the influence of the superordinate or the superordinate group as the latter seeks to expand its influence.

Third is *systems* conflict between individuals and groups at the same level of the hierarchy. Two high school departments or several teaching teams who share books, rooms, learning centers, and other resources frequently experience systems conflicts in squabbles over scheduling and territorial rights. In Pondy's words, "If in turn two subunits having differentiated goals are functionally interdependent, then conditions exist for conflict. Important types of interdependence matters are: (1) common usage of some service or facility, (2) sequences of work or information flow by task or hierarchy, and (3) rules of unanimity or consensus about joint activity."[27]

Pondy identifies five stages to a conflict episode.[28] The first is *latent* conflict and is concerned with the conditions which are underlying sources of conflict. Competition for scarce resources, drives for autonomy, and contradictory subunit goals are conditions which ripen the possibility of conflict.

The second stage is *perceived* conflict whereby principal parties (individuals or groups) cognitively are aware of conflict conditions. Sometimes perceived conflict exists in the absence of latent conflict. That is, some misunderstanding or muddled communication channel leads the primary teachers to believe that they may lose importance to the special education teachers when such is not the case.

The third stage is *felt* conflict whereby knowledge of a conflict condition becomes translated into feelings (hatred, jealousy, withdrawal, anxiety, self-pity, and rivalry, for example). In this stage, conflict becomes personalized. It is not teacher A against teacher B or department against principal but me against him and my department against her. The management of conflict implications at the felt conflict stage are important. In stimulating conflict, for example, ethics requires that the school executive be concerned with tension reduction and with depersonalizing the nature of the conflict. The strength of the school's ideological and social subsystems, as suggested earlier in this chapter by Rogers, will determine the extent to which felt conflict can be successfully managed.

The fourth stage is *manifest* conflict, which includes the actual display of conflict behavior. At one extreme the behavior is very obvious (physical and verbal violence) and at the other end very subtle (implicit bargaining during a group decision-making activity of an administrative team). The less intense is felt conflict and the more explicit do norms in the ideological and social subsystems frown on hostility, the more likely is conflict behavior toward the polite end of the continuum.

The fifth stage is conflict *aftermath*. In Pondy's words:

Each conflict episode is but one of a sequence of such episodes that constitute the relationships among organization participants. If the conflict is genuinely resolved to the satisfaction of all participants, the basis for a more cooperative relationship may be laid; or the participants, in their drive for a more ordered relationship may focus on latent conflicts not previously perceived and dealt with. On the other hand, if the conflict is merely suppressed but not resolved, the latent conditions of conflict may be aggravated and explode in more serious form until they are rectified or until the relationship dissolves. This legacy of a conflict episode is here called "conflict aftermath."[29]

Much remains to be learned about the constructive use of conflict in organizations. Recognizing first that conflict can have constructive consequences for schools is in itself an important contribution of the political systems view of schools. Indeed, viewing the school as a political system adds a rich dimension to understanding how schools operate. But as enhancing as these glimpses of reality are, serious caveats are in order. Political systems views are largely descriptive, not prescriptive. That is, they attempt to describe and understand what is actually occurring, and these are important undertakings.

School executives err, however, by assuming that because events are as they are, the name of the game is only to learn the rules and play by them. The rules themselves are at issue and must be evaluated for goodness of fit to the unique values of the school as a particular kind of organization. In educational enterprises, means and ends are indistinguishable. Teachers and students alike learn as much from how we organize and behave in schools as they do from the official educational program. Management and organization are part of the school's hidden curriculum and daily teach important lessons to students and teachers.

Notes

1. Graham T. Allison, "Conceptual Models and the Cuban Missile Crisis," *The American Political Science Review* 63, no. 3 (1969): 689–718.
2. Ibid., p. 707.
3. Ibid., p. 710.
4. James G. March, "The Business Firm as a Political Coalition," *The Journal of Politics* 24, no. 2 (1962): 662–678.
5. See, for example, our discussion of differences between public and private organizations, which appears in Chapter 4.
6. Richard M. Cyert and James G. March, *A Behavioral Theory of the Firm* (Englewood Cliffs, N.J.: Prentice-Hall, 1963), p. 26.
7. March, "The Business Firm as a Political Coalition," p. 674.
8. Ibid.
9. Ibid.
10. Ibid.
11. J. Victor Baldridge, "The Analysis of Organizational Change: A Human Relations Strategy Versus a Political Systems Strategy." R & D memo no. 75. Stanford Center for R & D in Teaching, Stanford University, 1971, p. 14.

12. This discussion of the school as a political system follows closely sections of Chapter 7, "Power, Authority and Conflict in Supervision," in Thomas J. Sergiovanni and Robert J. Starratt, *Supervision: Human Perspectives* 2nd ed. (New York: McGraw-Hill, 1979).

13. See, for example, our discussion of power and authority, which appears in Chapter 10.

14. Stephen P. Robbins, *The Administrative Process Integrating Theory and Practice* (Englewood Cliffs, N.J.: Prentice-Hall, Inc.: 1976), p. 64. This discussion of organizational politics follows Robbins, pp. 64–66.

15. Both the school and the individual benefit on the assumption that increasing school interest results in intrinsic satisfaction for many individuals. Further, to the extent that extrinsic rewards are associated with one's contribution to school effectiveness, the relationship also holds.

16. Louis R. Pondy, "Beyond Open System Models of Organization. Paper presented at the annual meeting of the Academy of Management, Kansas City, Mo., August 12, 1976, p. 33.

17. See, for example, Kenneth Boulding, "General Systems Theory—the Skeleton of Science," in Walter Buckley, ed., *Modern Systems Research for the Behavioral Scientist* (Chicago: Aldine Press, 1968), pp. 3–10, particularly his discussion of system levels five through eight.

18. See, for example, our discussion in Chapter 3 of Etzioni's compliance theory for an elaboration of normative compliance.

19. Of course, it should be noted that the establishment of organizational myths and metaphors is in itself a political process.

20. James G. March, "Education and the Pursuit of Optimism," invited address, Texas Tech University, Lubbock, Tex., October 18, 1974, p. 18.

21. Rolf E. Rogers, *The Political Process in Modern Organizations* (New York: Exposition Press, 1971). This reference is the source for the discussion which follows.

22. Lewis A. Coser, *The Functions of Social Conflict* (New York: The Free Press, 1954).

23. Stephen P. Robbins, *Managing Organizational Conflict: A Non-traditional Approach* (Englewood Cliffs, N.J.: Prentice-Hall, 1974). It may be that the "domesticated" native of schools is such that with survival guaranteed, adaptation is less important.

24. See, for example, Robert Blake, Jane Mouton, and Herbert Shepard, *Managing Intergroup Conflict in Industry* (Houston, Tex.: Gulf Publishing Col, 1964); Jay Hall, *Conflict Management Survey*. Houston, Tex.: Teleometrics, Inc., 1968); and Alan C. Filley, *Interpersonal Conflict Resolution*, Glenview, Ill.: Scott, Foresman & Co., 1975).

25. Robbins, *Managing Organizational Conflict*, pp. 78–89.

26. Louis R. Pondy, "Organizational Conflict: Concepts and Models," *Administrative Science Quarterly* 12, no. 2 (1967): 296–320.

27. Ibid., p. 318

28. Ibid., pp. 300–306.

29. Ibid., p. 305.

Chapter 13
The School Executive and External Relationships

As delineated in Chapter 11, one of the subroles in the role set of the school executive is that of community liaison. Depending on the position and the nature of the community, this subrole occupies more or less time and may or may not dominate the job-related activities of the incumbent. Those two factors, administrative position and nature of the community, also influence the way in which that executive subrole is performed. It is the case, of course, that large school organizations, especially those in urban areas, have personnel who are community relations specialists. This chapter is prepared with the generalist school executive in mind. It may be of interest to the specialist but is not written for the specialist's perspective.

The community liaison subrole did not suddenly appear in 1954, 1962, or 1976. Public education developed as a local function in the United States, and principal and superintendent roles were shaped in the crucible of community expectations and interactions as was the teacher role which preceded them. From inception, school executive positions have been inextricably linked to the immediate school community, directly or through town selectmen and later boards of education. As the state claimed its partnership rights in the conduct of public elementary and secondary education, the external community of concern for school executives increased in magnitude and complexity. The addition of the federal government as an active partner, since about 1960, added to the intensity of concern for external relations as well as exploding the magnitude and complexity of the school executive's community. Attention to the external-relations dimensions of role performance in education literature also is not a phenomenon of the mid-1970s. The responsibility of administrators for the operationalization of the community school is abundant in educational administration textbooks for the period 1945–54.[1] Texts and courses in school-community relations have been available for administrators and prospective administrators for decades.

In recent years the politics of education has developed as a methodological and substantive specialization within educational administration. The flowering of the specialization results from continued application of a subset of concepts and investigative methodologies from the social and behavioral sciences to the field of education, an application that began in earnest in the late 1950s. For the most part the researchers and writers in the area draw more extensively from political science than sociology or social psychology, although anthropology and economics have contributed concepts and methodologies. Increased national visibility of public education and the questioning of its impact and role in societal and individual development and functioning is no doubt a major factor that explains the emergence of the politics of education.

The special plight of the quality and governance of public education in the big cities, the rise of collective bargaining in public education, general societal conditions and movements in the 1960s and early 1970s, and economic conditions are associated with the prominence of politics of education. From Gross's *Who Runs Our Schools?*[2] in 1962 to the 1977 NSSE Yearbook, *The Politics of Education*,[3] there is an important, interesting, and immensely helpful literature for the school executive.[4] That literature and the significant issues to which it is addressed serve as the frame of reference and major source of ideas for this chapter.

THE SCHOOL EXECUTIVE IN SCHOOL GOVERNANCE

The school executive is formally linked to school governance from within the managerial level of the school organization.[5] As the agent of the board of education, a state-created body, the executive

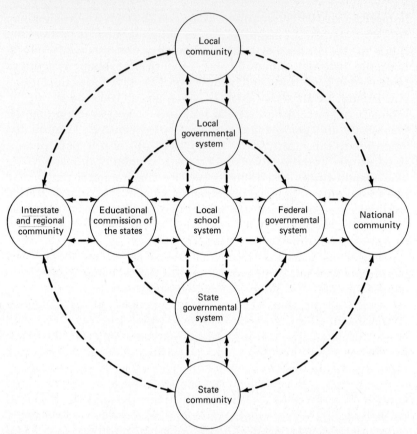

Figure 13-1   Model of the policy-making system of American education. (Source: John Thomas Thompson, *Policymaking in American Public Education: A Framework for Analysis,* © 1976, p. 30. Reprinted by permission of Prentice-Hall, Inc., Englewood Cliffs, New Jersey.)

comes under the direct authority of local and state laws and regulations concerning the governance of schools. Federal support for elementary and secondary schools has increased the sense that the school executive is involved in a national governance system for education. Federal and state court decisions impact on school governance and the school's (and, hence, the school executive's) relationships with individuals and groups external to the school. The complex of factors in the policy-making system for American public education is presented in Figure 13-1, with the local school system as the focal element in the system.

Local district policies and operating procedures affect the degree to which the school or school district extends participation in school governance to parents and other citizen groups. Subdistrict boards of education and/or school councils in big-city school districts such as Chicago, New York, and Detroit, responses to demands for community control of schools, are visible examples of school district actions that place the school executive in a direct governance relationship with citizens other than members of the local board. Thousands of schools and districts utilize citizen committees in addition to or in lieu of the subdistrict boards and councils.

The nature and importance of schools cause them to be of interest to various organizations, groups, and individuals. The school executive is constantly interacting in terms of additions or deletions to the school program, school rules and regulations for pupils, and behaviors of school personnel. Parent/citizen interactions that occur as a part of the normal, healthy operation of an educational system are additional points of external relationships for the school executive (and for teachers) and informally impact on that role's effectiveness in local school governance.

Although the functions of principals, superintendents, and other central office personnel vary with district size, board expectations, and style of the superintendent, direct contact with the board of education is an important, albeit indirect, external relationship.[6] In an earlier era in public school management, and today in many school districts, the school executive's major external relationships revolved largely around and through members of the board of education. The school board was perceived to be the community's voice in school policy matters. That boards may not have acted in a manner satisfactory to all groups is perhaps one reason for the expanded external relations role of the school executive. Changes in society in the past quarter-century, including power gains among community groups as well as the ever-expanding mission of public schools, have produced the situation where boards of education are not accepted as *the* public agent for education; indeed, the board of education may not be the arena for the resolution of even local conflicts that affect policies and conditions in public schools. Desegregation, pupil rights, and the use of certain books in schools are examples of conflicts that have been removed from boards of education to courts, chief state school officers, or legislatures. The local school community, although not exclusively the board of education, remains the primary focus of external relations for the school executive, however. That is particularly true with regard to analysis as a guide to executive behavior and ultimately, system response.

COMMUNITY CHARACTERISTICS

Three frameworks are presented in this section that can serve as beginning points for the school executive who would examine the environment as the community liaison role is performed.[7] The first relates to the configuration of community power structures, the second is based on the macrovalue orientation of the community, and the third is derived from change theory.

COMMUNITY POWER STRUCTURES

Since the publication of Hunter's work on the power structure in Regional City,[8] social scientists and others have been concerned with the identification of who holds and utilizes power in communities. Investigators of community power structures, though not currently spotlighted in the politics-of-education drama, produced a body of knowledge from which has emerged four basic types of community power structures.

Carver and Crowe[9] summarized these four as pyramidal or monolithic, factional or caucus, coalitional or polylithic, and amorphous. The pyramidal structure is characterized by a single group of individuals who make major decisions. At least two relatively durable groups vie for decision-making power in the factional or caucus type. In a coalitional or polylithic community, the nature of issues to be decided determines the interested individuals and groups who form coalitions that shift and/or disappear over time. "Amorphous" is the term used to describe the absence of any persistent pattern of individuals or groups who make/control decisions.

Walton[10] performed a meta-analysis of 39 studies covering 61 communities based on the same four-type framework, although he combined factional, coalitional, and amorphous for statistical treatment. He tested a total of 21 hypotheses, 8 relating to methodological and 13 relating to community characteristics. He concluded that most of the confirmed hypotheses related type of community power structure to methodological bias—for example, reputational versus decision method of identifying leaders, public versus private issues, definition of power, and discipline of researcher. Community characteristics that were found to be related to community power structure type were: Population growth was moderately associated with more concentrated power structures—pyramidal; competitive party politics was highly associated with less concentrated power structures; a high proportion of absentee ownership was highly associated with less concentrated power structures; and power

Table 13-1 COMMUNITY POWER STRUCTURE, SCHOOL BOARD
STRUCTURE, AND ROLE OF SUPERINTENDENT

COMMUNITY POWER STRUCTURE	SCHOOL BOARD STRUCTURE	ROLE OF SUPERINTENDENT
Dominated	Dominated	Functionary
Factional	Factional	Political strategist
Pluralistic	Status congruent	Professional adviser
Inert	Sanctioning	Decision-maker

SOURCE: Donald J. McCarty and Charles E. Ramsey, *The School Managers: Power and Conflict in American Education* (Westport, Conn.: Greenwood Press, Inc., 1971), Data Tables 1, 2, 3. pp. 200–203. Reprinted with permission of the publisher.

structures were changing in the direction of a greater dispersion of power.[11]

McCarty and Ramsey[12] investigated the modal behavior of boards of education and superintendents in four types of communities. Their four community types, which approximated the four previously defined, were: dominated, factional, pluralistic, and inert. They observed clear patterns, although not total congruence, between type of community structure, board of education, and superintendent behavior—see Table 13-1.

Of particular interest to us is the model role of the superintendent in the different community and board situations. In dominated communities with a dominated board the superintendent's role in board matters was that of functionary. In factional communities and boards, political strategist was the superintendent's role. Professional adviser was the role for the superintendent in a pluralistic community and a status-congruent board whereas the superintendent was decision-maker in an inert community in which the board of education played a sanctioning role for the schools in the community.

Sacred and Secular Communities

In the development of their framework for explaining local school board and superintendent behavior, Iannaccone and Lutz explicate two ideal-type communities based on fundamental value orientations.[13] These bipolar concepts, sacred and secular, were used by Becker[14] to summarize societal classification systems. After noting that sacred and secular are not adjectival concepts synonymous with other more or less bipolar pairs, including holy and profane, Becker defines the two societies as follows.

> A sacred society is one that elicits from or imparts to its members, by means of sociation, unwillingness and/or inability to respond to the culturally new *as the new is defined by those members in terms of the society's existing culture.* Otherwise put, a network of sociation that develops, among the personalities weaving and woven by it, a high degree of resistance to change, particularly in their social order, is a sacred society.
>
>   A secular society is one that elicits from or imparts to its members, by means of sociation, willingness and ability to respond to the culturally new as the new is defined by those members in terms of the society's existing culture. Stated in another way, a network of sociation that develops, among the personalities weaving and woven by it, a high degree of readiness and capacity to change, particularly in their social order, is a secular society.[15]

School districts that tend toward the sacred end of the sacred-secular continuum are likely to emphasize public consensus politics that continue to characterize rural school districts in the United States.[16] Conflict is kept from the public by working our disagreements in private. This is the natural and functional way of managing affairs because of the shared values and commitments of those in power. And although policies, facilities, personnel, and programs change overtime, they occur in such a way as to produce relatively little occasion for conflict, that is, through death, retirement, and routine updating.

In a pure sacred school district change of any type—for example, board membership administrators, programs, school practices—is very slow to come barring highly unusual circumstances. Successful changes in the schools are minor indeed and/or are presented as logical extensions or variants of existing programs and practices.

Secular communities, on the other hand, are more likely to have mechanisms that permit, even encourage conflict over major educational issues. The school board is, in part, a public forum for the discussion of major policies and decisions confronting schools. Conflict is seen as inevitable and functional in the decision-making process and, thus, does not have to occur only in private.

Changes in schools are more probable in secular communities, at least those that deviate significantly from current practice. Because of the "willingness and/or ability" to accept the new, there may be a tendency to prefer, even seek the different.

Iannaccone and Lutz[17] point out that the big-city school district would appear to be the best example of the secular school district in terms of the range of social groups present. They further point out, quite accurately we believe, that the decision-making processes and patterns of big-city school districts resemble those of sacred communities, thereby producing an incompatibility that leads to or exacerbates problems facing the school. It is ironic that this incompatibility gives rise to a level of conflict as severe as that which the district works to avoid.

Of course, there are no school districts that are perfectly sacred, any more than there are pure secular school districts. It is a matter of degree. There are, however, school districts that are more or less sacred or secular. The lighthouse school districts that always seem to emerge every few years are probably the clearest examples of districts whose educational practices reflect the core value associated with secular communities, that is, a willingness and/or ability to accept the new. Paradoxically, those districts tend to be predominantly homogeneous in terms of social and/or ethnic groups.

The point of the sacred-secular continuum for the school executive is that it helps to explain citizen and community attitudes as well as suggest, at least in broad strokes, more and less effective ways to approach the community liaison subrole. Also, there are "sacred" school communities within "secular" districts and vice versa. The effective management of external relations in district situations with significant variability requires intraorganizational understanding and response as well as external structures and procedures.

Placid and Turbulent Environments

In an attempt to increase understanding of organizational change, Emery and Trist applied the psychologically developed concept, the causal texture of the environment, to organizational analysis.[18] They consider four areas of knowledge essential for understanding organizational behavior: intraorganizational interdependencies, two-way interactions between the organization and its environment, and the interdependencies within the environment itself; the fourth area they term the causal texture of the environment.[19]

Four types of environments (causal textures) are identified, ranging from *placid, randomized* through *placid, clustered* and *disturbed-reactive* to *turbulent fields.* Differences between the two placid environments are not nearly so great as between them and the other two. Essentially, the continua from placid, randomized to turbulent field are complexity and uncertainty.

Placid environments are relatively stable and fundamentally

predictable. The ideal placid, randomized environment would be characterized by individuals who interact about and with the school organization on specific issues and in a disorganized fashion. Parents and other citizens take an interest about a child or a school building site, but there is no attempt to maintain the position on similar issues nor to expand the issue to include broader support. This causal texture type, although a logical alternative, has probably never existed since education came within the purview of school government.

The placid, clustered school environment is relatively stable and predictable. It is characterized by individuals who share, in some generally recognized patterns, interests, goals, and concerns for the schools. The Chamber of Commerce, the PTA, the Council for Basic Education, taxpayer groups, and racial and ethnic groups are examples of organizations with which the school organization, and thus the school executive, regularly interacts. This type of school environment may well be the type with which most of us are familiar and prefer.

A disturbed-reactive environment is like the placid, clustered one except that there are multiple groups and/or organizations of the same kind but not necessarily desiring the same input or outcome from the school organization. If the placid, clustered environment creates a potential conflict for the school analogous to multirole conflict for the school executive, the disturbed-reactive environment complicates the potential for conflict by adding multiple role-definer groups for each of the roles. Further, the competing organizations are aware of each other and are generally known to the school organization. Two organizations vying for teacher memberships and bargaining rights and two or more citizen groups seeking recognition to represent a school neighborhood in district program planning are simple examples of competing groups. Also, fluid coalitions of organizations are formed, which increases the uncertainty for school executives.

Turbulent fields are school environments that have the characteristics of the disturbed-reactive kind, plus the nature of the issues and processes for settling them are constantly changing as well. That is, not only are the actors changing but so is the script and art form. The school organization is confronted with a complex of groups/organizations that may change frequently, and the input/ outcome issues move from expenditures to program to treatment of pupils—and the strategy fluctuates from discussion to picketing to legal action. Wirt's analysis of core groups and issues that impact on the political authority of school board members and school administrators is a cogent description of the complexity of the current environment for public schools, especially in urban areas.[20] He identifies parents, students, teachers, taxpayers, and minorities as the core constituency making issue demands on the board of education, which in turn focuses the turbulence on administrators.

Terreberry[21] explicates the four types and argues that organizational environments are increasingly moving in the direction of turbulent fields. She suggests that this movement, with its dominant characteristic of uncertainty, explains the change in decision-making approaches from essentially rational models to more open and/or less "rational" approaches. Further, she suggests that the more environments assume the characteristics of the turbulent field, the more important information (especially advance information) becomes, thus adding to the importance of the liaison subrole of the school executive. Gaynor, citing both Emery and Trist and Terreberry, hypothesizes "that many school organizations, especially many urban school organizations, have or are moving from a 'placid-clustered' environment to a 'turbulent field' environment."[22]

CURRENT ROLE PERFORMANCE MODELS

Citing big-city superintendency turnover in the 1960s as one outcome of political turbulence in schools, Wirt identified ineffectiveness of the extant role model as the specific cause for the turnover.[23] The administrative chief or manager role with its emphasis on centralization and efficient management is under attack by parents, students, teachers, taxpayers, and minorities. His characterization of the superintendent as administrative chief is from Cuban,[24] who identifies three basic superintendent roles, with direct relevance to external relations, that have emerged over the past century. The three types, described in the first person for Cuban's stylistic reasons, are teacher-scholar, administrative chief, and negotiator-statesman.

> *The Teacher-Scholar*—I am the professional educator. Any question that directly concerns children and schools I decide. If it involves other, less important matters, I delegate the decision to my staff. As for outside involvement, what do laymen know? The less outside involvement the better. Nor do I care for conflict. Conflict interrupts the educational ·process. It upsets children and teachers. I work hard to exclude it from the board, staff and schools. Cooperation and unity are essential to progress. As for change, if it is instructional or curricular, I direct teachers and principals to begin working on it. I'll provide help to make the change work, but there is no question that it must begin.
>
> *The Administrative Chief*—A school system is a large organization.

System and order are necessary. Good management is essential. After careful study, I make the important decisions. Staff does the gathering and sorting of information and takes care of routine decisions. There are standard procedures for staff, but when the big decisions arrive at my desk, the buck stops there. With respect to external participation in school affairs, a certain amount is probably unavoidable. I try to control the level and direction of the involvement. Too much participation leads to conflict and that's bad. I can't get my job done. Unity among board, staff, and community leads to improved education. Conflict breeds disunity. As for change, I plan it with my staff. Change should come about in an orderly, sequential manner so that it enhances rather than disrupts the organization. All major changes, of course, must be approved by me.

The Negotiator-Statesman—We make decisions cooperatively. Many groups are interested in what happens in schools. On any single issue I have to meet with the board, teachers, parents, civic officials, and even students. We then hammer out a compromise acceptable to all. It's important that each group feels that it has some influence over the final decision. In this process there has to be much outside participation. We don't see folks as outsiders. All groups should be involved in decision making. That's why conflict doesn't scare me. It's the name of the game. Since there are many divergent interests, conflict is bound to occur. I have to handle it. Similarly, change results from conflicting interests being negotiated and satisfied. It goes on all the time. As conflict is inevitable, so is change.[25]

Cuban's analysis includes three important elements with respect to the dominant role models. The first is that the three styles are not mutually exclusive. It is the case that school executives in any position exhibit teacher-scholar behavior on certain issues or with some role referent groups, and act as administrative chiefs on some occasions and as negotiator-statesmen on still others. There is a tendency to see the three as appropriate for (a superintendent especially) functioning within educational, managerial, and institutional level (including external relations).[26] Reality is not so sharply differentiated, however. External groups are concerned with educational issues, for example, curricular and instructional questions, and teacher organizations are increasingly interested in managerial-level matters, for example, the scheduling of work and the assignment of personnel.

The second analytic element is that survival and/or effectiveness is related to a reasonable matching of external conditions and expectations and modal performance. This is analogous to the empirically verified point about the nature of environmental demands and internal organizational structuring for responding to those demands found in the works of Lawrence and Lorsch[27] and Lorsch and Morse.[28] School community environments comprised of individuals, groups, and organizations clamoring for influence in school decision-making require behavioral and structural responses different from those with only occasional questings for input.

The third and final analytic element is that significant shifts do occur in environmental conditions although the changes vary by communities in rate and intensity. The increasing pervasiveness of turbulence in society generally suggests that all school environments are targets for many of the school-related conditions found in the big cities. This is, of course, the reality noted at the beginning of the chapter that accounts in large part for the importance of the community liaison subrole and the prominence of the politics of education as a specialization in educational administration.

Mann constructed a three-role model typology and empirically verified it in an interview study with 165 school administrators in New York State.[29] The typology was developed around the concept of representation on the view that administrators represent the community in the conduct of schools. Two basic representational styles and one in-between style were utilized: trustee, delegate, and politico.

> Briefly, a *trustee* is someone whose decisions are based on his own values, even though the represented may disagree. A *delegate* reverses the priority and is guided by expressed citizen preferences even at the expense of his own best judgment. A third position, somewhat between the trustee and delegate decision-making styles, is usually called a *"politico."* A politico borrows from either the trustee or delegate styles as dictated by situations but has some internally consistent rationale for doing so. The politico does not merely waffle but rather enacts a trustee or a delegate orientation according to the dictates of circumstances.[30]

Superintendents, principals, and central office personnel with major community relations responsibilities were interviewed in four urban, three suburban, and three rural school communities. Of the 165 administrators studied, 15 were in private schools. He reported the following percentages for the three representational roles: trustee, 61 percent; delegate, 30 percent; and politico, 9 percent.[31]

A number of personal, school, and community characteristics were correlated with role type. The most interesting and immediately relevent of the findings involved public-private school, elected-appointed boards, administrative role, school size, and community type. All of the politicos were public school administrators, and private school administrators were slightly more likely to be trustees than their public school counterparts. Administrators working in districts with an appointed board were more likely to be trustees (74 percent) than those in districts with elected boards (61 percent). Superintendents were more likely to be responsive to the community—(as reflected in a smaller percentage of trustees) than were principals and central office administrators; 60 percent, 66 percent, and 83 percent, respectively. In general there appeared to be a curvilinear relationship between the size of school and the trustee administrator; the politico orientation was positively related to school size. Suburban school communities had a higher percentage of trustees (81 percent) than either urban (64 percent) or rural (60 percent) communities. When he considered only the principal role, Mann found that middle-class rural and urban nonworking and working-class poor-school-attendance areas had a smaller percentage of trustee principals, 54 percent and 48 percent respectively, than attendance areas with other socioeconomic characteristics and community type.[32]

All of the representative types were found to involve parents in school matters. The major difference was in the manner and impact of the involvement. By definition the delegate and politico recognize the legitimacy of and work to make possible the substantive involvement of parents. The trustee is more likely to see the involvement as a necessary evil and keep it to the lowest possible level.

THE SCHOOL EXECUTIVE AS COMMUNITY RESOURCE DEVELOPER

School executives can better determine the nature and extent of interaction with the school community and the perspective from which the community liaison subrole is performed by examining their communities against the ideas discussed in this chapter. We suggest such individual analysis. Further, contingency thinking about external relationships is strongly suggested. The selection of a dominant orientation to external relationships, like the choice of a basic approach to working with teachers and students, involves working through forces in the school executive, forces in others, and forces in the environment. The values perspective of this book, however, suggests parameters for preferred patterns of performance. In this concluding section we briefly discuss the school executive's performance of the community liaison role.

We begin by suggesting that *community resource developer* is an appropriate concept from which to begin. It holds open the potential for growth and development of individuals and groups external to the school but with legitimate interests in school affairs as well as providing for attitudes, processes, and structures defined in the negotiator-statesman role model. Concern for development of human resources in the community is the base against which the politico might move between trustee and delegate representational roles.

Performing the subrole of community resource developer rests on three sets of assumptions that are restatements of those delineated in Chapter 10.

1. Assumptions about the interests and capabilities of individuals and groups in the community:
   a. Most parents and citizens have legitimate interests in the effective and efficient functioning of schools.
   b. A majority of the individuals and groups are capable of increased understanding of and contribution to policy making for schools.
2. Assumptions about school executive behavior:
   a. The school executive's task is to help the board of education and other educators create an environment that facilitates the involvement of individuals and groups in the definition of education in schools and means to obtain resources to operate schools that approximate that definition.
   b. The school executive should lead in the development of structures to mediate conflicts in the definition of education and ways in which that definition can be implemented.
   c. The school executive should attempt to expand the opportunities for individuals and groups to increase their knowledge of schools and to engage in reciprocal influence exchanges with educators in the schools.
3. Assumptions about expectations for processes and ends:
   a. In the long term the quality of community and school interaction will improve as individuals and groups increase understanding and engage in reciprocal influence exchanges.
   b. Parents and citizens will exercise responsible self-direction and control and will increase their overall support for the school policies and programs they have helped to develop.
   c. Overall satisfaction with the schools will increase as community-school interaction improves the quality of schooling for pupils and, concurrently, helps individuals and groups grow and develop.

Of course the environment is turbulent. And yet schools experience difficulty in attracting parents and citizens to participate in school affairs, in some instances even to visit schools. Groups of parents and citizen and community organizations elect instead to engage only in power politics in the school community. The concept of community resource developer serves as the benchmark against which the superintendent or principal works as conflict is confronted and power coalitions countered. Parent groups at the school level and parent and other citizen groups at the district level form both the first line of defense against total disruption of the schools as well as the creative, often underutilized resources from which to construct more effective schools to serve children and young people.

Not all parents and other citizens individually hold the same degree of interest in participating in or influencing the formation of school policy. Similarly, total school communities vary, thus permitting significant variation in the formal structures created to effect participation. The performance of the community liaison role from the perspective of the community resource developer will provide a growth context for future interactions however frequent and conflict laden. It does not suggest the avoidance of considering conflicting views; rather, it accepts them as inevitable and treats them as educational experiences for participants.

Notes

1. See Fred D. Carver, "A Return to Rhetoric: School Administration Textbook Literature from 1946 to 1955," a paper presented at the 1978 annual meeting of the American Educational Research Association, Toronto, Ontario, March 27–30, 1978, 15 pp.
2. Neal Gross, *Who Runs Our Schools?* (New York: John Wiley & Sons, Inc., 1962).
3. Jay Scribner, ed., *The Politics of Education: The Seventy–sixth Yearbook of the NSSE, Part II* (Chicago: NSSE—University of Chicago Press, 1977).
4. See, for example: Warner Bloomberg, Jr., and Morris Sunshine, *Suburban Power Structures and Public Education* (Syracuse, N.Y.: Syracuse University Press, 1963); Robert S. Cahill and Stephen P. Hencley, eds., *The Politics of Education in the Local Community* (Danville, Ill.: The Interstate Printers and Publishers, Inc., 1964); Ralph Kimbrough, *Political Power and Educational Decision* (Chicago: Rand McNally, 1964); Nicholas Masters et al., *State Politics and the Public Schools* (New York: Knopf, 1964); Harman Zeigler, *The Political World of the High School Teacher* (Eugene: CASEA, University of Oregon, 1966); Lawrence Iannaccone and Frank Lutz, *Politics, Power and Policy: The Governing of Local School Districts* (Columbus, Ohio: Charles E. Merrill Publishing Co., 1970); Harry L. Summerfield, *The Neighborhood-Based Politics of Education* (Columbus, Ohio: Charles

E. Merrill Publishing Co., 1971); Frederick Wirt and Michael W. Kirst, *The Political Web of American Schools* (Boston: Little, Brown and Company, Inc., 1972); Michael Kirst, ed., *State, School, and Politics* (Lexington, Mass.: D. C. Heath and Company, 1972); Harry F. Wolcott, *Man in the Principal's Office: An Ethnography* (New York: Holt, Rinehart and Winston, 1973); William R. Miles, *Home-School-Community Relations as a Political Process: Four Exploratory Case Studies of the Implementation of Individually Guided Education (IGE) and Home-School-Community Relations* (Madison: Wisconsin Research and Development Center for Cognitive Learning, The University of Wisconsin [Technical Report No. 360, 3 vols.], 1975); Dale Mann, *The Politics of Administrative Representation* (Lexington, Mass.: D. C. Heath and Company, 1976); Louis H. Masotti and Robert L. Lineberry, eds., *The New Urban Politics* (Cambridge, Mass.: Ballinger, 1976), especially chap. 3.

5. Parsons differentiates between/among levels within organizations in terms of functions, placing the managerial level between the technical level (where the purposive activities are performed; in schools, the teaching-learning activities) and the institutional level (where the organization is formally linked to its environment; in schools, the board of education is the structural role at this level). Roles at the managerial level organize and direct the tasks of roles at the technical level and mediate between that level and the institutional level. See Talcott Parsons, "Some Ingredients of a General Theory of Formal Organization," in Andrew W. Halpin, ed., *Administrative Theory in Education* (Toronto, Ontario: Macmillan, 1969).

6. See, for example, Donald J. McCarty and Charles E. Ramsey, *The School Managers* (Westport, Conn.: Greenwood Publishing Corporation, 1971).

7. As used in this section and throughout the chapter community is not used in a precise definitional sense. The commonplace meaning of a (school) community is intended: individuals, groups, and institutions that exist within the geographical area identified with/by a school district. For a discussion of definitions of community, see Luvern L. Cunningham, "Community Power: Implications for Education," in Robert S. Cahill and Stephen P. Hencley, eds., *The Politics of Education in the Local Community* (Danville, Ill.: The Interstate Printers and Publishers, Inc., 1964), pp. 29–31.

8. Floyd Hunter, *Community Power Structure* (Chapel Hill: University of North Carolina Press, 1953).

9. Fred D. Carver and Donald O. Crowe, "An Interdisciplinary Framework for the Study of Community Power," *Educational Administration Quarterly* 5 (Winter 1969): 50–65.

10. John Walton, "A Systematic Survey of Community Power Research," in Michael Aiken and Paul Mott, eds., *The Structure of Community Power* (New York: Random House, 1970), pp. 443–64.

11. Ibid., pp. 452–53.

12. McCarty and Ramsey, *The School Managers.*

13. Lawrence Iannaccone and Frank Lutz, *Politics, Power and Policy: The Governing of Local School Districts* (Columbus, Ohio: Charles E. Merrill Publishing Co., 1970), pp. 29–35.
14. Howard Becker, *Through Values to Social Interpretation* (Durham, N.C.: Duke University Press, 1950), especially chap. 5.
15. Ibid., pp. 252–53.
16. See, for example, Alan Peshkin, "Whom Shall the Schools Serve? Some Dilemmas of Local Control in a Rural School District," *Curriculum Inquiry* 6, no. 3 (1977):181–204.
17. Iannaccone and Lutz, *Politics, Power and Policy*, p. 34.
18. F. E. Emery and E. L. Trist, "The Causal Texture of Organizational Environments," *Human Relations* 18 (1965):21–31.
19. Ibid., p. 22.
20. Frederick M. Wirt, "Political Turbulence and Administrative Authority in the Schools," in Louis H. Masotti and Robert L. Lineberry, eds., *The New Urban Politics* (Cambridge, Mass.: Ballinger Publishing Company, 1976), pp. 61–89.
21. Shirley Terreberry, "The Evolution of Organizational Environments," *Administrative Science Quarterly* 12 (March 1968): 590–613.
22. Alan K. Gaynor, "The Study of Change in Educational Organizations: A Review of the Literature," a paper presented at the UCEA—Ohio State University Career Development Seminar, Columbus, Ohio, March 27–30, 1975 (37 pages), p. 21.
23. Wirt, "Political Turbulence and Administrative Authority," p. 81.
24. Larry Cuban, "Urban Superintendents: Vulnerable Experts," *Phi Delta Kappan* 53, no. 4 (December 1974): 279–282.
25. Ibid., pp. 280–281.
26. See note 5.
27. Paul R. Lawrence and Jay W. Lorsch, *Organizations and Environment: Managing Differentiation and Integration* (Boston: Division of Research, Graduate School of Business Administration, Harvard University, 1967).
28. Jay W. Lorsch and John J. Morse, *Organizations and Their Members: A Contingency Approach* (New York: Harper & Row, Publishers, 1974).
29. Dale Mann, *The Politics of Administrative Representation* (Lexington, Mass.: D. C. Heath and Company, 1976).
30. Ibid., p. 11 (emphasis added).
31. Ibid., p. 38.
32. Ibid., pp. 30–65.

Part V
THE ACTION
SYSTEM

Chapter 14
The School Executive and Leadership

Leadership, leader, leader behavior, leadership functions, leadership styles, and leader-group relations—all are concepts which call attention to a dual concern of the school executive: that there is forward movement in the organization and that the executive is instrumental in effecting the progress. To be characterized as a leader is, implicitly, to be complimented. The obverse is equally true. Thus the message is clear: "Demonstrate leadership." Several obvious questions follow, however. What is leadership? What are its ends? How is it demonstrated? What is appropriate behavior for the leader? What is effective leadership?

In this chapter we discuss these questions. We begin by offering some definitions of the concept of leadership, and by examining ways in which scholars have studied leadership. We then focus on the leadership concerns of the school executive, and analyze the behavior and style of those engaged in leadership activities. We conclude the chapter by suggesting a synthesis of those ideas that seem to us to serve as benchmarks for the school executive as efforts are made to meet the demand for leadership.

Although it will become obvious that we do not conceive of leadership so narrowly as to restrict its exercise only to specific positions within formal groups, we should restate that we are concerned primarily with persons who are designated as administrators in formal school settings.

DEFINITIONS

According to Katz and Kahn,[1] there are three major meanings attached to the concept of leadership in the social science literature: a positional attribute, a personal characteristic, and a category of behavior. These three major meanings are implicit in certain of the definitions which follow and are generally observed in the subsequent discussion of the history of scholarly investigation of leadership.

Pigors, in 1935, defined leadership as "a process of mutual stimulation which, by successful interplay of relevant differences, controls human energy in the pursuit of a common cause."[2] Explicit in the definition is the notion of dynamic interaction between a leader and followers working toward agreed-upon goals. The same themes are evident in Stogdill's definition, "the process (act) of influencing the activities of an organized group in its efforts toward goal setting and goal achievement."[3]

A more action-oriented definition of leadership is the one proposed by Hemphill, the initiation of "a structure-in-interaction as part of the process of solving a mutual problem."[4] Lipham, in differentiating leadership from administration, modified the Hemphill definition only slightly. He defined leadership as "the initiation of a new structure or procedure for accomplishing an organization's goals and objectives or for changing an organization's goals and objectives."[5] As Lipham observes, this definition calls attention not only to action but to specific kinds of action: goal attainment or goal change. If one adds the adjective "educational" before "organization's" in the definition, one has what is perhaps the most commonly used definition of leadership in educational administration. One final definition of leadership is offered for its brevity as well as potency. Wilson, Ramseyer, and Immegart define leadership as "a directed social force."[6] In a recent commentary on leadership, Cunningham explicates the complexity as well as the directedness of leadership: "It (leadership) is the curious blending of leading and following, provoking and calming, disturbing and stabilizing, but always in a posture of movement, generating new strength and capability along the way."[7]

All of the definitions just presented were deliberately selected for their focus on leadership as a process, to the exclusion of the individual engaged in the process. Obviously, though, the process involves people who are leaders. Somewhat more clarity regarding the process of leadership is obtained by attempting to arrive at a definition of leader.

Halpin notes that the most common usage of the term "leader" is in relation to "an outstanding member of a class."[8] The school executive qualifies as a leader, according to this definition, by virtue of assigned responsibilities. Interestingly, it would be possible to convert any of the preceding definitions of leadership to definitions of leader by single-word changes. Thus the leader is the individual responsible for "the process of mutual stimulation" (Pigors); "the process of solving a mutual problem" (Hemphill); "the initiation of a new structure of procedure" (Lipham); or "a directed social force" (Wilson, Ramseyer, and Immegart). Fiedler, after reviewing the definitional problems, settled on a definition which is generally consistent with our thinking. He defines the leader as "the individual in the group given the task of directing and coordinating task-relevant group activities or who, in the absence of a designated leader, carries the primary responsibility for performing these functions in the group."[9]

As will be apparent when we discuss functions of the leader, we are concerned that this definition should not be interpreted so as to rule out the leader's concern for activities other than those associated with task accomplishment (e.g., initiating action, keeping members' attention on the goal, clarifying the issue, developing a procedural plan, evaluating the quality of work done, and making expert information available).[10] Substantive matters underlying the task-oriented activities are, of course, those for which the school system exists. However, there is another important dimension of group behavior—group maintenance activities (e.g., keeping interpersonal relations pleasant when arbitrating disputes, providing encouragement, giving the minority a chance to be heard, stimulating self-direction, and increasing the interdependence among members).[11] Under our conception of leadership these two dimensions are not mutually exclusive and the leader has some responsibility for both. Perhaps what we are saying is that the school executive (as the leader) is "the individual charged with the tasks of 'directing and coordinating' the group activities necessary to achieve or change goals." In our view, this definition negates neither the necessity nor legitimacy of informal groups and leaders. Rather, it calls attention to the formal school organization and its task and maintenance needs and goals.

SCHOLARLY ROUTES OF INQUIRY

Initial attempts at studying the leadership phenomenon were aimed at personal attributes of leaders. The notion was that if one could identify the traits of successful leaders, then the selection of persons with those traits would ensure goal achievement. There is some face validity to this argument and approach. At the intuitive level it is still used in selecting persons to fill school executive positions. Intelligent, tall, well-dressed individuals with athletic-type physiques, for instance, are probably the preferred school superintendent type. Stogdill's conclusion, following his classic review of the leadership literature[12]—that it is not certain traits per se which make a person a leader, but these traits in combination with certain dimensions of the followers—summarizes majority opinion on the subject of leader determination by attributes. Furthermore, he suggested the second route for scholars studying leadership to follow—namely, consideration of the group or the situation.

Groups became the focus for researchers in the hope that one might identify conditions under which an individual could effectively function as a leader. Although perhaps never excluding characteristics of the leader to the extent that the earlier researchers had ignored the group, investigations into the setting for leadership led most to conclude that leader effectiveness depends on the meshing of leader and group characteristics. As a result, three approaches are present in most recent theorizing and research about leaders and leadership.

The first of these approaches focuses on the behavior of the leader in interaction with followers. That is, the concern is not with personal or psychological traits of the leader but with *how* the leading process is performed. Closely related to this approach which gives attention to leader behavior is an approach giving attention to the functions of leadership—the "what" with which leaders are concerned. The third and most recent approach, exemplified by Fiedler's contingency theory of leadership effectiveness[13] and Hersey and Blanchard's situational leadership theory,[14] seeks to isolate the "it-depends" variables in relation to some particular leader characteristic, style, or orientation.

After a brief treatment of the leadership concerns of the school executive and attention to certain of the behavior/style dimensions of leadership, we shall return to these three current emphases.

LEADERSHIP CONCERNS OF THE SCHOOL EXECUTIVE

There are three areas of concern for the school executive who would lead:[15] (1) the executive's behavior; (2) the development of others; and (3) group leadership functions. It is difficult even for analytical purposes to separate the three concerns. The importance of each warrants the effort, however.

The Executive's Behavior

Although the school executive who would lead must have subleaders and a receptive group, it is not possible to escape the spotlight. Subordinates expect acknowledgment of this key responsibility through modeling behavior. It is not that the executive must determine appropriate behavioral styles for all in the school organization. Nor should it be expected that only the executive can perform the more prestigious leadership acts although certain of the symbolic acts tend to be reserved for the executive of a unit, for example, a school or district. Failure, however, to direct and coordinate group activities necessary to change and/or achieve goals is an abdication of leadership responsibility. It should be noted that the school executive's leader behavior may well not affect specific activities, but rather the structures, processes, and procedures by and through which the activities are conducted. Positive action is required from the school executive to ensure that structures, processes, and procedures are present and functioning. To borrow an analogy from decision-making literature, concern for the executive's behavior is related to its affecting opportunities subleaders have for exhibiting leadership.[16]

There are activities within the immediate work context of the school executive which demand action. The school executive who forever fails personally to suggest "structures" for these activities is abdicating the leader role. For example, the principal or superintendent who persists in ignoring problems concerning staff morale, student behavior, or curriculum content—even after everyone concerned admits to their existence—is engaging in abdicating behavior. At least there might be an opportunity scheduled for the group to discuss the problem—at a faculty meeting, perhaps. Or the problem might specifically be brought to the attention of the faculty with a request for solutions. A third behavioral choice would be to suggest a procedure by which the problem could be attacked. Or, further still, the executive could offer alternative solutions to the group.

The Development of Others

This second concern of the school executive is for the development of leadership potential in others in the school system. For three different reasons this is an important concern. First, effective movement toward goal achievement requires the efforts of numerous groups. Energetic, positive personal leadership by a superintendent is thwarted—perhaps negated—by failures of principals to behave in a similar manner.

Second, the school's manifest function is the development of human resources, its pupils. Its professional employees should obviously enjoy some of the same attention. Indeed, the fact that the schools are staffed with professionally oriented individuals should suggest that they too are prepared to exercise leadership in selected areas of activities.

Finally, admitting a bias toward thinking of organizational leadership as a set of functions to be performed, we suggest that certain individuals are able to perform one kind of function better than other individuals. Since total organizational performance is related to the extent and manner in which all of the functions are performed, the school executive, as leader, must be concerned with the development of leadership potential in others in the school organization.

Consider the principal and the principal's assistants; principal A—who encourages his or her assistants to initiate action, shares needed information, and supports action once initiated—is more likely to effect goal achievement than is principal B—who does none of these things with his assistants. Perhaps the threat of competition for organizational rewards and affection prevents the "leader" from giving more attention to this concern.

Group Leadership Functions

There are two meanings attached to the concept of functions, as used in the leadership literature. The first relates to the two essential sets of conditions which must exist in any group (e.g., a formally organized school group) for its continued existence. We identified these, when we defined leader, as goal achievement and group maintenance activities. Likert describes the same activities as "group task roles" and "group building roles."[17] Scholars who focus on the behavior of leaders are concerned with the relative emphasis placed on "getting the job done" or "showing concern for people."[18]

The second meaning attached to the concept of functions refers to specific processes or steps required for action by a school group as it interacts with problem situations. (These processes or steps approximate Bales's "interaction" categories.)[19] That is to say, the leader is concerned with identifying and defining the problem; defining criteria for acceptable solutions; and providing information, seeking opinions, and the like. Wilson, Ramseyer, and Immegart[20] delineate 13 of these specific functions in 5 sequential steps. We have modified and merged the steps and specific functions into 7 functions. We shall return to these seven functions in the final section of the chapter. The 7 functions are:

1. Making the group aware of the need for new or different action—awareness.
2. Clarifying alternative ends and strategies—settling on action.
3. Accepting and initiating a preferred end or approach—implementing.
4. Monitoring the progress toward the preferred end or approach—procession.
5. Introducing evaluative data—evaluating.
6. Concluding group activity regarding the particular end or approach—concluding.
7. Making the group aware of its results—feedback.

We call attention to both meanings attached to the concept of functions at this point, for both are important to the success of the leader. The former reminds the school executive of maintenance as well as achievement needs of the group, and the latter calls attention to the multidimensionality of leading.

Putting aside for the moment the task or function the leader is engaged in, we may focus on how the leader behaves.[21] This approach assumes that the way individuals in leadership positions behave is related to effectiveness of performance of the group's goals. It also assumes that behavior can be dimensionalized sufficiently to enable the student of leadership to assess patterns of behavior of the leader.

Dimensions of Leader Behavior

Just as group activities can be compressed into two major dimensions—goal achievement and group maintenance—so can behavior of leaders. Researchers who have investigated the behavior associated with leadership typically end up with two major dimensions, factors, clusters, or categories: one set of behaviors related to the task of getting the job done; and one set of behaviors related to a concern for people.[22] Foremost among instruments to assess leader behavior is the Leader Behavior Description Questionnaire (LBDQ) developed initially by Hemphill and Coons at the Ohio State University.[23]

Halpin and Winer,[24] working from the original LBDQ, identified the two major dimensions tested by this instrument as initiation structure and consideration. A more recent version of the LBDQ (Form 12) has been prepared by Stogdill.[25] This newest LBDQ-XII, encompassing 12 subscales, was also found by Brown[26] to yield two major factors, which he labeled "system" orientation and "person" orientation. Brown concluded that the two factorial dimensions of leader behavior were "familiar and meaningful" and were "first cousins" of the two major dimensions previously identified by scholars, including Halpin's initiating structure and consideration.[27] Thus we conclude that the Halpin dimensions are representative of the various categorizations and are useful concepts to use in an abbreviated treatment of leader behavior. They are also probably the most widely known among educational administrators. Let us look at the specific behavior the LBDQ taps with the two dimensions and report the consensus findings with respect to effectiveness.

Initiating structure behavior "refers to the leader's behavior in delineating the relationship between himself and members of the work-group, and in endeavoring to establish well-defined patterns of organization, channels of communication, and methods of procedure."[28] Items which assess initiating structure behavior on the part of a leader are:

1. He makes his attitudes clear to the staff.
2. He tries out his new ideas with the staff.
3. He rules with an iron hand.*
4. He criticizes poor work.
5. He speaks in a manner not to be questioned.
6. He assigns staff members to particular tasks.
7. He works without a plan.*
8. He maintains definite standards of performance.
9. He emphasizes the meeting of deadlines.
10. He encourages the use of uniform procedures.
11. He makes sure that his part in the organization is understood by all members.
12. He asks that staff members follow standard rules and regulations.
13. He lets staff members know what is expected of them.
14. He sees to it that staff members are working up to capacity.
15. He sees to it that the work of staff members is coordinated.[29]

*Scored negatively

Behavior classified as consideration "refers to behavior indication of friendship, mutual trust, respect, and warmth in the relationship between the leader and the members of his staff."[30] Items on the LBDQ questionnaire which assess the extent to which a leader exhibits consideration are:

1. He does personal favors for staff members.
2. He does little things to make it pleasant to be a member of his staff.
3. He is easy to understand.
4. He finds time to listen to staff members.
5. He keeps to himself.*
6. He looks out for the personal welfare of individual staff members.
7. He refuses to explain his actions.*
8. He acts without consulting the staff.*
9. He is slow to accept new ideas.*
10. He treats all staff members as his equals.
11. He is willing to make changes.
12. He is friendly and approachable.
13. He makes staff members feel at ease when talking with them.
14. He puts suggestions made by the staff into operation.
15. He gets staff approval on important matters before going ahead.[31]

*Scored negatively

Respondents rate their leader's behavior on a five-point scale: always, often, occasionally, seldom, or never. It is possible, of course, for respondents to describe an ideal leader, or for leaders to describe their behavior as the way they think a leader should behave. Scores on the two dimensions are obtained by summing across items and respondents and dividing by the number of respondents (a teaching faculty, for instance).

Perhaps the most important point about initiating structure and consideration behaviors is that they are not arranged on one continuum. On the contrary, they are two separate dimensions which may range from low to high in any individual. The two types of behavior (or LBDQ scores representing the two) may be plotted on horizontal and vertical axes which intersect at the mean points to create four quadrants. A leader's scores place the leader in one of the four quadrants (e.g., if scores are below the mean on consideration and above the mean on initiating structure, the leader would

The Action System

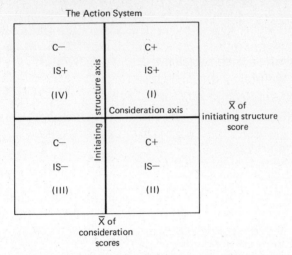

Figure 14-1   Quadrants depicting the two dimensions of leader behavior derived from the LBDQ. (Source: Adapted from Andrew W. Halpin, "The Superintendent's Effectiveness as a Leader," *Administrator's Notebook 7* [October 1958], p. 2.)

be in a different quadrant of the figure than if the scores were above the mean on both dimensions). Figure 14-1 illustrates the dual dimensionality of the behaviors.

The consensus of empirical researchers is that an individual who exhibits both dimensions of behavior—has high scores on consideration and initiating structure (Quadrant I in Figure 14-1)—is the most effective of any of the four combinations in accomplishing goals of the group. Members of the leader's work groups express a preference for this kind of leader also—that is, "ideal leaders" are described as scoring high on both dimensions. These findings are consistent furthermore with those of Blake and Mouton, who assess managerial behavior on two dimensions—concern for people and concern for production—and plot scores on an 81-celled grid.[32]

Theoretically, individuals might adjust their behavior to suit the particular situation. Thus unless a school executive was observed to be devoid of one of the two behaviors (consideration and initiating structure or whatever other typologies are used), it should be possible for the executive to move between the two to accomplish goals. Within reasonable limits, this position is probably sound. However, behavior tends toward consistency, and scholars concerned with identifying the ultimate in effectiveness of leader behavior have come to use the concept of leadership style or orientation in reference to the modal way in which a leader behaves. Describing leaders in style terms tends to mask the independence of the two dimensions of behavior and to force thinking into an either/or mold. Leadership style or orientation research, however, has been instrumental in helping to clarify conditions (the "it-depends" variables) under which one kind of behavior is more appropriate for goal achievement than another kind.

LEADERSHIP STYLES

With the Getzels-Guba social systems theory (see Chapter 9) as a referent, Guba and Bidwell[33] and Moser[34] derived three styles of leadership:

1. *Nomothetic* The leader emphasizes the demands of the organization—expectations for role occupants, rules, regulations.
2. *Idiographic* The leader emphasizes the needs of the individual—for being treated in a considerate manner, autonomy, doing "one's own thing."
3. *Transactional* The leader attempts to negotiate a course between the two extremes, at times engaging in nomothetic behavior and at other times engaging in idiographic behavior.

Although nomothetic style is not necessarily synonymous with initiating structure behavior, there is some definitional similarity. In the same sense, there are similarities between idiographic style and consideration behavior. Transactional leadership style, in its best form, seems to be a manifestation of the behavior of a leader who has considerable capacity for both initiating structure and consideration behavior. It should be noted that we are again speaking of the two major sets of activities essential to effective group functioning: goal achievement and group maintenance. In any event, leadership style research in ongoing organized groups has yielded essentially the same finding as leader behavior research: Group members prefer the transactional style of leadership, and it is generally the single most effective style.

Fiedler[35] has approached leadership style from a different perspective. Utilizing the concept of psychological orientation in preference to style, he classifies leaders as task oriented or interpersonal relations oriented on the basis of the way they describe the individual with whom they least like to work. Fiedler's conclusion, following dozens of investigations in controlled situations, is that the most effective leadership style is dependent upon three conditions:

1. Relations between the leader and group members.
2. Nature of the task to be accomplished—whether structured or unstructured.
3. Position power of leader.[36]

Our intent is not to delineate the Fiedler contingency model. The theory is of interest at this point because of the slightly different connotation it attaches to leadership style and its explication of specific "it-depends" variables relative to style and effectiveness. The leadership style variable in the theory is not directly based on behavior. It is, as already noted, inferred from psychological orientation as reflected in a description of the Least Preferred Co-worker.[37] The "contingency" variables are empirically derived situational determinants of effectiveness of leadership style in achieving group tasks. Thus the theory effectively combines the psychological and sociological approaches to the study of leadership. The assumption is not that leadership is or is not present in given situations. To the contrary, leadership acts are essential to goal achievement and the situational variables determine only what is the most effective leadership style. A simplified statement of the theory appears in the following equation:

$$\frac{\text{Appropriate leadership style}}{\text{Task-oriented style or inter-personal-relations-oriented style}} \; \text{for} \; \frac{\text{effective goal achievement}}{\text{organizational or group tasks}} \; \text{is a function of} \; \frac{\text{three variables}}{\begin{array}{l} 1. \text{ leader-member relations} \\ 2. \text{ task structure} \\ 3. \text{ leader position power} \end{array}}$$

Halal[38] suggests a metatheory of leadership that relates style, effectiveness, and situational variables. His theory is derived from a synthesis of the leadership literature and is similar to Fiedler's theory in its form, but it contains only two situational variables. These two variables, task technology and subordinate motivation, are conceived of as continuous variables, with the former ranging from simplicity to complexity and the latter from materialism to idealism. Leadership style is conceived to be continuous from directiveness to permissiveness. Leadership effectiveness, according to Halal's theory is a matter of congruence among the three variables.[39]

Situational leadership theory, developed by Hersey and Blanchard and applied to education by Gates,[40] singles out the maturity of followers as the contingent variable for task or relationship behavior. Reddin[41] related behavior of the manager, organizational effectiveness, and situational variables in a three-dimensional theory. Effectiveness, in the Reddin theory, is a function of the matching of behavior (style) with the situational variables of technology, expectations and styles of others, and organization traditions. Reddin's conceptualization is that there are eight basic styles (rather than four as derived from the initiating-structure–consideration quadrant and the Hersey and Blanchard frameworks): four effective and four ineffective.

We are now in a position to understand why group members generally prefer a transactional leader—a leader who is high on both initiating structure and consideration. Most administrative role occupants are expected to "lead" at all times. The conditions under which they operate, although modal in terms of situational variables, are constantly changing. There are times, for instance, when goal achievement needs to be emphasized. At other periods in the weekly, monthly, or yearly cycle of a school, group maintenance needs assume priority. Group members, therefore, when asked to describe the behavior of an "ideal" leader (principal, superintendent, or whatever) respond in a holistic sense. They prefer the individual who can emphasize task and interpersonal relations. Similarly, permanent leaders in groups with multiple tasks are most effective if they are able to exhibit both dimensions or both styles of behavior.

LEADERSHIP: A SYNTHESIS

After this brief look at the concepts of leader behavior and leadership styles, let us conclude by attempting a synthesis of the primary components of leadership. These primary components consist of four independent sets of variables: leader behavior, group tasks, specific leadership functions related to group tasks, and variables of intervention. All of the components of the synthesis were presented earlier in the chapter. One can derive most, if not all, of the conceptual tools surrounding the leadership transaction from the synthesis. The components will now be specifically identified and defined; they will then be summarized schematically; finally, we shall discuss them in direct relationship to the school executive.

Leader Behavior

The first set of variables comprises the specific behavioral tendencies of the leader. Consistent with and derived from the several formulations in the literature, we conceive of two kinds of behavior. First, there are specific behavioral acts which call attention to the accomplishment of whatever task the group is working toward—task behavior. An individual may exhibit little, some, or much task behavior. The second kind of behavior recognizes the presence of the human element and defers to the basic human considerations of security, respect, dignity, autonomy, and worth—person behavior.

Group Tasks

Paralleling the behaviors of the leader are the two perpetual group tasks: goal achievement and group maintenance. Goal achievement tasks refer to those tasks for which the group was formed and continues to exist. Schools exist to further the education of their students—through the teaching of reading, preparation for life, the learning of occupational skills, and the like. Group maintenance tasks refer to those tasks which keep the work group reasonably cohesive, thus enabling goal achievement. The line between group maintenance and goal achievement tasks becomes thin indeed in essentially human organizations such as schools. For example, in the sense that reasonable school-community cohesiveness is affected by transportation practices in a school district, a school executive's tasks related to transportation are group maintenance tasks. In general we would think that most staff personnel tasks are group maintenance tasks in character. Communication and coordination activities of the school executive clearly fuse the two tasks of group maintenance and group achievement. It should be noted that a major difficulty with the goal achievement–group maintenance dichotomy is the tendency to consider the former important and the latter unimportant. As we view the two, goal achievement is indeed prior and ultimate in importance, but only because without minimum level fulfillment there would be no group to maintain.

Leadership Functions

Leadership functions may be thought of as necessary events in the course of a group's movement from one task or set of tasks to another task or set of tasks. Similar to the more deliberate decision-making models, they are sequential and cyclical. That is, the functions occur generally in order and continually reoccur. Depending on the exigencies of the situation, one or more may occur naturally or be bypassed entirely. Although the school executive who is the "leader" of a particular group has responsibility for ensuring that these functions occur, we do not conceive of the executive necessarily performing all of them. The functions are:

1. Making the group aware of the need for new or different action—awareness.
2. Clarifying alternative ends and strategies—settling on action.
3. Accepting and initiating a preferred end or approach—implementing.
4. Monitoring of progress toward the preferred end or approach—processing.
5. Introducing evaluative data—evaluating.
6. Concluding group activity on the particular end or approach—concluding.
7. Making the group aware of its result—feedback.

Variables of Intervention

As Fiedler has so forcefully demonstrated, the effectiveness of a particular behavior orientation is related to three contingencies of the situation:

1. *Leader-member relations*—the state of the affect between the leader and members of his group; psychological togetherness.
2. *Task structure*—the nature of the structure of the task to which leadership is directed.
3. *Position power of the leader*—objectively, the amount of control the leader has by virtue of being designated leader.

In the event that a situation for leadership is so characterized that the designated leader could not provide effective leadership, others in the work group might be relied on to perform leadership functions. At another time, when the contingencies have changed, the designated leader could effectively perform the functions of leadership.

THE LEADERSHIP SYNTHESIS AND THE SCHOOL EXECUTIVE

Paramount in our concern in offering this synthesis is that leadership should not be conceived of totally as the prerogative of an individual, even if the individual is officially designated as responsible for acts of leading. Yet we recognize that the school executive has responsibilities—as this designated "leader"—for making sure that both goal achievement and group maintenance activities are effectively carried out. In one sense our synthesis confirms what insightful school executives have recognized for some time, namely, that there is more than one way of getting the job done— even the leadership job. It is intended to say more than that, however. Let us work through the framework systematically.

A school executive must be a leader of leaders. That is, the executive does not have to be personally and directly responsible for the performance of the seven leadership functions. Situational variables are not always arranged so that any one individual would be most effective all of the time. Even though a given school may be generally characterized as having good leader-member relations, structured tasks, and strong position power, there are times when subunits—departments, grade levels, or buildings—would not fit that modal characterization. Further, any one school executive would be hard-pressed to identify constantly the needed emphasis on the appropriate goal. Thus subleaders are essential; and the school executive, the designated leader, is a leader of these leaders.

Even if a school executive were sufficiently perceptive to identify the group task most in need of attention and were generally capable in the particular functional area, that individual's range of task or person behavior may be severely limited. For instance, an otherwise perfect leadership situation may be thwarted because a school executive who is strongly person-oriented blunders along or, worse yet, has no task-oriented subleader who can perform the leadership act. Thus the functions concept applied to leadership helps to clarify a phenomenon which is commonly observed. Some individuals are effective in creating awareness, others are expert at implementing, still others at evaluating, and so on. For optimizing leadership effectiveness and ultimately total school effectiveness, leadership functions call attention to the need for group leadership in addition to individual leader behavior on the part of the school executive.

The components of the synthesis, in our view, call attention to the appropriateness, for administrative effectiveness, of involving as many members of the group as possible in all activities, including leadership activities. Under those conditions, whether the school executive is task or person oriented is, thus, less relevant than whether that person insists upon being responsible for effective organizational functioning.

Notes

1. Daniel Katz and Robert Kahn, *The Social Psychology of Organizations* (New York: John Wiley, 1966), p. 301.

2. Paul J. W. Pigors, *Leadership and Domination* (Boston: Houghton Mifflin, 1935), p. 16.
3. Ralph Stogdill, "Leadership, Membership and Organization," *Psychological Bulletin* 47 (January 1950):4.
4. John K. Hemphill, "Administration as Problem Solving," in *Administrative Theory in Education*, Andrew W. Halpin, ed. (Chicago: Midwest Administration Center, 1958), p. 98.
5. James M. Lipham, "Leadership and Administration," in *Behavioral Science and Educational Administration: The Sixty-third Yearbook of the National Society for the Study of Education*, Part II, Daniel Griffiths, ed. (Chicago: The Society, 1964), p. 122.
6. Harold Wilson, John Ramseyer, and Glenn Immegart, "The Group and Its Leaders," Ohio State University, Department of Education, Center for Educational Administration, 1963 (mimeographed), p. 2.
7. Luvern L. Cunningham, "Educational Leadership: The Curious Blend" (editorial), *Educational Leadership* 33 (February 1976): 324.
8. Andrew W. Halpin, *Theory and Research in Administration* (New York: Macmillan, 1966), p. 81.
9. Fred E. Fiedler, *A Theory of Leadership Effectiveness* (New York: McGraw-Hill, 1967), p. 8.
10. Dorwin Cartwright and Alvin Zander, eds., *Group Dynamics*, 3rd ed. (New York: Harper & Row, 1968), p. 306.
11. Ibid.
12. Ralph M. Stogdill, "Personal Factors Associated with Leadership: A Survey of the Literature," *Journal of Psychology* 25 (January 1948): 35–71.
13. Fiedler, *Theory of Leadership Effectiveness*.
14. Paul Hersey and Kenneth H. Blanchard, *Management of Organizational Behavior*, 3rd ed. (Englewood Cliffs, N.J.: Prentice-Hall Inc., 1977); see Philip E. Gates, Kenneth H. Blanchard, and Paul Hersey, "Diagnosing Educational Leadership Problems: A Situational Approach," *Educational Leadership* 33 (February 1977): 348–54, for a specific application of the Hersey and Blanchard theory which was originally called "Life Cycle Theory of Leadership."
15. There are questions as to whether the emphasis on leadership and conditions in education have produced unrealistic expectations for educational administrators. See, for example, Robert J. Starratt, "Contemporary Talk on Leadership: Too Many Kings in the Parade?" *Notre Dame Journal of Education* 4, no. 1 (1974):5–15, and Francis J. Roberts, "School Principal: Minor Bureaucrat or Educational Leader," *The Urban Review* 8 (Winter 1975):243–250.
16. Diesing ascribes to the chief decision-maker the responsibility for the "political" decision-making structure which controls the other decision-making structures: economic, legal, and social. See Paul Diesing, *Reason in Society* (Urbana, Ill.: University of Illinois Press, 1962).
17. Rensis Likert, *New Patterns of Management* (New York: McGraw-Hill, 1961), chap. 10.
18. For an explication of nine sets of concepts related to these two

dimensions, see David G. Bowers and Stanley E. Seashore, "Predicting Organizational Effectiveness with a Four-Factor Theory of Leadership," *Administrative Science Quarterly* 11 (September 1966): 238–264, especially p. 248.

19. See R. F. Bales, "A Set of Categories for the Analysis of Small Group Interaction," *American Sociological Review* 15 (April 1950): 257–63.

20. Wilson, Ramseyer, and Immegart, "The Group and Its Leaders," pp. 14–16.

21. Actually, most of the instruments developed to assess the behavior of leaders are designed in reference to role occupants in formally organized groups. We point this out because it conforms to our belief that these persons are expected to engage in "leading behavior" and, thus, we need not isolate *pure* leaders or only those acts which are pure leadership acts.

22. See, for example, Bowers and Seashore, "Predicting Organizational Effectiveness"; Andrew W. Halpin, "A Paradigm for Research on Administrator Behavior," in *Administrative Behavior in Education*, Roald F. Campbell and Russell T. Gregg, eds. (New York: Harper & Brothers, 1957), pp. 155–99; and Thomas J. Sergiovanni, Richard Metzcus, and Larry Burden, "Toward a Particularistic Approach to Leadership Style: Some Findings," *American Education Research Journal* 6 (January 1969), 61–79.

23. Halpin, "A Paradigm for Research on Administrative Behavior," p. 170. The Leader Behavior Description Questionnaire is published by the Bureau of Business Research, Ohio State University, Columbus, Ohio. Persmission is required for its use.

24. See Andrew W. Halpin, *The Leadership Behavior of School Superintendents*, 2nd ed. (Chicago: Midwest Administration Center, University of Chicago, 1959; "The Leader Behavior and Leadership Ideology of Educational Administrators and Aircraft Commanders," *Harvard Educational Review* 25 (Winter 1955):18–32; *Theory and Research in Administration* (*supra*, n. 8), chap. 3; and "The Superintendent's Effectiveness as a Leader," *Administrator's Notebook* 7 (October 1958):1–4.

25. Ralph M. Stogdill, *Manual for the Leader Behavior Description Questionnaire—Form XII* (Columbus, Ohio: Bureau of Business Research, Ohio State University, 1963).

26. Alan F. Brown, "Reactions to Leadership," *Educational Administration Quarterly* 3 (Winter 1967):62–73.

27. Ibid., pp. 68–69.

28. Halpin, *Leadership Behavior of School Superintendents*, p. 4.

29. Halpin, *Theory and Research in Administration*, pp. 88–89.

30. Halpin, *Leadership Behavior of School Superintendents*, p. 4.

31. Halpin, *Theory and Research in Administration*, p. 89.

32. Robert R. Blake and Jane S. Mouton, *The Managerial Grid* (Houston, Tex. Gulf Publishing Co., 1964).

33. Egon G. Cuba and Charles E. Bidwell, *Administrative Relationships* (Chicago: Midwest Administration Center, University of Chicago, 1957).

34. Robert P. Moser, "The Leadership Patterns of School Superintendents and School Principals," *Administrator's Notebook* 6 (September 1957):1–4.
35. Fiedler, *Theory of Leadership Effectiveness.*
36. Ibid., chap. 9.
37. Instruments for measuring a leader's style—the Least Preferred Co-worker Scale (LPC)—and each of the intervening variables have been developed by Fiedler and are presented and discussed in *A Theory of Leadership Effectiveness.*
38. William E. Halal, "Toward a General Theory of Leadership," *Human Relations* 27 (April 1974):401–416.
39. Ibid., 409.
40. Gates, Blanchard, and Hersey, "Diagnosing Educational Leadership Problems."
41. William J. Reddin, *Managerial Effectiveness* (New York: McGraw-Hill, 1970).

Chapter 15
Educational Planning and
Systems Concepts

Planning is a process which precedes decision-making. The planning process is differentiated from other predecision activity in that it is systematic, deliberate, and continuous. A number of persistent educational dilemmas are associated with educational planning. The planning process, for example, can lead to democratic and open management or autocratic and closed management; to creativity and flexibility in organizational and human arrangements or rigidity; to more efficiency in utilizing financial and human resources or more wastefulness of these resources, particularly over a long period of time; to building identification and commitment among students and teachers to school goals or to having a demoralizing effect. Planning can further the development of the school as a professional organization or reinforce the school's bureaucratic tendencies. One's approach to planning as a process, the degree to which others are involved in planning, the extent to which discretion is maintained at lower levels of the school, and one's ability to maintain reasonable flexibility are determinants of whether one or another of the directions suggested previously is realized. Depending upon how it is implemented, planning is a powerful administrative tool with both desirable and dangerous, anticipated and unanticipated, consequences.

This chapter begins with an analysis of present approaches to planning in education. This is followed by a discussion of systems concepts and systems analysis—a relatively new and fashionable planning device for school executives. The effects of systems analysis on the school as a bureaucratic organization and as a professional organization are explored. The chapter concludes with a consideration of alternative planning strategies to formal systems analysis. These take the form of what we term a Management Systems Approach (MSA), a Cooperative Systems Approach (CSA), or a Technical Systems Approach (TSA)—each appropriate depending upon the nature of the problems and goals being considered, the persistence or longevity of the problem, the locus of ability authority in the school, and the appropriateness of centralized or decentralized decision-making. MSA is suggested when problems under study and goals being considered are more administrative than instructional, when problems are long range, when the primary locus of ability authority is with school executives rather than with teachers, support professionals, and community, and when centralized decision-making seems appropriate. CSA is suggested when problems and goals are more instructional than administrative, when problems are long range, when the primary locus of ability authority is with teaching and support professionals rather than school executives, and when decentralized decision-making seems appropriate. TSA is suggested for use under both MSA and CSA conditions but for short-term, ad hoc problems involving clear and precise goals and relatively fixed tasks. TSA would be an appropriate strategy for planning a summer workshop, for instance.

PRESENT APPROACHES TO PLANNING

Planning is often viewed as a luxury which few administrators feel they can afford. The stresses of the times, the urgency and complexity of problems facing schools, and the school's tendency to revert to satisfying its needs for survival, for the elimination of uncertainty, and for seeking and maintaining a comfortable state of equilibrium are all deterrents to planning. The highly stressful environment with which the school is faced, combined with its natural defensive tendencies, force school executives into reactive administrative behavior. Typically, reacting to external stimuli (phone, people, messages, etc.) and responding to the school's need to survive, to eliminate uncertainty, and to maintain itself day by day account for the major part of a school executive's time. Getting through the school day, week, or year is often a remarkable achievement indeed.

Dangers of Reactive Planning

A major problem with reactive planning[1] and decision-making is that school executives who practice such "planning" forfeit their right to decide the nature of the problems to which they will be responding. Once this right is forfeited, one begins to lose control over the nature and direction of the organization. The school as an organization, under such circumstances, largely determines the nature of goals school executives and others would pursue, the kinds of activities and behaviors expressed, and ultimately the solutions to these problems. Negative results, a number of which are described next, await schools and school executives who succumb to reactive planning.

1. *Stability is prized* Reactive behavior is inertia based. Periods of inaction are welcome, for they resemble equilibrium and satisfy the need to eliminate uncertainty. Stress is kept to a minimum. Innovation and change are not encouraged because they upset the state of equilibrium, result in stress, and require efforts to bring about a new level of equilibrium. The location, intent, or effect of this new level is often not as important as reaching some level somewhere. This is Management by Appeasement geared to bring about some semblance of calm and stability, with costs in quality and principle secondary.

2. *Defensive Management Is Encouraged* Reactive strategies often result in school executives evaluating decision alternatives in terms of their own safety, security, and status. One who continually responds to stress which is beyond his control soon becomes obsessed with his own survival. The school executive is pitted against a hostile organization and an unsympathetic environment in a win-lose contest.

3. *Paternalism Is Encouraged* Defensive management leads to the establishment of alliances. Decisions are often made on the bases of favoritism and protective trade-offs. Kingdoms are encouraged, and special-interest groups emerge as protective lobbies. Since little attention is given to future planning, uncertainty is actually increased. Information is scarce and prized. In effect, the communications network becomes a control mechanism and reward-granting device,

with school executives buying loyalty from subordinates by permitting them some access to the network. People feel safer when they have some notion of what is going on and will pay for this safety with loyalty.

4. *Long-Range Planning is Forfeited* Reactive strategies are short-term survival—and maintenance—oriented. Little attention is given to long-term goals and directions. Thus although the elimination of uncertainty is important for today, tomorrow's problems are guaranteed because no deliberate attention is given to the future.

5. *Educational Goals Assume the Lowest Status* The most serious result of reactive planning and decision-making is implicit in each of the dangers just discussed. In each case educational goals and the welfare of students are displaced by organizational and administrative needs, goals, and demands. School executives and teachers become defense bound and react to stimuli primarily in terms of promoting their own safety, security, and status. Self-actualization of students and commitment to other educational goals are indeed luxuries under such conditions.

NORMATIVE AND DESCRIPTIVE VIEWS OF PLANNING

Most authorities agree that educational leadership requires proactive postures from school executives. Indeed, it is recognized that a good leader *plans* in advance what to do, how to do it, and when to do it. Further, he *organizes* the means to achieve these ends, provides the necessary personal leadership to others who will perform the activities necessary to achieve goals, and *evaluates* progress. Accordingly, reactive behavior as described previously is viewed as pathological and proactive behavior is prescribed as a remedy. This proactive view with its emphasis on planning is a normative theory of administration—one which specifies or prescribes what school executives should do. Descriptive theories, on the other hand, attempt to provide a more accurate picture of what administrators actually do. Reactive planning is more familiar to administrators because it is a more realistic portrayal or description of their world. Robbins contrasts key elements of normative and descriptive views of planning in Figure 15-1.

To most, the proactive indicators seem clearly superior to the reactive indicators though the latter seem clearly more descriptive of reality. Mintzberg[2] and Bridges,[3] for example, have provided lucid portrayals of the real world of administration clearly in accord with the descriptive indicators. March and his colleagues, accept-

VIEWS OF PLANNING	
Normative (Proactive)	Descriptive (Reactive)
Setting of optimum objectives	Setting of satisfying objectives
Decisions geared to maximizing organizational performance	Decisions geared to protecting one's self-interest
Quantitative techniques used to make quality decisions	Decisions made subjectively
Decisions that are socially responsible	Decisions made in the best interest of administrators and organizations
Strategies developed in response to forecasts and needs	Strategies developed in response to changes in the environment

Figure 15-1   Contrasting normative and descriptive views of planning. (Source: Adapted from Stephen A. Robbins, *The Administrative Process: Integrating Theory and Practice,* © 1976, p. 469. Reprinted by permission of Prentice-Hall, Inc., Englewood Cliffs, New Jersey.)

ing the realities of life in organizations, have proposed a useful, provocative, and challenging "garbage can" model of decision-making as an alternative to rational-planning models.[4] According to this model, planning is not viewed as a very useful exercise because of the unpredictable nature of organization and environment on the one hand and the rational limits on human decision-making on the other. Decision-making is likened to a "garbage can" into which various school problems are deposited. Solutions, too, are also deposited into this same can though they are typically mutually exclusive of problems or at best only loosely coupled to problems. March and his associates suggest that a better image of planning and decision-making than identifying problems and seeking solutions, is to assume that solutions exist which must be matched to problems. Educational program decisions for example are often made on the basis of faculty interests and strengths rather than student or community needs. In school A strengths such as aesthetic education interests and skills among the faculty, become matched with an existing or invented problem—the need, for example, to broaden the curriculum to include the arts. Basic skills strengths and interests of faculty in school B might lead to discovering or identifying different problems. In each case the respective strengths of faculty are "solutions" in search of "problems."

Finally, according to March, teachers, administrators, students, parents, state department officials, and others are also deposited into this "garbage can." As a result of mixing people, solutions, and problems, fixed patterns of interaction occur which result in decisions.

Planning of any duration or of any detail, according to this view, is considered an academic exercise without much utility to school executives. Further, political and human limitations are seen to play a key role in decision-making. A better position, we think, is to accept the rational limitation of planning suggested by March and his associates but to view them as a *limitation to an otherwise purposive and rational-striving process.* We believe that people can share together, develop common commitments, have values, and strive to articulate these characteristics in the form of organizational objectives. In this spirit, then, planning is viewed as an important and helpful process which can improve effectiveness, but at the same time school executives need to acknowledge that this planning process is severely limited by human fraility on the one hand and the political process on the other.

In the sections that follow, ultra-rational views of planning will be criticized for not taking cognizance of human and political limitations, and a more moderate approach to planning is suggested.

SYSTEMS ANALYSIS

In recent years a new planning technique called "systems analysis" has captured the imagination of many educational administration theorists. Systems analysis as a strategy-planning and decision-making tool has its origins in operations research, a technique developed prior to and during World War II to apply radar research technology to military problems. The use of system techniques was accelerated in the United States when Robert McNamara became Secretary of the Department of Defense in 1961. Systems analysis was introduced into that department as a means of upgrading planning. The systems concept soon spread to other governmental agencies, including the U.S. Office of Education. Many state and local governments, including school districts, have adopted the systems analysis concept or suitable variations. In this section we examine what this new planning approach is, why it is so popular, and what we believe to be its most serious shortcomings.

Systems Analysis Defined

The systems concept is a very powerful one, referring to a complex of interdependencies between parts and processes which involve predictable or at least identifiable regularities of relationships between and among these parts. If one part of the system is altered in some way, each of the other parts makes a theoretically predictable adjustment. A similar type of relationship exists between the system and its external environment. We are in this case describing a theoretical system.

Systems analysis, then, can be defined as "an attempt to define carefully and map each of the interdependent parts of the whole so that one part can be manipulated with full awareness of the effects on each of the other parts internal to the system and the effects of this system on its environment." Systems analysis assumes that administrators emphasize control of performance toward specific goals, as well as channeling human and material resources with maximum efficiency toward those goals. Moreover, a key aspect of systems analysis is the evaluation of progress toward goal achievement; thus goals need to be operationalized so that they are readily measured.[5]

A model of a systems approach to problem solving is presented in Figure 15-2. Note that this model makes rather clear and specific demands in terms of the sequencing of events and activities. In discussing this model Miller delineates the following steps:

1. The assessment and justification of needs in terms of validity criteria leads to the structuring of new and/or redefinition of existing goals.
2. The definition of goals stimulates policy formulation and the resulting policy decisions establish performance requirements which are assigned to management.
3. Management must analyze performance requirements in order that it can define a complete array of performance specifications which can be used to explain the performance requirements.
4. The specifications are classified and categorized according to levels of organization and a hierarchy of performance objectives can be defined in measurable terms.
5. Performance objectives are the fundamental basis of plans—each plan outlines a course of action and details appropriate management controls.
6. Plans must be verified in terms of the performance context and the action sequence (strategy) which has been developed to accomplish the objective.

   It should be noted that a plan is the best alternative solution which will fully satisfy the specifications. A strategy, on the other hand, embodies the communication elements (information, education and motivation) required to make the plan work in terms of required compromises, adaptations, adjustments and concessions.
7. A strategy which has been validated through feedback and control is a reliable management procedure for the achievement of objectives.
8. The establishment of a management procedure facilitates the achievement of performance consistency in spite of the internal and external constraints on performance.

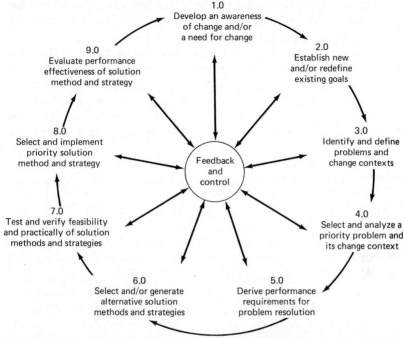

Figure 15-2   A Model of a systems approach to problem solving. (Source: Donald R. Miller, "Policy Formulation and Policy Implementation in an Educational System," *Strategies of Educational Planning,* Richard H. P. Kraft, ed. [Tallahassee: Educational Systems Development Center, Florida State University, 1969], p. 37.)

9. The resulting performance can be evaluated to determine the effectiveness of performance in terms of previously specified criteria and specifications.
10. The achievement of desired levels of performance proficiency procedures change. Such change will produce new needs, which when justified, will stimulate the formulation of new goals, and the cyclic phenomenon will continue.[6]

A number of critical requirements must be satisfied in order for strict systems analysis to work as a planning device in education. By "strict" systems analysis, we mean literal usage of the device in the engineering sense. Objectives must be stated explicitly, behaviorally, and in measurable performance terms. Specific criteria must be identified which can be used to measure the degree of change in performance. Required performance should be clearly described. Administration must gear itself to assure that performance moves according to plans. Feedback mechanisms are needed which will permit revision of performance standards and, if necessary, goals.

Ideally, systems analysis helps the school executive more clearly to identify the nature and scope of his problems, to generate operational and specific goals and objectives, to evaluate these goals and to arrange them in priority, to search for all alternative solutions within the limits of available resources, to examine each of these alternatives or options in terms of performance criteria, to assign each alternative or option a weighting score of some kind, and finally to select the best alternative. This process, when linked to others like it, forms building blocks for long- and short-range planning.

Popularity of Systems Analysis

Systems analysis and related approaches often appeal to school executives for a number of reasons. We are in desperate need of improved planning efforts in education; many school executives are aware of this and naturally look to systems analysis. Further, planning offers some relief in dealing with the realities of tight budgets. The concept of educational accountability is still another stimulant of systems analysis. Systems analysis, many educators feel, will discipline us to look more systematically at our present educational effort, our goal priorities, and the ways in which we allocate resources as a means of responding more adequately to the concept of accountability.

Additional reason for the popularity of systems analysis among school executives revolves around the concept of role attrition and the tendency of many executives to oversimplify problems related to role attrition as a defensive management strategy. The teacher militancy movement, combined with an increase in specialization in education and the urbanization of our society, has resulted in a change in administrative roles and relationships. School executives often cannot operate as instructional leaders in the superteacher sense, but rather must operate as those who are responsible for the emergence of this needed leadership from the staff. Many school executives, however, have not been able to make the adjustment from superteacher to human resource developer. Others have *incorrectly* interpreted this role change as one which pushes them out of the instructional system of the school. The effect in each case is the loss of previous role dimensions. Specialization has resulted in the emergence of a new caste of educators in schools—staff people, consultants, directors, coordinators, and other specialists. Further, urbanization and consolidation have caused role attrition from the top. Central office staff have increased in numbers dramatically, and the maintenance demands (usually in the form of paper work) have become more pressing each day, with the result being less opportunity to operate within one's administrative role as defined at an earlier time.

Thus the systems analysis movement is seen by many school executives as an opportunity to regain stature, autonomy, power, and control. After all, why can the school executive not become a specialist too? Systems analysis techniques of the engineering variety fit the bill perfectly, for specialized knowledge, codified language (input, output, etc.), technology, and the like, are the rudiments of a new management science "for administrators only."

Others look to systems analysis as a means of escaping reality. One way to deal with the multiple and conflicting problems (economic, philosophic, political, professional, sociological, psychological, and educational) facing school executives is by simplifying them. Systems analysis requires that problems and problem components, goals and goal components, and inputs and input components be reduced to their lowest denominators before they are dealt with. Problems are decomposed into subproblems, which are then solved more or less independently. Total solutions to major problems, then, take the form of collections of smaller or subsolutions. The problem with this approach is that although systems analysis is a linear technique, life is nonlinear. In commenting on this problem, assistant secretary of the Navy, Robert Frosch, notes:

> This criticism is frequently answered by the comment that problems are unmanageable unless sliced up and, therefore, the procedure is used though we know it may be seriously in error. This is the case of the man who played in a poker game that he knew to be crooked, because it was the only game in town; or the drunk who looked for his ring under the street lamp even though he has lost it a block away in the dark—the light was better under the street light. I have some difficulty seeing that a bad analysis is really better than an informed judgment, especially since faith in the analysis (and/or the decomposed solution to the problem) is frequently, nay, usually, used as a substitute for seeking or applying any judgment at all. I am often faced with a result that seems absurd, and can even produce a quick analysis that at least makes it obvious that the solution is absurd, but am then given the answer, "Well, that's what the analysis showed."
>
> Such a situation usually indicates room for deep criticism, either of the way in which the problem was divided up, or of peculiarities of the assumptions that drive the problem in curious and unsuspected ways, particularly through the unsuspected (by the systems man) nonlinearities of the problem. It sometimes appears that the only rational subdivision of the problem is to fractionate the blame to the point where approval is sought by default.

I would argue that careful attention to the parts of the problem that do not seem to be easily decomposable into semi-independent parts might be one very good guide to areas involving high risk, since these are likely not to be amenable to our usual rules, procedures, and technologies, and hence probably will have to be approached rather empirically.[7]

We are of the opinion that systems thinking has great promise in promoting administrative effectiveness for school executives. We do, however, have reservations about the enthusiastic and literal adoption of systems analysis and other systems engineering techniques in education. Some dangers of systems analysis are examined in the next section before some modified systems approaches are presented for those with responsibilities in human organizations such as schools, hospitals, welfare, and other social agencies.

Dangers in Systems Engineering

We have already commented on the problems of using a linear technique for nonlinear situations, as well as the problems of meeting the system's demand for specificity and measurability. One obvious danger is to prize those things (goals, purposes, criteria, standards, activities, and behavior) which readily fit the systems analysis model rather than those which are judged to be important. A number of other objections and dangers of a literal use of systems analysis in education are as follows:

1. *Overplanning and Overcommitment* One hazard of defining objectives too specifically, of deciding on narrowly defined alternatives, of establishing rather clear-cut procedures and arrangements for implementing alternatives, and of creating specific structures and forms to facilitate these arrangements is that the mold remains long after its usefulness or desirability diminishes.

   Educators and publics, for example, who are sure that the answer is a small-group, large-group, and independent study plan for the high school and who build a multimillion-dollar plant specifically to house this educational structure may well be victims of overplanning. This grouping program is "locked in," for the building will probably continue to influence the structure for some time, perhaps long after the professional staff's interest in the plan diminishes. The price we often pay for planning too specifically is the loss of flexibility.

2. *Emphasis on Mechanistic Dimensions* Systems analysis techniques, if taken literally, are by definition geared to bring out the highest production at the lowest cost. Production, in order to meet the demands of strict systems analysis, usually takes some quantifiable form such as how many students graduate, how many points on an achievement test, how many dropouts, and so on. In our earlier discussion of Hage's axiomatic theory of organization we noted that production and efficiency are goals best achieved by organizational structures characterized as being highly centralized, highly formalized, and highly stratified. In this mechanistic organization, goals such as adaptability and satisfaction are de-emphasized; complexity and other dimensions of personal specialization are discouraged.[8]

Schools in the United States are committed to the education of the masses, and, of course, some concern must be given to numbers and monies. The problem is one of balance, however, and the danger is that strict systems analysis will likely tip the balance in favor of mechanistic dimensions.

Schools are vitally concerned with the quality of life that they can bring to each of their "numbers" and to the nation at large. They are committed to pursuing vague and ambiguous goals such as creativity, adaptability, emotional and psychological quality, intellectual excitement, social awareness, and individual self-actualization. According to Hage's framework, schools should be much more interested in satisfaction and adaptability—goals which would be best achieved through organic structures whereby the school would *de-emphasize* centralization, stratification, and formalization (all key aspects of strict systems analysis) and emphasize personal specialization and autonomy.

3. *Reduction of Discretion* Systems analysis, if applied literally, is an extreme form of centralization which increases control of top management and reduces discretion at lower organizational levels. Schools are in many respects unique kinds of organizations. Litwak would refer to them as professional bureaucracies.[9] They pursue two kinds of goals—professional and bureaucratic. Professional goals legitimize the school as a societal institution (educating youngsters in basic skills, developing problem-solving skills, and preparing students for jobs are examples of professional goals). Bureaucratic goals tend to maintain the environment so that professional goals may be pursued

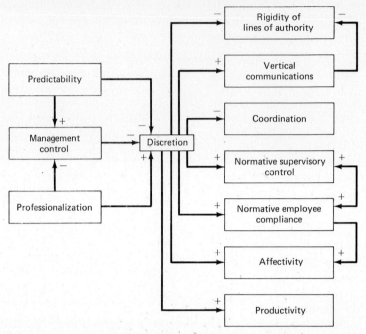

Note: The arrow lines in the chart indicate the assumed casual direction of the relationships; and the plus and minus signs represent positive and negative associations, respectively. For example, when predictability is high, discretion is low.

Figure 15-3   A discretionary model of organizations. (Source: Gerald D. Bell, ed. *Organizations and Human Behavior: A Book of Readings* [Englewood Cliffs, N.J.: Prentice-Hall, 1967], p. 101.)

more effectively (building schools, mowing lawns, busing students, changing light bulbs, and preparing budgets are examples of bureaucratic goals). Centralization (removing discretion from lower levels) places an inordinate amount of attention on the bureaucratic goals. These relationships are illustrated by Bell in his discretionary model of organizations, which appears as Figure 15-3. Bell hypothesizes that an increase in management control through increased predictability decreases discretion of teachers and other professional workers. The result of this decrease is an increase in rigidity, a decrease in vertical communications, an increase in administrative coordination, a decrease in self-control and group supervision, a decrease in voluntary, internal, or professional compliance, a decrease in satisfaction and consideration, and a decrease in goal attainment.

ALTERNATIVES TO SYSTEMS ANALYSIS

Our criticism of systems analysis is not with the concept of system, systems thinking, or systems approaches, but with the narrow and rigid application of the systems concept in the engineering tradition. As an approach to thinking that represents an extension of the scientific attitude and method in education, we endorse the concept. A systems approach is one which relies upon model building and the development of conceptual frameworks which help facilitate decision-making by providing bases for sorting variables and for showing relationships between and among variables and components. In this sense, systems thinking is intellectual technology which can be implemented without reference to computers or to other forms of quantitative or mathematical analysis. Indeed, machine-computer-mathematical technology may be helpful on occasions, but systems thinking is not dependent upon them and in some instances is better off without them. Systems thinking, then, is really the generation of intellectual maps with which we are better able to engage in planning, problem solving, and decision-making.

Systems concepts have the potential to modify significantly present organizational structures. Drucker suggests: "Authority and responsibility may well be the wrong principles of organization. It may be that we will have to learn to organize not a system of authority and responsibility—a system of command—but an information and decision system—a system of judgment, knowledge, and expectations."[10]

Much depends upon whether systems applications in education (1) are able to permit broad discretion at lower levels when needed; (2) can remain general enough so that we do not get bogged down in pursuing narrow educational objectives; (3) will remain flexible enough so that feedback is not a test of the success or failure of one's plans and strategies, but rather, feedback is input which can modify present operations and if necessary reorder goals; and (4) are able to bring students, teachers, school executives, and community together in search for common ground and commitment rather than serving as a device for clouding communications, building mistrust, and increasing estrangement.

Different situations require different applications of systems concepts. In the next section three approaches to systems thinking are described; one more appropriate for bureaucratic goals and functions; another, for professional goals and functions; and a third, a technical approach which can be used to supplement the others.

A Management Systems Approach (MSA)

The MSA follows closely planning and decision-making patterns typically associated with systems analysis.[11] It is a model through which plans and decisions are made within the limitations of inputs such as available resources and talents, predominant and competing value systems, needs, pressures, and other constraints. This model is illustrated in Figure 15-4.

Within constraints, problems are analyzed; new and existing goals are defined and ordered; through developing priorities and goals, problems are further narrowed and focused; performance standards are developed; alternative courses of action are generated and evaluated; decision rules are formulated; and sample solutions are developed as exemplars for action.

At this point our plan or blueprint for action is stored either mentally, or in a rule or policy book, as a standard operating procedure. When one is confronted with a problem which resembles the problems or goals treated in this planning model, he selects one solution from the limited range of sample solutions. In this sense decision-making is programmed. Reliability in decisionmaking is increased. This reliability provides school executives and others who occupy higher levels in the organization with more control over decisions and actions. Furthermore, since the decision-maker need only search the model for an appropriate solution from a limited range, less resources are expended and efficiency is increased. Those who occupy positions at lower levels of the organization, however, are not provided with much leeway in implementing the model. Thus participation and discretion are decidedly reduced.

A Cooperative Systems Approach (CSA)

The CSA departs considerably from planning and decision-making patterns typically associated with systems analysis. Although this approach is also a model through which plans and decisions are made within the limitations of given inputs, the purpose of the CSA is to promote flexible rather than programmed decision-making. This model is illustrated in Figure 15-5.

Within constraints problems are analyzed; new and existing goals are defined and ordered; consensus is sought on general goals; action guides are developed and evaluated; decision guides are formulated; and sample solutions are developed as exemplars for action. Sample solutions resulting from use of the CSA offer a broad range of alternatives and are only rarely complete or pack-

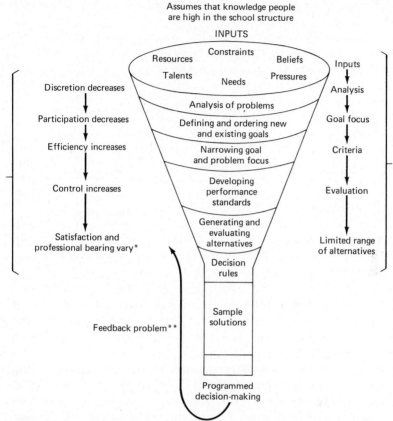

Assumes that knowledge people
are high in the school structure

INPUTS

Constraints
Resources   Beliefs   Inputs
Talents   Needs   Pressures
                            Analysis

Discretion decreases

Participation decreases

Efficiency increases

Control increases

Satisfaction and
professional bearing vary*

Analysis of problems

Defining and ordering new
and existing goals

Narrowing goal
and problem focus

Developing
performance
standards

Generating and
evaluating
alternatives

Decision
rules

Sample
solutions

Feedback problem**

Programmed
decision-making

Analysis

Goal focus

Criteria

Evaluation

Limited range
of alternatives

*Satisfaction and professional bearing vary depending upon whether problems are within
the area of concern of teachers or not. School bus routing may not be in the area of concern
but changes in the reading program may be in the area. If MSA is used in the first instance,
satisfaction and bearing may not be affected or may be positively affected. In the second
instance, however, use of MSA will result in a decrease.
**The downward nature of the MSA model creates a feedback problem when the funnel is
inverted.

Figure 15-4   The management systems approach.

aged. Thus they are not ready for application to preconceived or
canned situations but are guides and maps which help the
decision-maker formulate solutions.

CSA decision-making is more flexible than MSA decision-
making. Reliability in decision-making and control of top management are decreased. More time, energy, and money are spent on the
decision-making process—thus efficiency is also decreased. Participation and discretion at lower levels of the organization, however,
are decidedly increased. The MSA, in using a funnellike model,

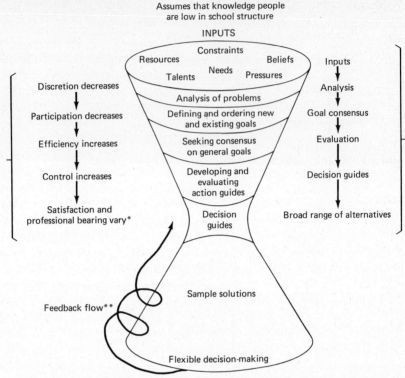

*Satisfaction and professional bearing vary according to the pattern described in Figure 15–4.
**When the hourglass model for CSA is inverted, the feedback flow is of the same intensity
as the downward flow.

Figure 15-5   The cooperative systems approach.

seeks to narrow and focus planning and to program decision-
making. The CSA, in using an hourglasslike model, does require
some goal consensus and focus but is open at top levels and remains
flexible at bottom levels. Furthermore, by inverting the hourglass,
feedback flows freely. Inverting the MSA funnel, on the other
hand, causes serious feedback problems, for the system is geared to
flow downward.

Satisfaction and professional bearing of the staff is a particularly crucial dimension in human organizations such as schools. It is
well to be aware, therefore, that satisfaction and professional
bearing increase or decrease depending upon (1) the location in the
hierarchy of people with knowledge relative to the kinds of goals or
problems being solved, and (2) the zone of difference in terms of
interest of those low in school organization. For example, if
teachers recognize and concede that on issue or problem A ad-

ministrators high in the school organization have superior ability and knowledge, or if teachers are relatively indifferent to issue A, then the MSA approach to issue A will increase the satisfaction and professional bearing of teachers. Indeed, the CSA approach to issue A will likely result in a decrease. On issue B, where teachers are not indifferent and perceive that they have superior knowledge, the opposite result with reference to satisfaction and professional bearing can be expected if MSA is used.

Additional Guidelines for Selecting an Approach

We have previously suggested, at some risk of oversimplification, that the CSA is more appropriate for goals generally associated with the professional or instructional system of the school and that the MSA is more appropriate for goals generally associated with the bureaucratic or management system of the school. Transportation, food service, inventory management, building program, and demand studies are examples of the latter, whereas teaching-learning, curriculum development, race relations, and student militancy are examples of concerns associated with the former. In Table 15-1, we present a checklist which may be useful in determining which approach to planning is most appropriate.

Technical Systems Approach (TSA)

The TSA is a method which may be used in conjunction with planning efforts of both the management and cooperative variety. This is a supportive approach usually associated with short-term projects with clearly defined goals and definite time constraints. TSA refers to technical processes whereby goals and objectives are pursued as efficiently as possible by plotting sequentially, tasks and steps. TSA is not a decision-making process in the strictest sense but rather a decision implementation strategy.

Planning evaluation and review technique (PERT) is an example of a TSA. PERT is basically a process which facilitates an organized attack on a project by breaking up and charting the events which must be completed in order for the project to be completed.[12] Usually starting in a reverse direction, one identifies each critical event or milestone which must be accomplished. These are then arranged in a sequence of prepotent steps so that one can see what needs to be done at a given time or before he can proceed with further steps. A sample PERT network appears in Figure 15-6.

Each of the events or milestones is represented by circles. The

Table 15-1   SELECTING AN APPROPRIATE STRATEGY

TEND TOWARD MANAGEMENT SYSTEMS APPROACH	TEND TOWARD COOPERATIVE SYSTEMS APPROACH
1. For administrative and management functions	1. For instructional and curricular functions
2. When dealing with things	2. When dealing with people
3. When control of activities in pursuit of goals is needed	3. When the focus is on problem solving and creative solutions
4. When problems are easily quantified	4. When problems are difficult to quantify
5. When goals are simple and readily specified	5. When goals are ambiguous and complex
6. When you want the plan to take control—automatic pilot	6. When you want people to take control—live
7. When the consequences of error are small and not serious	7. When the consequences of error are large and very serious
8. When you need a plan which is enduring	8. When you need a plan which is responsive to change
9. When ability and knowledge are high in the organization	9. When ability and knowledge are low in the organization
10. When programmed decision-making is needed	10. When flexible decision-making is needed

order in which one must progress through each event to reach project termination on time is represented by a number. The lines which connect circles represent activities which must be accomplished in order to move from event to event. Time demands may also be represented on the connecting lines. A variation of PERT which gives particular attention to time demands is called the Critical Path Method (CPM).

PERT has great utility in project management but is much too narrow or rigid an approach to be used as a general planning device. Projects which might readily lend themselves to PERT include moving administrative offices from one building to another, planning the get-ready countdown for the two weeks prior to school opening in the fall, setting up orientation programs, workshops, or conferences, planning the Christmas program, arranging the administrative aspects of a curriculum project, and planning a regional basketball tournament.

PERT techniques, like other planning techniques, involve intimate knowledge of the content of planning. It is for this reason, therefore, that we believe it easier for school executives and their staffs to learn and develop planning skills than it is to buy or rent the skills from a PERT or other expert, who must then become familiar with educational problems.

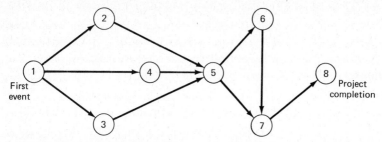

Note: In this case, events 2 and 3 may be pursued at the same time but completed before events 4 and 5. Events 6 and 7 may be pursued at the same time although 6 will need to be completed before 7. Operationally one moves from events 1 through 8 but in planning the network one moves from events 8 through 1.

Figure 15-6   A sample PERT network.

Planning: A Neutral Concept

We have argued in this chapter that planning is an essential requirement in building administrative effectiveness for school executives. Since planning may take several forms, each of which has anticipated and unanticipated consequences, some risk is involved. Bluntly, poor planning or choosing inappropriate planning approaches may be worse than not planning at all.[13] Of particular concern is adopting a highly formalistic planning strategy which does not match the unique characteristics of educational organizations. To be sure, a literature exists which demonstrates that in many cases formal planning can be more effective than informal planning. One study, for example, shows clearly that business organizations with formal planning procedures outperformed those which relied on informal planning on performance indicators such as earnings on common equity and earnings per share.[14] Another study shows a 130 percent increase in profits for business organizations with formal planning, compared with 59 percent over the same period for those that relied on informal planning.[15] Studies of this sort are often viewed as convincing by policy makers in this day of accountability and cost-benefit analysis. But the evidence in favor of a formal planning emphasis in public organizations is not forthcoming. The more structured the organization, the more standardized and reliable the work process, the more agreement on goals, the more obvious and refined the technology, the more insulated the organization from its environment, and the more authority vested in management, the greater the payoff in emphasizing formal planning. Contrast these characteristics typical of business organizations with those of schools and other public organizations presented in Chapter 4.

The next and final chapter of the book is concerned specifically with decision-making in education and represents a natural extension of this chapter. Planning issues and the decision-making process are conceptually distinct but in operation they are interdependent.

Notes

1. In a sense reactive behavior is not planning behavior—for by definition it tends not to be deliberate or systematic.
2. Henry Mintzberg's analysis of how administrators spend their time and the administrative roles inferred from patterns of time distribution is classic. Several replications of his work in educational settings are needed. See Henry Mintzberg, *The Nature of Managerial Work* (New York: Harper & Row, 1973).
3. Referring to school executives Bridges notes: ". . . on the one hand, he earnestly aspires to lead his subordinates to what he considers to be the promised land; on the other hand, the organizational realities are not conducive to the fulfillment of this leadership fantasy." See Edwin Bridges, "The Nature of Leadership," Conference on Educational Administration Twenty Years Later: 1954–1974," Ohio State University, Columbus, Ohio, April 1975, mimeo., p. 31.
4. See, for example, James March and Johan Olsen, *Ambiguity and Choice in Organizations* (Oslo, Norway: Universiitet Sforlaget, 1976), and Michael Cohen, James March, and Johan Olsen, "A Garbage Can Model of Organizational Choice," *Administrative Science Quarterly* 17, no. 1 (1972):1–25. The "garbage can" model has a number of shortcomings, one of which is its heavy reliance on exotic organizations for theoretical and empirical support. But over all this is an exciting and fresh idea which redeems the authors' use of such a garish metaphor. This approach to decision-making is explored in further detail in the next chapter.
5. One respected writer in curriculum and educational supervision feels that if educational goals cannot be operationalized behaviorally in a fashion which permits them to be readily measured, the school has no business pursuing them. John McNeil "Antidote to a School Scandal," *Educational Forum* 31 (November 1966):69–77. This view is further articulated in his *Toward More Accountable Teachers* (New York: Holt, Rinehart & Winston, 1971.)
6. Donald R. Miller, "Policy Formulation and Policy Implementation in an Educational System," in *Strategies for Educational Planning*, Richard H. P. Kraft, ed. (Tallahassee: Educational Systems Development Center, Florida State University, 1969), p. 36.
7. Robert Frosch, "A New Look at Systems Engineering," *IEEE Spectrum* 6 (September 1969): 29.
8. Hage's theory is discussed in detail in Chapter 7 of this book. That discussion is based on Jerald Hage, "An Axiomatic Theory of Organi-

zations," *Administrative Science Quarterly* 10 (December 1965): 289–320.

9. Eugene Litwak, "Models of Bureaucracy Which Permit Conflict," *American Journal of Sociology* 67 (1961): 177.

10. Peter F. Drucker, "Managing the Educated," in *Management's Mission in a New Society*, Dan Fenn, ed. (New York: McGraw-Hill, 1959), p. 147.

11. We use the term "management" in this title rather than the term "administration" as a convenient label for differentiating between organizational concerns involving primarily *things*, and administrative concerns involving primarily *people* or *educational programs* directly. It should be noted, however, that business administrators and writers in that field see management as a general effort directed at achieving objectives through others. In this sense, management includes administration (managing the details of executive affairs) as well as leadership (influencing people to accomplish desired objectives). See, for example, R. Alex Mackenzie, "The Management Process in 3-D," *Harvard Business Review* 47 (November-December 1969):80.

12. See, for example, Ralph Van Dusseldorp, Duane Richardson, and Walter Foley, *Educational Decision-Making Through Operations Research* (Boston: Allyn and Bacon 1971).

13. The following references will be helpful in developing a more thorough understanding of planning and planning systems that we are able to provide in this book. *Administrative Technology and the School Executive: Applying the Systems Approach to Educational Administration* (Washington, D.C.: AASA Commission on Administrative Technology, American Association of School Administrators, 1969); Frank Banghart, *Educational Systems Analysis* (New York: Macmillan, 1969). Stanley Elam and Gordon Swanson, eds., *Educational Planning in the United States* (Itasca, Ill.: F. E. Peacock, 1969); Richard Kraft, ed., *Strategies of Educational Planning* (Tallahassee: Educational Systems Development Center, Florida State University, 1969); Ralph Spencer and Donald Walters, eds., *Systems Analysis Symposium* (Philadelphia: Department of Educational Administration, Temple University, 1969).

14. Stanley Thure and Robert House, "Where Long-Range Planning Pays Off," *Business Horizons* 13, no. 4 (August 1970):15–24.

15. David Herold, "Long-Range Planning and Organizational Performance: A Cross-validation Study" *Academy of Management Journal* 15, no. 1 (March 1972): 91–105.

Chapter 16
A Social Humanities View of Educational Decision-Making

This last chapter is based on our premise that decision-making is at the center of administrative and educational activity and is a key concept in understanding administrative effectiveness. Traditional approaches to educational decision-making assume that rationality prevails for both decision-makers and those who are affected by decisions. More recent advocates, largely basing their speculations and propositions on the Nobel Prize winning work of Herbert Simon,[1] suggest that rational decision-making theories may be more normative than descriptive.[2] Each of these perspectives is discussed in this chapter and a social humanities approach to decision-making, one which attempts to integrate both science and value, is proposed.

RATIONAL DECISION THEORY

This discussion of rational decision-making and our discussion of systems in Chapter 15 are related. It is difficult to separate planning from decision-making, particularly if one uses a systems approach.

Systems thinking as applied to decision-making in education can readily be traced to John Dewey's scientific method of solving problems. This approach is based on the concept of rationality. Rationality in decision-making is expressed in the following assumptions: (1) problems can be clearly defined and delineated; (2) complete sets of alternatives can be discovered and described as a result of extensive search; (3) a set of consequences can be attached to each alternative; (4) consequences can be weighted according to some objective formula in terms of the probabilities of success in solving the problem; (5) this weighting procedure permits cardinal ordering of alternatives.

James March and Herbert Simon point out numerous difficulties with rational decision-making models. For example, the occasions when educators have complete and accurate knowledge of consequences which follow alternatives are rare. Indeed, most educational decision-making involves high risk and a good deal of uncertainty. Thus judgments, consensus, beliefs, experience, and professional and human intuition become critical, for fact and knowledge of consequence are unknowns.

> One can hardly take exception to these requirements in a normative model—a model that tells people how they ought to choose. For if the rational man lacked information, he might have chosen differently "if only he had known." At best, he is "subjectively" rational, not "objectively" rational. But the notion of objective rationality assumes there is some objective reality in which the "real" alternatives, the "real" consequences, and the "real" utilities exist. If this is so, it is not even clear why the cases of choice under risk and under uncertainty are admitted as rational. If it is not so, it is not clear why only limitations upon knowledge of consequences are considered, and why limitations upon knowledge of alternatives and utilities are ignored in the model of rationality.[3]

March and Simon argue that except under routine or simple circumstances most organizational and individual decision-making seeks the discovery and selection of satisfactory alternatives—those which will do the job, as opposed to optimal alternatives—those which will do the job best. Administrators seek to find a needle in the haystack which will work rather than the best needle.

Perhaps the most classic statement of limits on rational decision-making can be found in Simon's work *Administrative Behavior: A Study of the Decision-Making Processes in Administrative Organization*. Simon notes:

> The limits of rationality have been seen to derive from the inability of the human mind to bring to bear upon a single decision all the aspects

of value, knowledge, and behavior that would be relevant. The pattern of human choice is often more nearly a stimulus-response pattern than a choice among alternatives. Human rationality operates, then, within the limits of a psychological environment. This environment imposes on the individual as "givens" a selection of factors upon which he must base his decisions. However, the stimuli of decision can themselves be controlled so as to serve broader ends, and a sequence of individual decisions can be integrated into a well conceived plan.

The deliberate control of the environment of decision permits not only the integration of choice, but its socialization as well. Social institutions may be viewed as regularizations of the behavior of individuals through subjection of their behavior to stimulus-patterns socially imposed on them. It is in these patterns that an understanding of the meaning and function of organization is to be found.[4]

In recent years March and others have been expanding the concept of cognitive limits of human rationality to include limits which characterize the organization itself and limits of the political context in which the organizations must function.[5] Their thesis is simple. Everywhere within organizations one encounters nonrationality. Consider, for example, the extent and frequency with which each of the following examples is true. In school districts decisions are made after tedious study and large expenditures of resources only to remain unimplemented. After teachers struggle to win decision-making prerogatives, they show indifference toward participating in the general governance of the school. Decisions on major issues having far-reaching consequences for the whole school are often made on the spur of the moment and with only limited participation. An administrative team gets together to tackle one problem but instead winds up dealing with a host of other and unrelated problems.

March and his colleagues maintain that organizational defense mechanisms operate to confuse the decision-making process still more. The past, for example, is *fictionalized* to correspond with present circumstances. By the same token, present circumstances are *rationalized* to match past history. We assume, for example, that goals attained were actually intended, and what appears to have happened has actually happened.

"Ambiguity" is the word March uses to describe the environment for decision-making within educational organizations, and the organizations themselves are labeled as organized anarchies. Organized anarchies, according to March and his colleagues, are characterized by three general properties: disagreement over and difficulty in articulating goals and preferences, unclear technologies, and fluid participation.[6] One axiomatic characteristic of schools is their inability to articulate clearly and obtain wide-spread consensus on goals and objectives. Since the beginning of recorded history people have argued over issues such as what knowledge is worth knowing and what functions the schools should serve. The second property, unclear technology, is also a widely accepted characteristic of schools. Not only is there disagreement over school goals, but means are uncertain and highly idiosyncratic. Teacher-preparation programs vary widely, and issues of pedagogy are widely debated within the profession. The final property, fluid participation, is evidenced by widespread differences in commit-ment levels which teachers, students, and parents bring to the school, rapid turnover of school boards, mobility among adminis-trators and teachers, a highly mobile client group, one-twelfth of which turns over every year merely by graduating, and rapidly changing community pressure groups.

In an organized anarchy, March and his colleagues maintain, decision-making is more akin to a "garbage can" than to a com-puter. The computer metaphor suggests a highly programmed, objective, scientific, rational process. The "garbage can" metaphor, by contrast, suggests a sloppy, accidental, more pungent process. To some the label "garbage can" seems both distractive and frivolous. Though we would have preferred a more staid label (perhaps decision exchange arena), the label is far less important than the underlying phenomena it intends to communicate.

The "garbage can" conceptualization of decision-making was briefly discussed in chapter 15.

Let us now examine in more detail how decision-making occurs in "garbage cans." Three things are deposited in the can. First are *problems* which arise from nowhere and everywhere. They may be related to issues of curriculum, discipline, parent interference, reduction in force, competency testing, careers, frus-tration at work, interpersonal relations within the school, adminis-trative styles, jobs, money, and ideology. All of these problems are legitimate and require attention. Next, *solutions* are tossed in the can as well. Solutions are products of people within the organiza-tion. They are answers to particular problems *but are generated separate from problems.* Assigning spaces in the parking lots, using parents to monitor the playground or supervise the lunchroom, redecorating the teachers' lounge, departmentalizing science and math teaching in the sixth grade, purchasing a series of objective tests and scoring manuals from a publisher, giving teachers one hour a day for preparation time, and mainstreaming the arts into the elementary school basic curriculum are all solutions in search of problems. Often the real reason for offering a solution will not be acceptable and thus must be matched to a more legitimate problem. Few would accept the reason that the teacher's job would be easier if math and science were departmentalized in the sixth grade. Advocates, therefore, must search for a more acceptable and legitimate problem to match this solution. Declining test scores becomes the problem and the need for concentrated basic skill teaching by specialists (departmentalization) is offered as a solution. As a further example, consider a group of junior high school students who would like to have a jukebox or stereo system installed in the school cafeteria (a solution). It would be naïve to approach the principal with this idea without some sort of justification (a problem). Thus the students pool their collective wisdom and invent a problem. They note a general disorder in the cafeteria characterized by litter, noise, and horseplay and difficulty in keeping students within the cafeteria boundaries. Appreciating their concern for the problem and its alleviation, the principal discusses with students several alternatives and together they stumble on the solution—install a jukebox or a stereo system.

Finally, following March's reasoning, participants "jump" into this "garbage can" as well. Participants come and go however. "Since every entrance is an exit somewhere else, the distribution of 'entrances' depends on the attributes of the choice being left as much as attributes of the new choice. Substantial variation in participation stems from other demands on the participants' time (rather than from features of the decision under study)."[7] To many who are familiar with the workings of schools, March's portrayal of decision-making rings true.

MUDDLING THROUGH

Charles Lindblom proposes an alternative to rational decision-making which is based on successive limited comparisons.[8] A comparison of this intuitive approach with more rational decision-making approaches appears in Table 16-1.

The successive limited comparisons or intuitive approach builds out continually from current situations, step by step and then only slowly. It is incremental in nature and is aimed at arriving at agreed-upon policies and procedures based on past experience. A number of limitations of such "muddling through" becomes quickly apparent.[9] The strategy is conservative, with so much depending upon the adequacy of present policy and procedures. Incremental change will not encourage significant departure from present practice in a short period of time. Moreover, this approach fails unless reasonable continuity exists in the nature and scope of

Table 16-1 THEORETICAL AND INTUITIVE APPROACHES TO DECISION-MAKING

THEORETICAL APPROACH: RATIONAL-COMPREHENSIVE (ROOT)	INTUITIVE APPROACH: SUCCESSIVE LIMITED COMPARISON (BRANCH)
1a. Clarification of values or objectives distinct from and usually prerequisite to empirical analysis of alternative policies.	1b. Selection of value goals and empirical analysis of the needed action are not distinct from one another but are closely intertwined.
2a. Policy-formulation is therefore approached through means-end analysis: first the ends are isolated, then the means to achieve them are sought.	2b. Since means and ends are not distinct, means-end analysis is often inappropriate or limited.
3a. The test of a "good" policy is that it can be shown to be the most appropriate means to desired ends.	3b. The test of a "good" policy is typically that various analysts find themselves directly agreeing on a policy (without their agreeing that it is the most appropriate means to an agreed objective).
4a. Analysis is comprehensive; every important factor is taken into account.	4b. Analysis is drastically limited: (i) Important possible outcomes are neglected. (ii) Important alternative potential policies are neglected. (iii) Important affected values are neglected.
5a. Theory is often heavily relied upon.	5b. A succession of comparisons greatly reduces or eliminates reliance on theory.

SOURCE: From Charles E. Lindblom, "The Science of Muddling Through," *Public Administration Review* 19 (Spring 1959): 81.

the problems that school executives face and in the goals and objectives that schools pursue. Technology, means, and procedures through which goals are achieved must also be stable over long periods of time for this approach to succeed.

A number of approaches to planning and decision-making are appropriate in educational settings—depending upon time, the nature of the problem, the distribution of ability, and the desirability of centralized or decentralized decision-making. In most cases, however, the pure types—such as a scientific, rational decision strategy or an intuitive decision strategy—are not completely satisfactory in school settings. Educational decision-making as an applied science is dependent upon hybrid strategies which can mesh and synthesize scientific and intuitive approaches.

CRITIQUE OF THE NONRATIONAL THESIS

Undoubtedly, the recent work of March and his colleagues has provided expansive insights into the real world of organizational decision-making. But how this work is viewed can have telling effects on educational practice. As with most descriptive theoretical work, a tendency exists to take what is as a given that cannot be changed and thus behave accordingly. This theme was discussed in Chapter 12, where we viewed the school as a political system, and in Chapter 4, where we discussed administrative values as they relate to decision-making. March and his colleagues seem to suggest that nonrationality is a basic characteristic of organizational decision-making and limitations which exist stem from attempts at rational decision-making. Our view is that nonrational features of organizational life are real and cannot be underestimated or ignored, but they are limitations on a potentially purposive and rational process. To restate our position given in Chapter 4, *though it is not realistic to see goals as unduly fixed and operational and to develop stepwise plans and strategies, persons, though quite complex and difficult to label, are capable of valuing, agreements are possible, goals can be determined, and persons as individuals and the human system of an organization as a whole are capable of intrinsic, goal-seeking behavior.*[10]

TOWARD A SOCIAL HUMANITIES VIEW OF EDUCATIONAL DECISION-MAKING

One test of leadership in an applied field such as that of the school executive is the ability of the leader to sort through both perspectives of science and value (descriptive and normative) in a fashion which provides some balance and permits reasonable action. Questions of philosophy, ethics, and values have not been examined formally in educational administration with much intensity. Yet a vast normative literature does exist which tells administrators what they ought to do. Often this literature takes on missionary or ideological perspectives and in its enthusiasm neglects or distorts more scientific and more realistic or descriptive views of the world. For example, nonrational views of decision-making discussed in this chapter are simply ignored by many advocates of shared decision-making, management by objectives, and team administration. Often advocates of power-equalization strategies seem to ignore evidence which suggests that the more equal the distribution of power among groups, the more political and zero sum the game.[11] The result is often less principled decisions—exactly the opposite of what power-equalization advocates might desire. Taking the other side of the coin and focusing on only what is, however, offers little insight into how school executives might better function. Normative views are necessary as well, for it is from them that we derive our standards, make explicit our values, and select our goals.

Future work in the field of educational administration and indeed in the broader field of educational policy is likely to focus on the theoretical and practical problems of integrating the two perspectives.

Social Humanities as a Discipline

Descriptive views of educational policy and administration are frequently derived from the social sciences and other related fields such as management science and systems analysis. Normative views, by contrast, seem more imbedded in the humanities. Questions of purpose, mission, values, ethics, right, wrong, good, and better are examples. Statements of philosophy and underlying models of humanism and assumptions about how humans behave and of what they are capable, though often portrayed in a "scientific" manner, are typically more hopes and ideals, statements of value, than accurate descriptions of reality.

The social and managerial sciences received a great deal of attention in educational administration during the sixties and seventies and evidence for this exists in the fact that we now attract unprecedented attention from social scientists who represent an array of fields (anthropologists, organizational behaviorists, sociologists, psychologists, social psychologists, management scientists, policy analysts, ethnographers, political scientists, legal scholars, economists, and so on). The humanities, by contrast, have not been as formally or extensively examined.

The question remains, how might insights from the humanities, particularly value issues, and those from social science be meaningfully integrated? The need for integration is generally undisputed but has not been systematically studied. Gastil has suggested that a new discipline be established to work out this problem and to offer decision-makers a set of guidelines for action.[12] He coins the discipline the social humanities. Following his work, let us examine how a social humanities view of educational decision-making might take shape and how such a view might be used to improve educational decision-making. This discussion will be in an *invitational* mode. No pretense is made that the ideas are fully developed. Our purpose is to present an abbreviated set of ideas for examination, discourse, and elaboration. If the social humanities concept is usable, widespread further study will be needed and many more proposals must be considered before a workable methodology can be developed. Our commitment to searching for a means to integrate the social sciences and humanities is sufficiently strong, however, for us to offer this modest proposal knowing well it is underdeveloped and tentative in nature.

Applying the Social Humanities View: One Possibility

Applying the social humanities view to educational administration requires that we accept two assumptions as being characteristic of the nature of humankind. The first, a biosocial view, assumes that humans are basically self-interested and self-serving. As such, they assume a calculative posture responding to the costs and benefits of various situations. Their biological capabilities and cultural conditioning determine what is of value and the nature of desirable interchange between cost and benefit. The goal of such interchanges is to maximize one's advantage. This view provides much of the impetus for scientific-descriptive study of educational administration and indeed is the target of such inquiry. How can we understand better and predict human behavior under these conditions?

The second, a humanistic view, assumes that humans are capable of reflection, responsible action, and valuing. Further, it is assumed that agreements are possible, goals can be determined, and persons as individuals and as human systems of an organization are capable of intrinsic, goal-seeking behavior. This in turn implies the ability of people to commit themselves to action.

To many, the assumptions seem contradictory but if we can accept that the human being is complex and only partially understood,[13] the two assumptions can be considered as alternating and somewhat competing moods of human nature rather than as mutually exclusive entities.

Educational decision-making, whether viewed as rational or not, requires that one give some attention to problem analysis and to selecting from among alternatives. If each of the assumptions is to be reflected in an evaluation of several decision alternatives or in an analysis of a problem in search of alternative solutions, then we need a set of pluralistic criteria to help guide this analysis and evaluation. The guidelines would be pluralistic in the sense that *both* descriptive and normative views of human nature and administrative action would be taken into account. Following Gastil,[14] four dimensions will be considered in developing a pluralistic framework for analysis and evaluation:

1. *Utility* This dimension is concerned with the practical, with social maximization, with cost/benefits and with other standards of production and achievement. Utility contributes to the goals of a good society by expanding its wealth and other aspects of material production. As educational executives evaluate decision alternatives, they give attention to the practical utility of each to the school, the community, and society in general.

2. *Transcendence* Though the practical matters suggested by utility are important, they bespeak routine and have an instrumental view of achievement without necessarily considering growth in new understanding or in establishing higher standards of achievement. Transcendence is going beyond the ordinary, to creativity and excellence. From a psychological point of view, transcendence refers to the capacity of a proposal or alternative to build esteem, autonomy, and self-actualization. As educational executives evaluate decision alternatives, they give attention to the potential of each to help individuals, organizations, the community, and society to move beyond the ordinary, to grow to new levels of understanding, to higher standards of operating.

3. *Justice* This dimension is concerned with equity in the distribution of benefits accrued by each decision alternative. Utility and transcendence both require benfits to the school and society but do not speak-to their equitable distribution. As educational executives evaluate decision alternatives, they give attention to the extent each provides for a just distribution of benefits.

4. *Ethical Limits* In this proposal justice is considered as a universal ethical concern and therefore present in all decision settings. Ethical limits, on the other hand, refers to other moral questions raised by or germane to the problems at hand. Lying and deception, for example, are often ethical considerations which surface in problems. Consider a school executive who wants to do everything he or she can to help pass a school tax increase. Is it okay to deceive the public a bit by exaggerating the school's fiscal plight?[15]

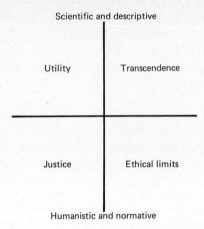

Figure 16-1   A pluralistic framework for evaluating educational decisions. (Source: Adapted from Raymond D. Gastil, *Social Humanities* [San Francisco: Jossey-Bass Publishers, 1977], p. 111.)

Obviously, passing the tax increase means much more for students. No easy answer exists to this ethical dilemma or others. But they must be addressed nevertheless. As educational executives evaluate decision alternatives on the basis of utility, transcendence, and justice, they should consider as well other ethical questions which surface.

Each of the four dimensions of this pluralistic framework for analyzing and evaluating educational decisions is illustrated in Figure 16-1. Note that the dimensions are grouped by the extent to which they represent scientific and descriptive criteria as opposed to humanistic and normative criteria. Scientific and descriptive dimensions tend to be instrumental and achievement oriented, suggesting action or moving ahead. Humanistic and normative dimensions tend to be substantive and value oriented, suggesting guides to action rather than action itself. Within these categories some dimensions are more abstract than others. Utility and justice are more concrete and more easily described than transcendence and ethical limits. They are often routinized and can be expressed in formal terms as in a legal code or a managerial plan of action. Transcendence and ethical limits, on the other hand, are typically abstract, and metaphysical.

The Limits of Choice Among Alternatives

Basic to this formulation is that problems can be analyzed and alternatives can be considered on each of the four dimensions—

utility, transcendence, justice, and ethical limits. Ideally, a proposal would maximize each of the four. Realistically, however, each of the four should be viewed as having an acceptable range. A curriculum proposal, for example, might have only marginal utility with regard to increasing the basic skills but offer a great deal of transcendence potential, and be considered both just and ethical. If this proposal had very, very little utility, it would likely be found unacceptable regardless of its ability to meet other criteria. It follows that a second proposal which offers a great deal of utility and was found as well to be just but only marginally strong in the areas of ethical limits and transcendence might be found acceptable but another with less than marginal strength in one or both of these areas would not. Though a perfect balance among the dimensions is the ideal in evaluating decision alternatives, it is likely that decisions will be made on the basis of acceptable limits.

We would propose further that a serious excess in any one dimension is likely as well to upset an acceptable level of balance among the four. An overemphasis on justice (equal treatment of individuals and equal distribution of resources and benefits), for example, could negatively influence the transcendence potential of a proposal. Sameness often discourages creativity and blunts the edge of individual initiative. Further, commitment to organizational purposes would likely be bland and the organizational incentive system dulled. This dullness of transcendence, persisting over time, would eventually lower the more routine performance capability (utility) of the organization and would raise as well a series of ethical questions. Is it fair to treat everyone equally when their contributions are differential? Should we persist in distributing resources equally even though the need may be greater in one area than another? As utility, transcendence, and ethical limits are weakened, the organization's health and productive capability are endangered. This, then, could lead to a decline in organizational productivity and esteem—the raw materials of a just distribution system. Having less to distribute, justice itself suffers from its initial excess.

We offer, then, a limits proposition to help guide one's efforts in maintaining an acceptable level of balance among the four dimensions. *Over time, a serious deficit or excess in any one dimension of the pluralistic framework for evaluating educational decision alternatives negatively influences each of the other dimensions.*[16]

A STRATEGY FOR DECISION ANALYSIS AND AN EXAMPLE

The analysis of problems and the evaluation of alternatives can take a variety of forms. This process is typically implicit and informal but if made explicit, the process, regardless of form, is likely to include some concern for or statement of a problem, a descriptive account of relevant information, a search for theoretical or intuitive frameworks to help understand and clarify the problem, a values analysis whereby the evaluators' preferences, biases, and assumptions would come into play, and finally some decision intended to improve things would be made. The steps are not necessarily executed in order, but somehow all are typically called upon by the educational decision-maker.

For purposes of our discussion, we shall describe the steps more explicitly and arrange them in order, *recognizing, of course, their more implicit nature in reality.* Following Gastil,[17] the steps are as follows: (1) state the problem; (2) provide a narrative or descriptive account of the main facts and/or important information; (3) conduct a scientific analysis of this information; (4) conduct a humanistic evaluation using the pluralistic framework (utility, transcendence, justice, and ethical limits); and (5) propose solutions to improve future outcomes.

For purposes of illustration let us consider a *problem* already addressed in this book—centralization versus decentralization. We shall deal with this problem generally by raising this question: Under what conditions should centralization be emphasized and de-emphasized? To shape the problem, we could rephrase it as follows: To what extent should a high school principal emphasize centralization and decentralization with respect to departments and chairpersons?

The next step requires a scenario which details the facts as they pertain to the problem and provides other important information. The number of departments, type of school, quality of staff, existing organizational structures and school governance procedures, the political climate and training, disposition, motivation, and commitment of chairpersons might be issues included here. Obviously, situations vary and both scientific and humanistic evaluations should take into account these differences. The success of proposed solutions is typically contingent upon situational factors, and therefore a given solution might work in one setting but not in another. Thus describing the facts as they are defined by local circumstances is an important part of the process whether implicitly or explicitly conducted.

The third step requires that the educational decision-maker

take into account what "science" has to offer. For brevity, we shall limit this "scientific" analysis to Hage's Axiomatic Theory of Organization[18] (see Table 9-1 and the accompanying discussion for details) and March and Simon's discussion of unanticipated consequences[19] (see Figures 9-1 and 9-2 and the accompanying discussion for details). We could as well use Lawrence and Lorsch's concept of differentiation and integration[20] or one of several other "scientific" analyses of the subject of centralization in organizations.

Hage's framework suggests that increased centralization is usually accompanied by an increase in the school's status system and by more reliance on standardization and reliability. Routines become established and codified, and the number and use of rules increase. He proposes further that these are likely to have positive effects on the school's productivity (defined as producing large numbers of standard outputs—i.e., tests, curriculum formats, field trip procedures, chaperoning routines, and graduating students with similar but minimally oriented competencies) and on efficiency (favorable cost-benefit ratios). The theory does point out, however, that increases in centralization are accompanied by decreases in emphasizing personal and professional specialization. The decline tends to result in less job satisfaction among teachers and in a decline in the school's ability to be innovative and responsible. It follows that decentralization would honor the personal and professional specialization of teachers more adequately and would improve job satisfaction and the school's ability to respond to the changing conditions. The price for these gains would be less routine production and more costs. Further, standardization and stratification would increase.

March and Simon's concept of anticipated and unanticipated consequences of decisions points out some of the hazards of assuming that things progress as rationally as we would like. They note that decentralizing of departments often results in the emergence of subgoals not consistent with the overall school goals and in general in the splitting of interests among school groups. Further, as power is distributed among groups and they become relatively equal in strength, competition often increases and an undue emphasis is placed on winning and losing.

This sort of "scientific" analysis of the real world and how it seems to work is useful to but not directly usable by educational executives. Too many other factors must be taken into account— many of them quite subjective but real nevertheless.

The fourth step requires that a humanistic evaluation be conducted using, for our purposes, the pluralistic framework, which includes the dimensions of utility, transcendence, justice, and ethical limits. This analysis will of necessity be general, since we are dealing with the abstract question of decentralizing authority by making high school departments more influential and not a specific problem facing a given principal in an actual school.

With respect to utility, since schools are committed to the mass education of society and resources are limited, some attention will need to be given to maintaining minimum standards and assuring some reliability in school outputs. Schools are accountable, as well, to a public that wants some assurance that units within the school are functioning satisfactorily and that administrators maintain control. Further, funding problems are sufficiently severe that sound fiscal practices should prevail and that resources are used wisely. New programs, for example, cannot be "added on" at will but are typically financed by money freed from programs that are discontinued. This, in turn, requires a degree of coordination which must of necessity frequently override the preferences of individual departments and teachers. It follows that centralization will likely remain a part of the picture in any decision a school executive makes if utility is to be honored.

Following Hage's theory, centralization is negatively associated with personal and professional specialization, with job satisfaction, and with the school's ability to adapt and respond. But it is precisely these variables which have the potential of transcendence, for over time they contribute to higher standards of achievement, higher levels of understanding, and higher levels of performance for the school as well as more intrinsic satisfaction for individuals. Thankfully, the issue we are discussing is not answered in terms of yes or no. If both utility and transcendence are to be honored, the variable centralization needs to be considered as elastic and thus capable of being stretched in one or another direction to achieve enough utility without severely endangering transcendence and vice versa. Perhaps considering each of the other two dimensions can shed further light on what the nature of this stretching might be.

The dimension of justice is often honored by strategies which are designed to increase the distribution of power and authority in organizations. In a just society, according to Rawls, a full range of political and civil liberties would prevail, equality would be complete and would therefore include equal access to positions of status and opportunity.[21] It is just, we would agree, to give people control of that aspect of their government which affects them, to honor their competence with sufficient authority to act, to permit them access to information, and to otherwise honor their right to professional destiny. But justice too must be balanced against other concerns. Like others, this is an elastic concept from complete equality on the one extreme to injustice on the other. The range of just acceptability within these extremes is, however, large.

In considering ethical questions other than justice, for example, one views the case for and against centralizations more moderately. We should take into account, for example, that the equal distribution of power among groups in time increases the amount of intraschool competition as each department vies to increase its strength. Decision-making can become more political, with winning and losing being emphasized. Indeed, goals of increased power and the status of subunits can come to replace, or at least to compromise, the more altruistic school goals, and decision-making can as a result become less principled.

Following another line of reasoning, the school belongs to the community and its people. The more simple the structure of the school, the more coordinated its efforts and the more centralized its authority structure, the easier it is to influence. Decentralization makes the school more complex and thus often less susceptible to community influence. To what extent should organizational arrangements which work against easy access and influence from the community be encouraged?

The fifth step requires that the educational executive propose a solution. In our case, since we are dealing with a general concept rather than a specific problem complete with scenario, we shall discuss solution possibilities. As the principal emphasizes decentralization with respect to school departments, the "score" on each of the four dimensions would, in our view, be as follows:

Utility would be low. The principal would have less control over school events. Routine school production is likely to plateau or decrease, but cost would increase. It would be difficult to coordinate things and to maintain a uniform stance on issues. Low utility does not mean the absence of utility. The principal, being conscious of the limits of the propositions discussed earlier, must maintain a sufficient margin of utility to keep the school operating smoothly and with some impunity from outside forces.

Transcendence would be very high. Teachers and other professionals would be more committed to work and enjoy more intrinsic satisfactions. The school itself would become more adaptive and responsive. But the principal will need to maintain some control over this trend.

Teachers can "turn on" to things not directly related to school effectiveness. The cost, number, and types of innovations can get out of hand. One group of teachers pursuing its own interests might actually create problems for teachers in another department.

Justice would be high, since the principles of autonomy and power equalization would be honored.

Ethical limits would be moderate. Though decentralization has a number of ethical virtues, the caveats of increased competitiveness, politicizing internal decision-making, and insulating the school from the public are important ethical questions.

In the absence of a particular problem in a specific setting, it is not possible to give an answer to the problem of centralization or to propose and evaluate specific alternatives. But this discussion can help principals and others to find that point of elasticity in the concept of centralization to emphasize and indeed can provide some guidelines to help him or her decide when to expand further or restrict the level of centralization as situations change.

Obviously, more work must be done on refining the process of analysis and evaluation we portray, and more models need to be developed and shared for discussion and trial. Nonetheless, we believe that a social humanities view is worth considering. Further accelerated development of thought and practice in educational administration awaits the better integration of scientific and value ways of knowing.

ADMINISTRATIVE EFFECTIVENESS FOR SCHOOL EXECUTIVES: A SUMMARY

In the final analysis, judgment is the important determiner of effective educational decision-making. Yet responsible judgment cannot be exercised unless the basis for judgment rests upon a storage of conceptual capital. This capital needs to be comprised of insights from both the scientific and artistic aspects of administration; indeed, synthesis of the two aspects forms the substance of an applied science of educational administration. The social humanities view we propose is one way in which this applied science might develop.

When this storage bank of conceptual capital is properly arranged in one's mind, its application to educational problems takes the form of an intellectual or mental systems approach. Within this approach, five systems, each of which forms a distinct part of this book, can be identified: the belief system, the human system, the organizational system, the political system, and the action system. The first four systems are substantive in nature in that their complex interdependencies form the model structure, the theoretical approach, and the content through which school executives move in developing action strategies for administrative effectiveness. Each of these systems will now be summarized.

The Belief System

Values and beliefs form a crucial part of educational planning, decision-making, and implementation. All educational activity needs to be guided by a value system unique to educating youngsters in a free society. Not only is it important for school executives to examine carefully and evaluate their values and beliefs about people, education, and administration, but they must also develop awareness for the beliefs of others—including students, teachers, and the community. These are developed in the form of educational and management platforms. It is through the belief system that administrative and educational goals are generated.

The Human System

It is useful to think of dimensions and variables of the belief system and the organizational system as being *initiating* variables. Dimensions and variables which comprise the human system, on the other hand, are *mediating* variables. Output or school *success* variables are those associated with the achievement of educational and school goals.[22] Conceptually, initiating variables such as administrative assumptions, values and beliefs, power distribution, and organizational arrangements frequently do not *directly* affect school success variables. Rather, initiating variables have a strong effect on the mediating variables, which in turn influence school success variables.

The growth and development of the human organization receives primary attention by school executives interested in administrative effectiveness. Indeed, if growth is valued in youngsters, the school will need to become a growing organization for all. These remarks should not be interpreted as a pitch for developing the human relations skills of administrators, but rather as support for the development of human resources.

The Organizational System

Schools are formal organizations. Like other formal organizations, schools have "needs" over and above those given to them by people. For example, schools tend to seek and pursue survival goals, to eliminate uncertainty, and to maintain present equilibrium. Society gives schools additional goals, and these tend to legitimize schools as official societal institutions. Schools achieve their purposes through people who are differentiated by task, role, and function. People and schools are put into motion by power and authority—both internal, such as motivation, and external, such as coercion. Certain organizational personalities emerge—based on how the school is organized, how power is distributed and used, and what goals enjoy a privileged position—which help identify one school from another. The interface between person and organization varies from school to school and from person to person, depending on a number of factors. Dimensions of organization, power distribution and use, and the character of interaction between human being and organization have critical effects on the nature and quality of organizational effort, educational decision-making, and administrative effectiveness.

The Political System

Schools operate in a political environment and are themselves political organizations. Of concern to school executives is the school's vulnerability to outside political forces. On the local scene, for example, communities are more diverse, expectations and demands for resources are more ambiguous and vocal, power and authority are more diffuse, and public participation in the affairs of schools is more intense. At a broader level, the strengthened role of state education departments, increased federal influence through mandated legislation and the courts, and shifts in school-funding patterns which reduce local influence are all in evidence. These forces increasingly require that the school executive be portrayed as a politician. Though political roles are legitimate and necessary, the bottom line for school executives is the authority they are able to muster as educators. Forsaking educational leadership roles, we believe, removes distinctive qualities which school executives enjoy and will seriously erode their ability to influence events.

Internal politics are greatly magnified these days. They force the school executive into the role of bargainer and negotiator rather than leader. Again the problem, as we see it, is not one of either/or but one of balance. Political behavior within schools can be managed, we believe, by building and nurturing organizational patriotism. This requires closer matching of individual goals and aspirations with those of the school—a leadership, not bargaining, task.

The Action System

Planning, deciding, and leading are the main components of the action system. This system provides insight into developing action strategies which are directed toward the achievement of people's goals, educational goals, and school goals. We argue that action takes place as a result of forces which exist in each of the other systems.

Leadership is an important aspect of administrative effectiveness. We do not subscribe to a "great man" theory of leadership. The complexities of life and leadership in educational organizations are such that administrative effectiveness depends upon one's ability to see that leadership functions are performed, that leadership emerges from a variety of sources and is not held to be the exclusive province of school executives. But important differences exist between professional administration and educational leadership. Leaders bring to their jobs a sense of vision and purpose which adds rich meaning to their lives, the lives of others, and the activities of the school. In Starratt's words:

> A critical quality of any leader is that he is profoundly convinced that his vision of what ought to be or could be has a dramatic significance for the lives of those for and with whom he works. He is caught up with the drama and excitement of what he and his subordinates are doing, and he communicates and shares them with subordinates.
>
> When speaking of educational leaders, we must add to the above quality, a continuous, lived experience of learning, in which the educational leader shares with his subordinates his own zest for expanding his own understanding and appreciation of the human epic.[23]

It is our hope that this book has contributed in a small way to instilling in readers this sense of drama and vision so essential to educational leadership.

Notes

1. Herbert A. Simon, *Administrative Behavior: A Study of Decision-Making Processes in Administrative Organization* (New York: Macmillan, 1945), pp. 108–9. This classic is now in its fifth edition.
2. Normative theories are statements of what ought to be. They set the

standards for our behavior as administrators and provide us with value perspectives upon which to judge administrative and organizational functioning. By contrast, descriptive theories focus on what is actual and real. This dimension of reality provided by descriptive theories provides administrators with a map which can help them understand more accurately the world within which they must work.

3. James March and Herbert Simon, *Organizations* (New York: John Wiley, 1958), p. 138. See also chap. 6.

4. Simon, *Administrative Behavior*, pp. 108–9.

5. See, for example, Richard Cyert and James G. March, *Behavioral Theory of the Firm* (Englewood Cliffs, N.J.: Prentice-Hall, 1963). Michael D. Cohen and James G. March, *Leadership and Ambiguity the American College Presidency* (New York: McGraw-Hill, 1972), Michael D. Cohen, James G. March, and Johan P. Olsen, "A Garbage Can Model of Organizational Choice," *Administrative Science Quarterly* 17, no. 1 (1972):1–25, and James G. March and Johan P. Olsen, *Ambiguity and Choice in Organizations* (Oslo, Norway: Universitet Storlaget, 1976). On the political context see our Chapter 13.

6. Cohen, March, and Olsen, "A Garbage Can Model of Organizational Choice," p. 1.

7. Ibid, p. 3.

8. Charles E. Lindblom, "The Science of Muddling Through," *Public Administration Review* 19 (Spring 1959):79–88.

9. See, for example, Yehezkel Dror, "Muddling Through—Science or Inertia?" *Public Administration Review* 24, no. 3 (September 1964): 153–157.

10. For an example of others who see a certain rationality to the nonrational view see Henry Mintzberg, Dura Raisinghani, and André Theóret, "The Structure of 'Unstructured' Decision Processes," *Administrative Science Quarterly* 21 (1976):246–275.

11. See, for example, Jeffrey Pfeffer, "Power and Resource Allocation in Organization," Barry Staw and Gerald Salencik, eds., *New Directions in Organizational Research* (New York: St. Clair Press, 1977), pp. 235–65.

12. Raymond D. Gastil, *Social Humanities* (San Francisco: Jossey-Bass Publishers, 1977). Gastil's pioneering proposal for establishing a discipline of social humanities is seminal to this discussion. The context of his analysis is broad policy particularly as it affects national and international development. These liberties are taken in articulating the social humanities view within the context of education.

13. See for example, Edgar H. Schien, *Organizational Psychology* (Englewood Cliffs, N.J.: Prentice-Hall Inc., 1965), pp. 47–63.

14. Gastil, *Social Humanities*, pp. 109–21.

15. Sissela Bok, *Lying: Moral Choice in Public and Private Life* (New York: Pantheon Books, 1978).

16. For an elaboration of the limits proposition, see Sergiovanni, "A Social Studies View of Educational Policy and Administration."

17. Gastil, *Social Humanities*, pp. 141–46.

18. Jerald Hage, "An Axiomatic Theory of Organization," *Administrative Science Quarterly* 10 (December 1965): 289–320. See also our discussion which appears in Chapter 9.
19. James G. March and Herbert A. Simon, *Organization* (New York: John Wiley, 1958), pp. 37–45.
20. Paul R. Lawrence and Jay W. Lorsch, "Differentiation and Integration in Complex Organization," *Administrative Science Quarterly* 12, no. 1 (June 1967):1–47.
21. J. Rawls, *A Theory of Justice* (Cambridge, Mass.: Harvard University Press, 1971).
22. For a synthesis of relationships between and among initiating, mediating and school success variables, see Thomas J. Sergiovanni and Robert J. Starratt, *Supervision: Human Perspectives*, 2nd ed. (New York: McGraw-Hill, 1979), chap. 2.
23. Robert J. Starratt, "Contemporary Talk as Leadership: Too Many Kings in the Parade?" The *Notre Dame Journal of Education* 4, no. 1 (1973): 13.

Index